Praise for *Seeing Excellence*

"I wish I could have read this book years ago. I .... hallenges that I faced and every team member and leader faces... .... government and its velocity is accelerating. Jobs and skills are changing to meet new demands. Do you have the skills needed to be effective? Example by example, this book will help you improve your personal effectiveness and the effectiveness of those around you. If you want to make a difference in government, read this book."

From the Foreword by Dugan Petty,
Senior Fellow, the Center for Digital Government and the Governing Institute,
Former Oregon CIO and Purchasing Director,
Past President, National Association of State Chief Information Officers and
National Association of State Procurement Officials

"What a terrific tribute to those in public procurement who have been role models for excellence! I really liked the way you blended the theoretical understanding with proven implementation by agencies and teams. You have tons of examples and do a very nice job of lifting up these champions. This is an incredible piece of work."

Rick Grimm
Chief Executive Officer
NIGP – The Institute For Public Procurement

"I love this . . . What a wealth of information and great ideas!"

Carol Wills
Contract Specialist
P-Card Administrator
Academy School District 20, Colorado Springs, Colorado

"I started with the Art in the Procurement Manual story. Reading through it engaged me to read more. Sometimes most simplistic common sense approaches or creative approaches can make a huge difference in our 'perceived' bureaucratic environment. I especially liked the emphasis on the 'Art of Question,' the importance of talking to our customers, and face-to-face communication."

Carol Wilson
Director of Procurement, State of Connecticut
President, National Association of State Procurement Officials

Seeing
EXCELLENCE

Learning from Great Procurement Teams

Richard Pennington

HUGO HOUSE PUBLISHERS, LTD.

Seeing Excellence: Learning from Great Procurement Teams, by Richard Pennington

ISBN 978-1-936449-50-7

Library of Congress Control Number: 2013947047

Cover design: NZ Graphics

Interior Design: Taylor by Design

Hugo House Publishers
Denver, Colorado
Austin, Texas
www.HugoHousePublishers.com

Contents

PART I — EXPAND THE TEAM'S THINKING

PART II — FOCUS THE TEAM'S ATTENTION

PART III — SUSTAIN THE TEAM'S EFFORTS

List of Figures

Preface

The idea for this book started in the Summer of 2002 when the newly formed Colorado Division of Finance and Procurement was creating its own continuous improvement model: SCOPE—Systematic Controls, Oversight, and Policy Evaluation. I owe a special thank you to my colleagues there for helping develop the idea—Art Barnhart, the State Controller; Kay Kishline, State Purchasing Director; Larry Friedberg, State Architect; and Verneeda White and Greg Mechem, the Central Collections managers.

As we talked about the elements of continuous improvement and problem solving, we had some fun with scope imagery. I am an aviator, so the radarscope worked for me for project management. The gyroscope is also an especially important instrument in aircraft and to me symbolizes stability and purpose. The periscope came to symbolize the need to surface periodically and look around—an especially important concept in internal service organizations in government.

After we finished mapping out SCOPE over a few months, I recall Verneeda saying, "Richard, you should write a book." Well, it only took two tries and ten years. What started as a linear description of how organizations can improve ended up as a book about "seeing" excellence in teams. I used the scopes to look at great stories and learn from them.

To all my colleagues in the division, I owe a deep debt of gratitude. They endured a continuous improvement project during a national economic downturn that was making us do more with less, a common malady in state and local government offices.

I owe a special thanks to Sandy Montanez, our office manager, who helped create SCOPE. I still remember thinking we were on to something when Sandy asked me one day, "Richard, how do you get on the radarscope?" Sandy provided gyroscopic stability to me as we worked through difficult economic times in a new division finding its way. The division taught me a lot about purpose and life. Keep purpose in mind.

Fast forward to the summer of 2010, after I had left state service and retired (I thought) from the practice of law. The idea of the book's purpose was cemented at the annual conference of the National Association of State Procurement Officials (NASPO). That was when I heard Thomas Linley's presentation about the state of Ohio's multifunctional office machine project. Dr. Jack

Pitzer, like me a NASPO life member but unlike me a co-author of an NIGP foundational text *Fundamentals of Leadership and Management in Public Procurement*, heard the presentation also.

As serendipity would have it, I got a phone call while sitting in the NASPO audience from the staff at the National Institute of Governmental Purchasing (NIGP) asking if I'd be interested in submitting a story for their upcoming issue of *Government Procurement* magazine: we had a one week deadline! "Find opportunities," I say in this book. Well, this opportunity found me sitting alongside Jack. That story written with Jack about the Ohio project was my first. I'd like to thank Jack and Thomas for helping mold the basic approach to this book.

The stories about excellence are the heart of this book. To each of the "stars" in those stories who let me peer through my figurative telescope and spoke with me about their projects, thank you for letting me learn from you.

One integrating thread of excellence throughout this book is the role played by the national associations in promoting the profession and the professionals showcased here. I count the National Association of State Procurement Officials as the best professional association I have ever been in. The persistence, resilience, and commitment to excellence of state chief procurement officials is humbling, and NASPO's support to chief procurement officials is exceptional.

NIGP—The Institute for Public Procurement—has a first-class training program that satisfies the daunting task of educating procurement professionals from hundreds of government entities each having their own laws, policies, and culture. Among my best decisions ever was to get a certified public procurement officer (CPPO) certification that I proudly use along with my J.D. Rick Grimm, NIGP's CEO, offered special encouragement about whether this book added to NIGP's already robust professional library. Thanks Rick for your support.

The National Procurement Institute, an affiliate of the Institute for Supply Management, helps bridge the gap between government and our commercial supply chain colleagues. They helped me develop the lessons in this book by permitting me to speak at their annual conference in Denver. All of these associations supported the story spotting in this book and the evolution of the ideas in various ways. They exemplify the spirit of excellence illustrated here.

I had some special help sharpening the message of this book. Dugan Petty graciously agreed to write the foreword. He introduced me to catalytic leadership and spent considerable time helping me get the project management pieces of the book right. Thanks, Dugan, for sharing your time and special insight. So did Dr. Dan Price, a fellow Air Force Academy alumnus and B-52 pilot who I have worked with for about a decade. Dan in fact was my first co-instructor in a seminar—Launch!—where we test-piloted many of these ideas seven years ago.

Keep learning, this book counsels. Barb Johnson is a master contract instructor for NIGP and taught me how to engage classes without directive (make that "traditional PowerPoint") training. Barb gives back to the profession while she is incredibility busy practicing it, and she models effective learning and training like few others. Barb is a lateral leader.

I'd like to thank a few other lateral leaders. Douglas Richins, now the chief executive officer of the WSCA-NASPO Cooperative Purchasing Organization LLC, taught me what facilitative leadership means. Doug was at my side during what I call my successful failure, our innovative attempt at a two-state e-procurement system. Thanks for being a friend and mentor.

Ron Bell, thanks for your special leadership in NASPO and encouragement on this book. John Utterback, thank you for showing me how to experiment with new ideas. I'll never forget your 1996 call asking what a "BAFO" was! Or your support on the Colorado/Utah e-procurement project. Art Barnhart, I admired your resolute integrity in the face of trying challenges. Tom Jeter, I owe you a special thanks for the encouragement and time you spent the first time around on this book.

The middle of the book talks about focusing. It's funny where you find project management excellence. I was fortunate to practice law for about five years in the Denver office of the McKenna Long & Aldridge LLP. Not only is that firm chock full of gifted and smart professionals—I was awestruck really with their talent—Lisa King and her colleagues there taught me about organization, team work, and planning ahead. MLA supported me in my first book, the *Colorado Procurement Handbook*, and I thank them for doing what they do so well.

And thanks to my Mom and Dad, who not only endured the early flirtation with scopes. Dad also served in the Air Force and previewed an early version of the leadership chapter. He and Mom both exemplify the leadership principles in chapter 10. Mom and Dad have been special role models for my sisters and me.

About six months ago, I had my first conference call with my publisher, Dr. Patricia Ross, and my editor, Kay Kishline. They both have degrees in writing and bonded right away. My memory has jettisoned most of the details of that first call, except for one. During a conversation about inverted triangles (a writing thing) and my writing style, the word I do remember is: "circuitous." Thank you Patricia for reaching out at my first Colorado Independent Publishers Association meeting and making me feel I belonged. And thanks for bringing Chandra Wheeler to the team; her copyediting brought needed discipline to my writing. You and your design team were great finds!

And Kay, you gave the book a soul and made the stories dance off the page! Thanks for making this book so much better.

And finally, to my wife Maggie. I apologize publicly for the 2:00 a.m. wake-ups! Thanks for understanding and being so supportive. I went searching for excellence in procurement offices—I had it right at home.

Foreword

Richard Pennington was sitting on the other side of the bus during the NASPO conference in 1999 talking with a fellow Air Force Academy graduate. He was the new Colorado Procurement Director and faced a steep learning curve.

As I listened to them talk, I thought to myself, "Did this new procurement director know what he was getting into? Did he have the background and the patience to succeed in a state government environment that was more about finding consensus than being in command and in control?"

Since then Richard and I have worked together on several projects. First as our careers followed a similar path as state procurement officials and later as Richard moved into private law practice and my career path moved through Risk Management and ultimately into Information Technology as Oregon's State CIO.

However, as we moved toward the inevitable retirement, something became very clear to me: no matter what we do, Richard and I share a passion for excellence in public service and a deep commitment to public procurement that efficiently and effectively serves the public's interest.

Richard's leadership style and team-building skills became apparent to me in 1999. Doug Richins, the Utah Purchasing Director and Richard formed a strong collaborative partnership for the procurement of a system. It made great sense—leverage a single system in multiple states and aggregate the transaction volume to pay for the system. This provided an opportunity for both states to share project management resources, technology resources and build a system that was extensible to others.

As Oregon looked at joining the project, I found Richard to be inclusive, accommodating, and committed to the success of the project. He understood collaboration and practiced it. He was committed to achieving Colorado's needs, but he also understood the project had to be successful for each of the participating states. Richard was modeling the lateral leadership he writes about in this book.

You can find out more about this innovative exploration into multi-state IT system development procurement in chapter 7. While the example is nearly 15 years old, the concept is fresh and relevant today as states explore and pilot shared system partnerships.

I was fortunate to receive or sometimes choose a number of challenging and varied assignments during my public service in Alaska and Oregon. Ranging from facilities, procurement, risk management, and eventually to information technology, the successes were always due the work of effective groups or teams. One of the keys to team success in an ever-changing government environment is a positive shared vision of the future. While easy to talk about, the day-to-day execution is hard work. Chapter 8 provides helpful tools and examples.

In Alaska, I had my earliest opportunities to work with diverse stakeholder groups to achieve shared outcomes. Often each group from within or outside government had their unique interests and beliefs of what should happen. Finding consensus and reaching a shared solution was challenging. The principles and examples in chapter 4 on paying special attention to the early meetings to get the group off to a good start and decision making can make the difference between a successful group outcome and group that just spends and ultimately loses momentum and fails.

Another early lesson learned was that individually generated ideas seldom survived as solutions in government. Lasting solutions are developed in concert with people who care most and can act to make a solution happen. The early success of the Western State Contracting Alliance (WSCA) in the early 1990s is because of the collaborative decision model we followed. In more recent years, the rewrite of Oregon's procurement statute in 2002 would not have been possible without the hard work of a collaborative work group. Along the way, I learned from both success and failure. I wish I could have read this book years ago. It contains ideas and solutions to challenges that I faced and every team member and leader faces.

The best leaders I've seen in government are not necessarily the most polished or best communicators. They have the ability to adapt their approach to the situation, engender trust, and enable a group with different and often conflicting interests to achieve enduring outcomes that all can live with. Few if any people are born with those abilities. Leadership skills are acquired and perfected over time. Chapter 10 provides insight into many leadership models that can help tailor the right approach to meet a leadership challenge.

So what does it take to lead effective teams to move a project or initiative forward? It is not just luck. There are key ingredients that make teams successful.

As a reader, you will find insightful, practical examples mixed with just enough theory to help you or your team excel.

As Richard and I worked together through the years, the answer to the question I had on the bus years ago is a resounding yes. Richard's skills and ability go beyond his deep knowledge of procurement. This book is a result of that commitment and skill.

I know him as a collaborative leader who knows how to find consensus and achieve results. He is also an inquiring student of management and team dynamics. This book reflects more than just his interest in procurement but his understanding of what it takes for leaders and teams to excel in any field or discipline.

Above all, this book shines a light on excellence in public service delivered by effective teams with strong team leadership.

Change is the new constant in government and its velocity is accelerating. Jobs and skills are changing to meet new demands. Do you have the skills needed to be effective? Example by example, this book will help you improve your personal effectiveness and the effectiveness of those around you. If you want to make a difference in government, read this book.

Dugan Petty
Senior Fellow, Center for Digital Government
Senior Fellow, Governing Institute
Former CIO, state of Oregon
Former Director of General Services, Chief Procurement Officer, State of Alaska
Past President of NASCIO and NASPO
Founding Member and Past Chair, Western States Contracting Alliance
2011 "Top 25 doers, Dreamers, and Drivers" in *Government Technology*
Giulio Mazzone Distinguished Service Award—NASPO, 2004

Introduction

*Look around you. Learn from colleagues whose stories demonstrate the
essential elements of effective project and quality management.*

———◆———

Have you ever just opened a procurement manual and looked, really looked, at what was in it? Does anything catch your eye?

Public procurement is one of the most hidden and misunderstood functions in all of government. It operates at all levels of government: federal, state, and local levels. The public procurement function (sometimes called purchasing, acquisition, or government contracting) has a variety of organizational structures. It can be a small as an "additional duty" in a small city, to as large as thousands of people in the Department of Defense.

Somewhere in the middle, many states and larger municipalities have offices with dozens of procurement professionals. There are significant differences between government purchasing and that done by the American public who rarely sees these professionals. The amount of money involved is sometimes staggering. Statutes and rules are enacted to control funds and to promote fairness for industry, which competes for the contracts issued by federal, state, and local governments.

These laws and rules are commonly found in the manuals developed by these offices. They are some of the driest reads imaginable.

However, some procurement officer somewhere in the heart of the United States saw the potential in that most lowly of documents. That person asked what if I put art—literally—in that manual. So she did. The Procurement & Contracts Administrator in Montrose County, Colorado, had some kids enter a drawing contest, she put the best in the manual, and the results that manual produced were staggering.

That's the essence of "seeing excellence," in every aspect of the procurement process, and that is the heart of the matter of this book.

Story Spotting for Excellence

For the past two years, I have been spotting stories that illustrate project excellence. In chapter 10, I tell the Montrose County story about children who participated in a "request for poster" project that taught them about public procurement. They eventually contributed art to the county's procurement manual, which in turn had county commissioners seeking it out. Who would have thought!

For the most part, the stories I discovered are derived from procurement offices. Those offices are often unsung parts of government, but they, like perhaps no other offices, bridge organizational boundaries.

This book focuses on teams and small group excellence. Even readers who are not practicing public procurement can glean useful ideas from these professionals. If you are involved with groups where members have no formal supervisory or management authority, you are more like public procurement offices than you imagine!

There are several stories told here of groups that are not technically in government procurement offices, but they are familiar to those who are. The California Office of Systems Integration publishes best practices that touch many of the project management, quality management, and organization learning topics in this book. Other stories also resonate: A 501(c)(3) nonprofit organization that counsels companies on government procurement, an accounting team that forged a new way of organizing teamwork, and even a law firm that works in government contracting and helps educate companies about doing business with the government. All these stories have universal lessons.

The stories sharpen the lessons about effective teams, continuous improvement, and project management. I have told the Montrose County story in presentations at annual conferences of NIGP—The Institute for Public Procurement, the National Association of State Procurement Officials (NASPO), the National Procurement Institute (NPI), and the National Contract Management Association (NCMA). That story and others in this book illustrate many lessons, including the overarching theme of how all of us can be lateral leaders in the profession: leaders even though we may not be supervisors or appointed as formal team leaders. Almost all of the stories told here were written after talking to the leaders of those teams or observing first-hand what they have done.

The Focus of This Book

This book is a compilation of those stories and the lessons I have learned from them. Chip Heath and Dan Heath, co-authors of one of my favorite books *Made to Stick*, talk about the power of storytelling as a way of getting ideas to stick. I hope these stories give you some ideas about how to keep getting better as a team and an organization.

The surprising thing about this project was how well the stories and accomplishments illustrate timeless principles that others have researched and written about. I build on the learning available from the story narratives by providing references to other resources that I have found particularly useful. They provide the schema or conceptual structure for the lessons in these stories. I also identify practical behaviors to get you beyond theory to tools and practices you can use.

Ten years ago, the Colorado Division of Finance and Procurement developed visual metaphors of scopes, such as telescopes and gyroscopes, as a problem-solving approach in the division's Systematic Controls, Oversight, and Policy Evaluation process (SCOPE). I am not in procurement operations any longer, but I've continued to use these scopes as a framework for studying the essential elements of continuous improvement and effective projects. In this book, we see the metaphor in expanding the universe of ideas with the telescope, focusing on the details with the microscope, and sustaining success with the gyroscope.

As this book unfolded, there were expected and unexpected lessons. First, not unexpectedly, teams and collaboration are at the center of all of these stories. Nothing much is accomplished in today's organizations without groups and teams. Collective effort is the key to continuous improvement, managed change, and transformation of procurement offices. Collaborative effort is a key ingredient in activities like competitive procurements. We all work in groups, and a team is a type of workgroup commonly associated with continuous improvement and projects.

Second, while this book is organized generally in the order in which these considerations occur in a project, continuous improvement is not a linear process. You may start with a clear understanding of purpose, as on a procurement project. On the other hand, you may be looking for ideas about how to organize a function such as centralized versus decentralized procurement and want to start talking to people who have done it before. You may want to assemble a team to get a kaleidoscopic variety of perspectives and brainstorm ideas, or you may identify an important opportunity and then assemble a team. However, you are not likely to jump into sophisticated process mapping and other analysis at the beginning. Measurement sometimes is used at the beginning to identify opportunities. At other times, though, measures are used for analysis during the project or even become a "purpose" when a team develops measurement systems.

Still, there are overarching patterns in these stories that led to the book's three parts. Effective teams have a phase in which they expand the team's thinking. The team starts with expansive thinking during formation, eventually pivots to focusing the team's attention, and typically ends with a decision. The team's shared leadership, learning strategies, and risk and change management approaches help sustain the team's efforts. While these elements are not linear, successful teams touch each at some point in their life cycle.

The lessons here boil down to a few key concepts. Along with the indispensability of teams and the need not to be too linear in one's thinking, "focus on purpose" finally cemented itself as the gyroscopic, central concept throughout. Purpose is at the center of deciding who should be on a team. The purpose illuminates how and when project management is integrated into the group norms and how the component tasks are broken down to start making progress. The purpose of a project frames the relevance of measurement, what is measured, and how to approach analysis. The project's purpose also affects how risk management is addressed and whether the project implicates broader considerations of change management as well as the ultimate decision made or recommended by the team.

Another central concept is the importance of asking good questions. In the early stages of a team's formation, the ability to engage in humble inquiry—a term coined by MIT professor and psychologist Edgar Schein (2009)—is often the touchstone for engagement with stakeholders and customers. Early stages of team formation are fraught with some uncertainty that team leaders help mitigate through facilitative inquiry. "Stepping to their side" also involves the use of questions. This approach helps build trust in a team and permits stakeholders and customers to understand, anticipate, and control some aspects of change.

These themes weave themselves through the book and into the final chapter on lateral leadership. They are also important to a team's effective management of a traditional procurement project or efforts to improve their processes.

Develop Your Own Approach to Continuous Improvement

NASPO, NIGP, and NPI have accreditations or awards for organizational excellence and have established criteria that highlight essential elements of continuous improvement. Their standards value strategic planning, emphasize proper placement of the procurement office in the overall organization, and assess the use of procurement best practices by the agencies. They also consider the use of measurement by the agency, the use of automation, and evidence of continuous improvement. These accreditation and award standards are a good source for the elements of outstanding procurement organizations.

At its core, this book is about getting better as an organization from the team perspective. It looks at improvement in three dimensions. Chapters 1 through 8 examine the managed-change aspects of organization life: defining purpose, finding opportunities, looking for best practices, assembling teams, managing projects, performing analysis, measuring, and managing risk and change. These are commonly considered elements of problem solving, broadly moving organizations through change.

We also look at learning and leadership in the context of small group work. These dimensions have larger scales for bigger organizations, but we will focus on the small group or team. Chapter 9 provides food for thought on how to keep learning as a team and organization. Chapter 10 rounds out the book by looking at lateral leadership, which is particularly relevant to the team environment but also raises important issues for leaders where the scope of the leadership is greater.

For the most part, this book keeps its focus one level deeper than broad organizational performance. It looks at small group practices that illustrate how procurement offices continuously improve. Your office may use tools for identifying opportunities for improvement, mapping out a strategy for getting there, and then assembling a team to get the work done. This book uses stories to show how it is done.

Organizations sometimes have their own approaches to planning, execution, reporting, and improvement. NIGP refers to Total Quality Management (TQM) in its definition of "continuous improvement." TQM was a well-known quality management system used in the early 1990s. I was first introduced to systemic continuous improvement, what I call *quality management* in this book, through the ideas of Dr. W. Edwards Deming in the early 1990s with the Air Force's foray into Total Quality Management.

At about the same time, Motorola developed a process known as Six Sigma for improving manufacturing operations, and Six Sigma has been widely adopted in various industries. Japanese approaches to automobile manufacturing became synthesized into *Lean* principles, and before long, a more comprehensive approach to improvement, Lean Six Sigma, began to be used by industry and governments. It integrated the concepts of both Six Sigma and Lean.

The city of Punta Gorda, Florida, used Lean and Six Sigma in a procurement improvement project: looking at its payables process and eventually implementing a procurement card program.

Lean Six Sigma in Punta Gorda, Florida

"We are in the improve phase!" That's how Marian Pace, Procurement Manager for the city of Punta Gorda, Florida, described the status of their city's Six Sigma project. The Punta Gorda City Manager had hired a business management consultant to train city employees on Lean and Six Sigma principles and to help them select projects. Punta Gorda employees were challenged with finding ways to increase city revenues, improve efficiencies, and reduce costs, waste, and non-value added processes. Projects selected included commercial solid waste and fire department non-emergency services, and Marian saw an opportunity to apply these sophisticated techniques to procurement. In effect, she aligned with the city's chosen method of improving its operations in order to examine transaction processes and to evaluate the potential for a procurement card program.

Six Sigma is a business-improvement methodology developed by Motorola that uses rigorous processes to systematically eliminate defects and inefficiencies. Along with its cousin "Lean," it has moved into government.

The term "six sigma" is a statistical concept (sigma signifies the standard deviation) describing near perfection in process performance. The phases of Six Sigma are known as DMAIC: Define, Measure, Analyze, Improve, and Control. Lean principles were an outgrowth of manufacturing approaches used in Japan. Lean emphasizes process flow, waste, and time.

This detailed examination of the process resulted in a better understanding of the city's payables process and the identification of opportunities for improvement. Eventually, the project led to implementation of a procurement card program to streamline payments. In addition to the significant process efficiencies, Marian's team estimated that the city would receive between $49,000 and $57,000 in rebates under the card program. As will be told in chapters 7 and 8, Marian Pace is a fan of the Lean Six Sigma process!

Both NIGP and NPI place a great deal of importance on having a continuous improvement focus as an element of excellent organizations. Yet they do not promote any particular approach. The city of Fort Wayne, Indiana, was one of the earliest government agencies reported to use Six Sigma.[1] Colorado, Ohio, and Washington reportedly are now implementing Lean.[2] Effective continuous improvement does not require use of any of these models. In 2002, when the Colorado Division of Finance and Procurement was searching for an approach to continuous improvement, Six Sigma training was only just starting nationally. However, it was fairly expensive, and the division opted for a more "common sense" approach that used visual imagery to integrate these steps. As the division director at the time, I felt that we did not have the resources or time necessary to train people on the elements of Six Sigma, then receiving a lot of attention among quality professionals. We had a diverse group of managers and employees: attorneys, accountants, architects, procurement professionals, and debt collectors. I wasn't sure that Six Sigma's teaching about manufacturing process statistical variation, or grafting Japanese Lean manufacturing principles into a financial internal services organization, was going to be accepted by our people. So we developed SCOPE, Systematic Controls, Oversight and Policy Evaluation, as an adaptation of other quality management systems. SCOPE was our division's approach to revising the state's internal controls policies in a systematic way.

Nor did the Colorado state government use an agency-wide approach like Lean Six Sigma. The state used strategic planning and performance-based budgeting for performance measurement, but it did not have a statewide approach to organizational performance improvement and measurement that was widely taught and accepted.

In the three years that we used SCOPE, we revisited our small purchase procedures, mapped debt collection processes in central collections, and wrote statutory revisions. We also began revisions to the state's contracting policy and procedures, which first involved looking at contract-approval process measures. We'll learn more about that project in chapter 6.

Most of the structure to *quality management* comes from quality professionals. The American Society for Quality has a rich history of training and scholarship with regard to various quality management approaches. Perhaps the flagship publication of ASQ, now in its second edition, is Nancy Tague's *The Quality Handbook* (2005) that contains descriptions of various tools. The book describes, for example, brainstorming, some project management tools like project charter checklists, prioritization matrices, and process flowcharts. Many of the tools—especially the statistical tools—were created for manufacturing operations. But the second edition of *The Quality Handbook* reflects the growth of quality management system use in services and government.

In this book, we distinguish between continuous improvement and other kinds of projects undertaken by procurement teams. The next chapter draws that distinction, for example. The discussion explains how finding opportunities for improvement in procurement office operations is different than overseeing procurement planning on a request for proposal. While project management involving well-defined processes presents opportunities for improvement, there is a difference when compared to more traditional continuous improvement projects like that undertaken by Punta Gorda, Florida.

While we'll keep an eye on project management, the heart of this book is about continuous improvement. Not all projects involve the structured approach of Six Sigma, though. In 2012, the state of Oregon won the NASPO George Cronin Award for Procurement Excellence.[3] The award is based on assessment of a project's innovation, transferability to other states, extent of service improvement, and cost savings and efficiencies. Oregon teaches many lessons in this book, but the 2012 Cronin Award project is an excellent example of how to dive into continuous improvement.

Oregon's "Direct Dealership" Fleet Price Agreements

Oregon, like many other states, had a fleet problem. They spent an inordinate amount of administrative time managing fleet price agreements. The old approach to vehicle model year roll-over and bidding involved countless overtime hours. The procurement and program offices incurred significant legal costs executing almost 100 vehicle price agreements, and they had recurring customer complaints (an estimated 9–14 per day) from state agencies that claimed they were able to "beat" the agreement pricing. During the early evaluation phase of the project, the state learned that it cost approximately $2,000 per year to manage each price agreement. It took three months just to add a new vehicle to the contract, and it took three employees to manage the large number of statewide contracts.

One of the team's initial steps was to dig deeply into the industry practices and pricing structures. Through significant market research discussions with dealers, manufacturers, and agency fleet users, they learned that the traditional practice of annually bidding fixed vehicle specifications had downsides. The state did not have the flexibility to add new models introduced during the model year without significant administrative costs associated with contract amendments. Even more importantly, prices tended to be highest early in the model year. Prices declined as the model year went on, but the decrease was not reflected in contract rates. Moreover, throughout the course of the year, special pricing packages were available that provided often equivalent functionality at significantly reduced prices. Yet, the standard state price agreement format did not provide the flexibility to take advantage of these special value deals.

When the fleet program and the purchasing office started to discuss changing the contracting approach, they encountered resistance. Yet as the procurement analysts describe it, they benefited from the resistance. They became very data oriented, using: administrative costs, benchmarked costs, and tables showing how prices are broken down among dealers and vehicle models. The program credited the data-driven approach for overcoming the resistance among users.

They freely acknowledged that the program required additional work purchasing vehicles, but there was an offsetting advantage. The contracts included an "evolving technology" clause that permitted ordering of any models carried by a dealer. The solicitation permitted disclosure of pricing elements by individual dealers that enabled more effective negotiation. A key success of the project was a contractual mechanism allowing spot requests for quotations using the manufacturer's "build your own vehicle" websites for vehicle configuration. State fleet buyers could request quotes known as "price verifications" from dealers and take advantage of the most recent favorable pricing.

Oregon's project included clearly articulated goals. They sought to minimize administrative costs and reduce total cost of ownership by implementing largely self-managing, long-term fleet relationships.

(continued on next page)

> *Oregon's "Direct Dealership" Fleet Price Agreements, cont'd.*
>
> Their published goals emphasized customer focus and communication. Goals included: improvements in collaboration (especially with dealers in economically disadvantaged areas); better access to alternative fuel vehicles (the new approach facilitated purchases of more "green" vehicles); limiting to the extent possible over-specification of vehicles that reduced competition; and using "micro-level competition" that took advantage of favorable pricing available at the time of ordering (including purchasing "off the lot").
>
> Continuous improvement was baked into the new system. The program created a customer "complaint" mechanism for continuous feedback. The purchasing office monitored purchase prices and compared pricing with that available in other states and derived from other market analysis tools. As a result, Oregon's pricing averaged 3% less than that in other states studied by the project. Moreover, other states participated in Oregon's contracts because of its favorable pricing and innovative approach.
>
> The project required continuous analysis of pricing disparities, and how state-purchasing practices affected the overall value proposition. As those familiar with fleet operations know, the pricing structures for vehicles is complex and constantly evolving. Notably, Oregon succeeded in achieving a first: a manufacturer-direct contract that Oregon hopes will encourage other major manufacturers to do the same.

The Oregon project illustrates well the elements of continuous improvement. The project also demonstrates how these elements are nonlinear, in the sense that some are encountered earlier in the project than one might expect. The project team started by asking the question, "How can we improve?" Early on, before other teams might ever think about looking at measurement and data, they realized the value of collecting objective information about pricing and inefficiencies. They also cemented the project direction using clearly articulated goals, highlighted in this book as an early factor key in successful projects. Oregon's project may not have unfolded in the order of chapters in this book, but the elements are all there.

Your organization's approaches may vary. But most importantly, get started using an approach to continuously learning and getting better. Do not let the sophistication of these other models deter action. Starting can be as simple as documenting your processes.[4] Whatever the approach, it will have these elements:

1. Assessment of the current state[5] by periodically reviewing of the "as is" through some engagement with customers and stakeholders and comparison to the "should be" of the system.
2. Collaborative engagement to analyze the reasons for the gap.
3. Identification of barriers to improvement.
4. A plan for making the decisions and implementing the actions necessary to reducing that gap.
5. Development of an approach to monitoring those actions and the results to assess the need for further adjustment or change.

Six Sigma, Lean, Lean Six Sigma, business process engineering, and Total Quality Management are specific continuous improvement models. They may come and go. This book attempts to identify the underlying skills and strategies that teams and their leaders need that are common to all of these models.

Collaboration, having a clear purpose, and the effective use of questions are central concepts in this book. But at the end of the day, in any project, you will have at least touched on all of the considerations described in this book's chapters. The stories provide context, and the references give you more material for study if you like.

This book ends where the most personal exploration still needs to be done: sustaining our operations through effective organizational learning and cultivating leadership skills. Also called knowledge management, the challenge of organizational learning, for a while, was equated with information technology systems. Now, organizational culture and informal learning are more front and center. And this evolution requires the leader to keep at the process of improvement and learning. This book shows actual teams and their leaders who have achieved excellent results by using tools to connect knowledge to practice.

This book is about stories that illustrate excellence in action. And there was one final lesson that may be obvious to all readers. Building effective teams takes time and patience, as well as leadership contributions from everyone. We hope that this book may give you some ideas about how you can help your team succeed.

PART I

EXPAND THE TEAM'S THINKING

1 Focus the Team's Purpose

This book is about getting better as a team. Continuous improvement underlies many management systems, such as Six Sigma, Lean, and Total Quality Management; however, teams can develop their own approaches using the techniques in this book. It starts with purpose. A clear purpose provides context and orientation for a team's efforts and anchors every definition of success.

> *"How will we know we succeeded?"*
> —Anonymous

In the spring of 2011, I attended preliminary planning meetings at the Colorado Health Institute about health insurance exchanges. The Obama administration had passed health reform legislation that provides for the establishment by state governments of automated exchanges to serve as clearinghouses for small businesses and individuals seeking affordable health insurance. The meetings were the state of Colorado's first, informal effort to map out an approach to the health insurance exchanges.

The group was meeting to discuss the elements of the process relating to eligibility, verification, and enrollment. The attendees were representatives of different stakeholder groups: the insurance industry; persons familiar with the current state information systems used to determine eligibility for various entitlement programs; and groups representing the constituents and consumers of the programs. Any new health insurance exchange system designed to be used by businesses and individuals to provide affordable health care options would have to accommodate stakeholders in the state's existing systems.

I was a latecomer to the meetings and attending in my role as an interested member of the public. I had some experience in information technology systems procurement and forecasting possible public procurement issues in health insurance exchanges.

There were perhaps two dozen attendees at the meeting representing various constituencies: healthcare insurers, government entities, and representatives of groups reliant on Medicaid and other government assistance programs that might be affected by the exchange. The group obviously had met a few times before.

At the end of the meeting, when the facilitator asked whether there were any questions or comments, one gentleman raised his hand and asked, "How will we know we succeeded?"[1] "Good question," the facilitator replied. Apparently, at least one person in the group did not have a clear picture of what the group was trying to accomplish.

That question points the way to this chapter. To be effective, a team needs to understand where it is headed. Knowing how it will know success is a key ingredient in defining the team's purpose.

Purpose, Goals, Objectives, Values and Principles

Knowing success requires a clear picture of the purpose. "Purpose" is a concept that spans the space between individual effectiveness and broader organizational success. Individual purpose is embedded in Stephen Covey's second of his seven principles, "Begin with the end in mind."[2] The importance of organization objectives is not a new concept. Management guru Peter Drucker wrote about it. W. Edwards Deming—widely credited with spawning the Total Quality Management movements of the late 1980s—emphasized the importance of purpose in his 14 principles. Deming's first principle was to create constancy of purpose for the improvement of product and services. Those who have written extensively about leadership—Walter Bennis, Jim Kouzes and Barry Posner, and Ronald Heifetz for example—all include purpose in their lists of essential elements. NIGP's Outstanding Agency Accreditation Achievement Award (OA4) embraces a version of purpose in its criteria. Mission, values, and guiding principles all help frame purpose for organizations, and teams need to be aligned with the broader organizational goals, mission, and vision.

In a project-driven initiative—many procurement projects are formal projects in the *project management* sense—the purpose of the initiative must be well defined. The using organization may be primarily responsible for spending appropriated funds, perhaps implementing the terms of a grant, so the focus of purpose is driven by the program. In project-management parlance, that purpose is called the *objective*. A cross-functional group doing procurement planning may be assembled to create the statement of work and define performance measures that can be used to monitor contractor performance. Or the group may be focused on how to conduct the selection of the contractor to maximize the prospects of project success at the lowest cost or on terms that represent best value to the agency. These all can be underlying purposes of the group.

But where does one begin in a continuous improvement project? As has already been emphasized in this book, the process of continuous improvement is not a linear one with sequential, well-defined steps. Instead, teams should think of this as *flow*, to borrow the term used by John Kotter in his book, *Leading Change*. But the various descriptions all point in one direction, achieving some purpose. The threshold coalescence of a group around *purpose,* and how groups collectively turn purpose into results, is an important step in growing an organizational culture.[3] When teams develop, the early stages of a team's life are particularly important because members have not had the opportunity to get to know one another. During that early period, the team needs to determine whether it has a meaningful purpose and clear goals.[4]

Bellman and Ryan (2009) found that people participate in groups to fulfill a variety of needs. They want to grow as individuals, be part of a group that is pursuing a worthwhile purpose, and make a difference in the larger sense. Team leaders must not lose sight of the fact that the team's purpose and goals are framed around the broader context of individuals' motivations for being on a team. Individual motivations and expectations can be good topics for early team icebreakers, in fact.

There are subtle differences between purpose, goals, objectives, and values, common terms that describe the end products of strategic planning in organizations. A *purpose* is an end or aim to be kept in view in any plan, measure, exertion, or operation. *Goals* often are considered the next level of specificity, "Observable and measurable end results that help to further define an organization by giving it direction; long-term target and vision of the future."[5] Goals are often a byproduct of organizational strategic planning. An *objective* is even more discrete, often associated with project management. An objective is "a specific, measurable and observable result of an organization's activity which advances the organization towards its goal."[6] It is important to align with an organization's use of terminology, of course, but in many respects, these definitions all circle around *purpose*.

A purpose often includes value-associated elements. A continuous improvement project team might be aimed at eliminating unnecessary oversight or steps with questionable value in a procurement process, for example. At first, a team may be brainstorming and looking for opportunities, and the team's purpose is defined by overarching value concepts like "efficiency" and "effectiveness."

Efficiency commonly is associated with getting the most done with the least amount of resources or effort. Effectiveness, on the other hand, is a measure of the quality or degree to which objectives are accomplished. Team purposes and the ways that team performance later is evaluated often have components of both.

In large measure, the initial team activities may be driven more by values than specific goals. Sometimes, an organization's approach to centralization and decentralization, the predominance of internal controls, and the balance between cost and effectiveness represent values that a team must align with. The organization's strategic plan, performance-based budget submissions, or other similar documents may highlight key values.

Values are enduring beliefs or ideals, something that is considered intrinsically valuable. As the NIGP *Values & Guiding Principles of Public Procurement*[7] explains, values exert major influence on the behavior of an individual and serve as broad guidelines for action. They form a framework for professional behavior and the choices that professionals make. NIGP's values for public procurement include accountability, impartiality, ethics, professionalism, service, and transparency.

A principle is related to *value*. A principle is "a basic truth, law or assumption; a rule or standard of behavior; a rule of conduct that derives from ethical values."[8] Principles assist individuals in determining the rightness or wrongness of their actions, are more explicit than values, and are meant to govern action.[9] There are various guiding principles that relate to each of NIGP's values. For example, to satisfy the value of accountability, procurement professionals must be knowledgeable and practice due diligence. To act ethically and preserve the public trust, they act in ways that avoid the appearance of impropriety. To live the value of impartiality, professionals treat suppliers fairly and without imposing unnecessary constraints on competition. To uphold the value of professionalism, they seek personal, continuous improvement through education. To be of service to the public and other stakeholders, they develop constructive relationships and maintain a customer-service focus. To keep public procurement processes transparent, procurement professionals provide timely access to procurement policies, procedures, and records. These actionable principles reflect underlying values that guide the actions of public procurement professionals.

All of these terms are related and help inform the fundamental goal of keeping purpose in mind in teams and their projects. The team develops a clear, compelling purpose that guides it throughout the project.

Clarifying and Using the Team's Purpose

Sometimes an organization's purpose can be succinctly captured by a vision statement. It is a statement that clearly and concisely addresses the future nature and purpose of the entity; it is a short statement that tells who the organization is and where they are going.[10]

While vision statements are not often used by teams, they can learn from them. Those who write about vision statements recommend that vision statements satisfy certain criteria, criteria that can frame team purposes as well. They should create a compelling picture of a desired future. They should represent a shared vision, inclusive of the needs of all stakeholders. The statement should be achievable, but a challenging stretch. The vision ideally is vivid, creating an image of a collaborative future with a desired result.[11]

Richard Hackman (2002) maintains that, in addition to being challenging, a team's direction must be clear in order to align strategy and action. It also must be consequential. On the other hand, over-specification of the means to the end can have a de-motivating effect on teams.[12] Bellman and Ryan (2009) likewise emphasize the importance of team purpose, but they caution as well that too much structure can impede creativity.

Sometimes teams are assembled, but the team has no clear purpose. Team leaders at this point should reorient activities to achieve clarification of the purpose.[13] Alignment with organizational goals is important, and an organization's strategic plan or scorecards may provide some guidance. Consider also enlisting team members with relationships with senior management to help a team clarify its purpose. This takes a great deal of finesse often, balancing the responsibilities of reporting to managers and attempting to create a compelling, consequential, clear purpose for a team.

The stories in this and later chapters illustrate the importance of purpose in perhaps five main ways. First, a clear purpose provides overall orientation to a team's efforts to seek opportunities and implement continuous improvement initiatives, often serving as the beacon for development of change management strategies that may be required as a result of improvement opportunities. The central purpose and related strategies and objectives help reveal relevant measures of performance.

Second, a compelling purpose is commonly cited as a necessary context for success of teams. The purpose helps energize, orient, and engage talent.[14] According to Hackman (2002, 2011), a compelling purpose should satisfy three objectives. It is clear and helps orients the team. The purpose is challenging, energizing the team. Further, the purpose is consequential and meaningful, promoting team engagement. These essential ingredients are good touch points when defining a team's purpose. The purpose then assists a team in setting priorities in the face of limited time, resources, and competing activities.

Third, a purpose illuminates the goals and objectives for the project. It also provides the criteria for decisions related to the project. Indeed, in project management parlance, establishment of objectives is part of the planning process. In procurement projects, purpose frames contract performance measures and contract administration approaches. Options and decisions related to the project are tested against the original purpose.

Fourth, a knowledge-creation "vision" is a part of the equation for effective organizational learning. In government, given often-limited resources, the knowledge vision helps set priorities among activities that range from informal learning, to requirements for onboarding new personnel, to actions required to sustain improvements and learn from projects at the end of a team's lifecycle.

Finally, this book ends by touching on lateral leadership. Helping a group sharpen the purpose is a critical part of leadership, even on a team level.

Some teams spend a considerable amount of time developing their goals and purposes. Continuous improvement teams, for example, have to define the scope of their activities, clarify the guiding principles behind improvement, and align with other organizational initiatives. One technique is to use charters and other draft documents to clarify team purposes and even to facilitate dialogue with senior management. Recurring attendance by management or executives may not be possible during the early work of a team. But succinct charters, plans, or other documents approved by them can include mission or objectives statements that help clarify the purpose of a group.

In 2011, the state of Oregon won a NASPO George Cronin Award for Procurement Excellence for its disaster preparedness project. As you read this story, consider how the development of a clear purpose helped this team in its early, formative stages.

Oregon's Disaster Preparedness Workgroup

In 2007, Oregon experienced an unprecedented flood disaster. As the state marshaled efforts to respond, Marscy Stone, the Outreach Coordinator for the Oregon State Procurement Office, and her colleagues realized just how much there was to learn from the procurement response. As a result of those experiences, she formed a team from multiple agencies involved in statewide disaster response to improve the procurement process.

In its early meetings, the Disaster Preparedness Workgroup brainstormed about stakeholders and expanded membership. To avoid the tendency to expand beyond procurement response issues, they also developed a project charter, returning to the charter and goals whenever they started to get off track. The charter had written goals that were included on meeting agendas to help the team keep focused. To address good but out of scope ideas that came up during brainstorming, the team used a "parking lot" to capture thoughts and issues that might be of interest to the state's emergency management leadership.

As the project progressed, the team produced a comprehensive website and disaster management guidebook for agencies. They tested their materials in tabletop exercises using non-procurement personnel to ensure that the resources were intuitive and did not require procurement professionals to implement. In the final stage of the project, the team published its tools on their website.

After celebrating its achievements, the team began meeting quarterly. The goals of the project were reviewed with newcomers as they planned next steps for the group. Marscy characterized her team as "wonderful to work with." When asked to identify the most important tool the team used, Marscy was quick to answer. "The charter," she emphasized, " didn't just sit on a shelf. We used it continuously to keep focused."

The Oregon story illustrates a common problem in the early life of teams. Sometimes the enthusiasm overwhelms the team's capacity to focus and achieve its goals. Preparation of a team's project charter helps focus the group. Figure 1-1 shows the introductory paragraphs of Oregon's Disaster Preparedness Workgroup charter and how purpose was integrated.

Modification 1 – 5-12-2010

Charter: DPO Disaster Preparedness Workgroup (DPWG)

1. Context

SPO is committed to supporting the procurement activities necessary to respond to disasters when the Governor or his designee has proclaimed a state of emergency. The Governor's proclamation may include accidental, natural or terrorists incidents that would initiate a state of emergency situation. The scope of the state of emergency would be outlined in the Governor's proclamation.

The State Procurement Office (SPO) has been called to take a much more active role to assist Oregon communities and their citizens to address immediate needs and to stabilize the state of emergency so activities that support the recovery can be planned and initiated.

2. Purpose

The DPWG is a working team. The emphasis is to develop, recommend, and document processes to support procurement activities during a state of emergency event.

To accomplish this DPWG will:

a) Identify, recommend, develop and implement documents and agreements needed to support procurement activities during a state of emergency event.
b) Identify, recommend, develop and implement documents and agreements needed to support finance resources during a state of emergency event.
c) Identify, recommend, develop and implement a resource cooperation plan and approach to support a state of emergency event.
d) Identify, recommend, develop and implement training manuals/documents to enhance consistency during a state of emergency event.
e) Develop and contribute to a statewide communication plan for agencies to ensure consistent information and training is available to partnering agencies.
f) Identify and maintain a list of products and services available to support a state of emergency event.

3. Participation

The DPWG consists of Designated Procurement Officers (DPO) or designees, SPO, DAS Human Resources Service Division (HRSD) and Oregon Military Department to represent agencies that typically respond to state emergency events.

All DPWG members will:

- Participate and contribute from the perspective of creating success for procurement support tools needed to promptly assist affected parties during a state of emergency event.
- Ensure the charter is abided by.
- Identify a communication liaison to DPO Council and stakeholders.
- Identify and engage subject matter experts as needed to complete the work.

4. Decisions

The DPWG will take a poll of those present and prepare recommendations for DPO consideration with the pros and cons of the recommendation based on input and feedback of the workgroup and any sub-group or subject matter experts convened for specific focused work.

5. Workgroups

The DPWG may create work or sub-groups (Workgroups) to develop or research specific tools to assist the DPWG in its recommendations to the DPO Council.

Figure 1-1. Project Charter.

In Oregon's case, the charter framed what the project was intended to accomplish: development of intuitive procurement tools that could be used in the early phases of disaster response by personnel who may not have been procurement professionals. The team did not discount the importance of other ideas, but it used the "parking lot" approach to capture the ideas and eventually feed them to other parts of the state's emergency response network management. Note that the development of the purpose occurred in the early stages of the team's life. Marscy Stone kept the purpose visible by including it on project agendas during recurring meetings.

The Oregon story also helps introduce a tool used during the earliest stages of a project and assembly of the team: brainstorming. The team brainstormed to make sure the team had the right members. The workgroup eventually included members from organizations who had not been involved in the response to the flooding. But the team realized that other kinds of disasters—pandemics for example—required involvement of other organizations like the Public Health Division.

Brainstorming gets early treatment in this book because it is one of the most useful tools to teams. Projects involve three basic phases. First, there is an expansion period where teams try to capture as many ideas as they can. This is the *divergent* period of team thinking, when judgment is suspended for a period. Chapters 2–4, about finding opportunities, looking at best practices and the early stages of team formation, are associated with the divergent phase. Typically, there is a period of *emergence* when ideas are explored, perspectives shared, and analysis is conducted. The *focusing* or *convergent* phase of a project (or team problem solving) involves selection from among the ideas and mapping out specific actions necessary to achieve the objective or purpose. Chapters 5–7, that cover project management, measurement and analysis, and decision making, are generally associated with emergence and convergence (focusing). At the center of all of this is the purpose. It guides divergent thinking, analysis, and the decisions that eventually get a team to an objective.

Brainstorming is a tool used to generate ideas. Brainstorming can be used to identify values and purposes that frame a continuous improvement project. Teams brainstorm about possible values that frame a continuous improvement effort. Marscy Stone's team used this tool when they brainstormed other possible participants on the disaster-preparedness workgroup.

Brainstorming

Teams use brainstorming for planning and identifying risks. Plan the brainstorming session in advance and refer to it in meeting announcements. Let participants know that the meeting will be different. If you as team leader are an expert, consider asking someone else to facilitate the meeting so all members are encouraged to offer ideas. Effective facilitation keeps the session expansive in idea creation. These are typical steps in brainstorming:

1. Use large yellow self-stick notes and a whiteboard, flipcharts, or another surface to which they will adhere.
2. Set the stage by discussing the ground rules. Assumptions will be suspended, and all team members have an equal voice.

3. State the problem or question like, "Who are the various stakeholders or other participants who might be useful members of the team?" or "What are the elements of the purpose for this team?"

4. Go around the room to improve the statement of the problem or question by clarifying it. If a change is made, restate the clarification and the reason so there is common understanding.

5. After problem or issue clarification, have everyone reflect for 5–10 minutes and write down their top five ideas in short phrases.

6. Without discussion, have each in turn state the idea and put them up on the white board until ideas are exhausted. Take five minutes for the team to read the ideas.

7. Go around the room and provide an opportunity to ask clarifying questions: there is no discussion yet about the merits of the ideas.

8. If there are many ideas, have team members or groups go to the white board and group the ideas in clusters of related concepts, putting short titles on the white board to identify the clusters. Clustering is not intended to limit the discussion, it simply makes discussion easier.

9. Discuss then the relative merits of the grouping and ideas under each group.

10. Record the results, clarifying as necessary. It may be helpful to take a picture of the final clusters to assist with recording.

In a virtual environment, brainstorming poses challenges. In a telephone conference call, participants have to remember the ideas as they are proposed, and the leader has to rely on recording and summarization to capture the idea. Unless online collaboration tools are used to record ideas visibly in real time, such as mirrored desktop applications or rapid document upload capability, a team loses the ability to add a visual dimension to brainstorming. Summarization and then open discussion of clusters or themes may be the only option unless ideas are published for a later discussion, clustering, and discussions of priorities. The use of nontraditional meeting minutes may be particularly important. The grouping of ideas in meeting minutes may be useful for future discussions.

The Punta Gorda and Oregon stories told so far are examples of continuous improvement projects aimed at improving various procurement processes. The concept of purpose in these projects is related to improvement in procurement operations on a fairly broad level.

Procurement-planning teams supporting solicitation development are somewhat different. They have various purposes for existing, driven largely by the program mission that they are supporting. But they have common overarching objectives: they are assembled for the purpose of satisfying a procurement requirement by effectively using procurement tools to obtain best value at fair and reasonable prices. Procurement-planning teams look more like traditional project management. The objectives largely are defined by external users who bring their requirement to the procurement office.

Purpose still is key, however. The neighborhood-stabilization grant program in Port St. Lucie, Florida, illustrates the role of purpose in monitoring project progress and making adjustments as needed to account for unanticipated developments. In short, the purpose becomes the beacon for project learning. The story of this project was told in NIGP's *Government Procurement* magazine in its October/November 2010 edition. In addition, Port St. Lucie won NIGP's Innovation Award in August 2010 for the project. This narrative tells the back story of how Port St. Lucie achieved its success through execution of a complex project and how the project's purpose guided the team.

Port St. Lucie's Neighborhood Stabilization Grant Program

There were a lot of vacant houses in Port St. Lucie, and property values had declined severely. In response, the city's Community Services Department applied for and received a $13.5 million federal neighborhood-stabilization grant, designed to improve infrastructure in areas especially hard hit by economic decline. The objectives were to stabilize and stimulate the economy, keep Building Department personnel performing their important functions, and be good neighbors for surrounding communities. The companion goals were to increase local vendor opportunity and educate the vendors about the city's procurement system. Those purposes framed the project planning.

To initiate the project, Community Services personnel and Cheryl Shanaberger, deputy director of Port St. Lucie's Office of Management and Budget (OMB), met with stakeholders and brainstormed ways to satisfy the grant requirements. There was, as always, a very short time for performance.

The city's Building Department inspected foreclosed homes and worked with the Legal Department and Community Services Department to acquire the homes. OMB received the list of renovation requirements from the Building Department inspectors for bidding. Requirements later expanded from just repair to "improve and enhance" the salability of the homes.

As the stakeholders worked together and conferred with vendors, the team realized that procurement and contracting processes would have to be adjusted. The time required to conduct sealed bids, for example, would not satisfy the time constraints for expenditure of grant funds. The city developed an innovative process to pre-qualify vendors so bids could quickly be obtained for home renovations. Instead of waiting for the time required to procure using the traditional design-bid-build model, in which architects design the project and companies bid against detailed specifications, requirements were sent to pre-qualified vendors in the various trades who had been through rigorous training about the process. They submitted electronic proposals in a streamlined version of the sealed bidding process.

When the city opened its second phase of bidding, some vendors expressed hesitation about participating. According to Cheryl, some vendors thought the specifications were too vague. Also, some vendors had bid based on the renovations they thought houses needed rather than what was in the specifications. As a result, participation suffered and bid prices may have been inflated.

The city's team regrouped and revisited the way renovation estimates were established. They worked through the process using home inspectors versed in the process to better target repairs.

"What would we do to make these houses more livable to us personally?" Cheryl asked. "We weren't afraid to admit that something wasn't working. For example, at first we thought we could just pre-qualify two to three vendors in the various trades. We needed more, and we fixed the process." The process was changed to include a site visit to the homes and an open meeting with vendors with an opportunity for questions and clarifications of the requirements.

> There was a healthy tolerance of potential setbacks. Some properties were destroyed because they couldn't be economically renovated. This was an example of the learning environment, the tolerance for risk.
>
> "Sure, there was risk," Cheryl explains. "There was a possibility that the properties could not be restored and sold. But it was a risk the city decided to take collectively."
>
> What a success! By the time the city won the NIGP Innovation award, they had purchased and renovated over one hundred homes.

Purpose was central to the evolution of the Port St. Lucie project. They revisited the purpose after seeing that some vendors were no longer participating. The overarching purpose of the neighborhood stabilization grant project had not changed, but the events on the ground caused the team to clarify its concept of purpose. Oregon also saw the value of purpose early in the project to set priorities and develop its performance strategy.

Both projects illustrate the importance of clarifying and using the team's purpose effectively.

The Contours of Purpose: Practical Constraints on Decision Making

Purpose helps define the contours of decisions in a project. Along with the purpose of the group, teams should define the constraints on decision making. All teams have them. Few projects have unbounded charters.

The purpose of the group later becomes a litmus test for assessing recommendations and decisions. The purpose of the group not only provides the roadmap for further inquiry and analysis, the purpose provides some of the criteria against which later decisions are measured. Having a solid understanding of the group's purpose is critical. And understanding purpose means also understanding the constraints.

In traditional projects—procurements, for example—constraints often are expressed in the statement of work. In continuous improvement projects, on the other hand, the constraints may be less obvious and require significant effort to uncover.

The statutes and ordinances governing an organization may provide constraints. Ethics may be among the most well-known constraints on decisions. Aside from law, though, the strategic direction of an organization, perhaps found in the strategic plan, may identify priorities that are constraints on a project and decision making. A government may adhere to decentralization principles that practically limit some procurement initiatives aimed at improvement. Other policy-making offices often frame constraints to projects. In a procurement card program, for example, the controller or accounting department may set policies that have to be accommodated. In yet other cases, a team's leader may have to engage senior leadership to clarify the range of a team's freedom to act.

In Port St. Lucie's case, the federal grant financial requirements were constraints. Federal Office of Management and Budget Circular requirements would have imposed some basic competition requirements for awarding home-renovation contracts. In Punta Gorda's payables project, the city likely had legal constraints regarding how it could acquire a procurement card once it decided on that solution.

Constraints may also be perceived from organizational culture. In the case of Punta Gorda, conceivably there could have been some cultural resistance in the financial community to the use of procurement cards.

Some Key Questions about Purpose

In any project or continuous improvement initiative, ask yourself, "How will we know we succeeded?" Explore as a team its purpose. In early team meetings discuss:

1. Is the purpose clear enough that it can serve as a visible guide for future action?
2. How does the purpose meet the intrinsic needs of the team and the extrinsic needs of the organization?
3. Is there any value to reviewing the organization's current strategic plan or other documents that show how this project fits into the overarching goals, values, principles, and vision of the larger organization?
4. Does the purpose include a vision for the future that adequately embraces the team's values and guiding principles?
5. Is the purpose visible enough so it can guide the subsequent actions of the team through the expansion and focusing phases of creating, exploring, and selecting ideas?
6. What is the collective elevator speech that captures the purpose of the team?
7. What are the key legal, policy, and organizational constraints that may limit options or frame decisions?
8. Does the group have a process for revisiting the purpose and constraints at key times to see what has been learned and what needs to be adjusted in terms of project strategy?

How Will We Know We Have Succeeded?

Knowing how to evaluate success is the essence of purpose and the key to productive team effort. Continuous improvement is a non-linear methodology for enhancing organizational performance. It encompasses getting better as a team and is reflected in many management systems. Purpose anchors both continuous improvement and project management. A clear purpose provides the measure of success.

2 Find Opportunities: Practice the Art of the Question

"The seeds of change are implicit in the first questions we ask."[1]

———◆———

Continuous improvement starts with opportunities, and questions are the primary tool for uncovering those opportunities. Questions play a central role in expanding ideas, focusing objectives, fostering collaboration, and solving problems. The "art of the question" remains a key to effective change.

Continuous improvement, at its core, is about relationships with customers and other stakeholders. Find opportunities to deliver customer value through a focus on customer satisfaction, responsiveness to their needs, and delivery of timely, effective service.[2]

An opportunity is defined as a combination of circumstances, time, and place favorable for a particular action or activity. Continuous improvement is such an activity, a "process for improving an organization's performance along several criteria, particularly quality, over a period of time; an outcome generally included in a Total Quality Management program."[3]

Continuous improvement comes in various forms. Thomas Linley, then with the Ohio Office of Procurement Services, won a NASPO Cronin Award for Procurement Excellence for finding an opportunity for improvement. As the story unfolds, ask yourself what role "inquiry" played. As Thomas knew, going to see how the client works is an important part of inquiry. One gets a totally different perspective.

Ohio's Multifunction Copier Project

Thomas Linley is a lateral leader. Thomas joined the Ohio Office of Procurement Services in 2009. He assumed responsibility for the state's cost-per-copy office copier contract and wanted to better understand the contract, so he visited his clients. He discovered that many had numerous machines in their office suite: faxes, copiers, and printers. In some cases, the equipment was located near similar equipment

(continued on next page)

Ohio's Multifunction Copier Project, cont'd.

belonging to other offices. The variety of machines posed a user training challenge, and a few clients expressed frustration about having multiple maintenance contracts.

Thomas witnessed first-hand the way machines were used, and he saw an opportunity for improvement. As a result, the purchasing office decided to test consolidation in their department and in one local government. The pilot reduced 438 existing machines to 289 capable of processing the same annual volume, a 39% reduction in annual costs and an estimated $66,182 in annual savings. The successful implementation enabled Thomas to expand the program to other agencies that saw the value of consolidation.

Thomas eventually saved the state of Ohio more than $182,000 in the first year of a pilot project and received the Bronze award for procurement excellence from the National Association of State Procurement Officials (NASPO). The NASPO award evaluates projects nominated from state procurement offices for their innovation, transferability to other states, service improvement, and savings in terms of cost or efficiency.

According to Thomas, "The agency is the customer; we are their consultants. . . . The customers really helped identify the opportunity for improvement."

Thomas's project is an example of "internal consultancy," a concept used by McCue and Pitzer in the NIGP foundational text, *Fundamentals of Leadership and Management in Public Procurement* (2005). We borrow many concepts from consultants in this book. Internal consultants are a segment of the consultancy world, and they face special challenges.[4] Modern organizations are blurring the boundary lines, and some people like purchasing agents span across them, a hallmark of internal consultancy.

Thomas Linley's project was a good example also of effective use of project and quality management. We've learned already from Punta Gorda, Florida, that Lean Six Sigma—a successor in some ways to the earlier model known as Total Quality Management—is a process improvement method that is widely used in industry and some governments. Lean Six Sigma and TQM both focus on the customer.

At its core, achieving the "voice of the customer" in Lean Six Sigma requires inquiry and analysis across several dimensions that capture what the customer wants. Tague's (2005) description of Six Sigma tools includes one, the "house of quality," that is used in product development. It focuses on customer relationships and customers' preferences for things like accuracy, friendliness of staff, and speed of problem resolution. In the Fort Wayne, Indiana, Lean Six Sigma implementation described by George (2003),[5] he characterizes the "voice of the customer" process in Lean Six Sigma as a quest for alignment between an organization's priorities and those of customers.

Inquiry is central to TQM and its progeny. When one is spotting opportunities for improvements, the use of effective questions is particularly important.

The Art of the Question

There is no substitute for face-to-face conversations. Teams should go to the customer's place of business and ask them the key questions. Things like, "What one thing can I do or stop doing to help you be more successful?" Questions occupy a central role in expanding ideas, focusing teams on objectives, fostering collaboration, and solving problems. Again and again, one sees the use of questions as central to achievement of excellence by groups and individuals.

We'll see the importance of questions in various parts of this book. In this chapter, we see them in the expansion of ideas. In a later chapter, we see questions used to facilitate team activities and foster collaboration. Still later, questions are used to identify risks in project performance. Indeed, authors who have written about the opening, exploring, and closing phases of creativity devote significant time to developing skill in the use of questions.[6]

Fisher and Sharp (2009) emphasize the need for teams to use "real questions." Real questions are those that do not overtly promote an agenda but encourage sharing of ideas. Going to a client and saying, "We haven't had any issues with your agency, things appear to be OK, aren't they?" is a less effective way to learn. Leading questions, those susceptible of yes or no answers, tend to be closed questions and are less useful.

Edgar Schein is a well-regarded educator, researcher, and consultant who has studied organizational psychology, organizational culture and leadership, and process consulting. Schein (2009) concluded that "humble inquiry" is a necessary part of any helping relationship, including consulting. Understanding the client—their needs and how one can best contribute in the helping relationship—starts with pure inquiry. But inquiry loses its power if questions are used to disguise hidden agendas and don't promote active client engagement in identifying an opportunity or solving a problem.

There are various ways to disguise hidden agendas in questions. Clients even do it. Peter Block (2011) portrays some clients' "how" questions as not constructive. Clients often want to offload the problem on the expert, with questions that Block calls "warning signs." How long will it take? How do we get them to change? What are the steps? What do we measure? Jumping right to these questions externalizes the problem and changes the focus to others, to skills, and away from the purpose. And away from the relationship that is at the heart.[7]

Questions are more effective if they are open-ended, as in, "What one thing could we do better to help you succeed?" Frame dialogue with customers using open-ended questions.

Effective questions and inquiry have these characteristics:

- They provide enough context for the questions or inquiry to orient the listener.
- Questions are open-ended, using words like, "Can you describe?" and "What three things?" and "Who in your experience?"
- Where possible, keep imagery positive in questions, "Think about a positive collaboration with procurement in the past. What made that a positive experience?"

- Some negative responses will come out, but try to deflect as much as possible into positive imagery, e.g., "Imagine that those concerns with the procurement process were solved in three years. What would that process look like from your perspective?"

So instead of asking, "Is our process for starting the requisition process too difficult to understand?" ask, "What one thing could we do to make our requisition process more valuable to you?" This use of questions is a way of starting a conversation that gets customers thinking about possible improvements and being part of the solution.

Good questions promote divergent, expansive thinking. In her book on quality management tools, Tague (2005) generalizes these questions in a way that is very useful for meetings with customers, stakeholders, and among team members.[8]

- Who cares about what we do and what do they care about?
- What are we doing now and how well are we doing it?
- What can we do better?
- What prevents us from doing better?
- What changes could we make to do better?
- What worked, what didn't, and how can we do what worked every time?
- What did we learn?

Surveys also can be useful in helping identify areas that need improvement. Many surveys use questions that are formatted for numerical responses, however. Quantitative analysis has its place. But leave some questions open-ended to invite customer feedback. Ask them how you are doing and what they might suggest to improve your operations.

One current theme in organization development is a switch from problem-oriented inquiry, the focus of Six Sigma models, to questions with a positive orientation. The theory is that keeping one's focus on problems cements the established way of operating while a team searches for fixes to that method. Instead, positive-focused inquiry changes the perspective from problems to possibilities in the system. While the opportunity may begin with a problem, the positive method of inquiry finds possibilities for a positive future by building on the strength of the group or organization.[9]

Appreciative inquiry (AI) is a method of system engagement in change initiatives that emphasizes the positive and the importance of the question. In fact, the appreciative question is at the heart of the process. AI emphasizes inquiry that is grounded in positive experiences to inform present implementations and a positive vision of the future. AI's basic idea is that questions oriented around problems tend to be limited in their scope and what they achieve. They focus on the past way of operating. If a team asks for problems, they get problems identified. The ultimate objective is to achieve overall system improvement that accentuates positive change.

Appreciative inquiry uses three essential lines of inquiry. In the context of a procurement-improvement project, for example, questions would be used to describe an optimal experience with procurement collaboration in the past. How would what you learned from that experience be relevant to what we are discussing today? What would you imagine the perfect procurement collaboration to look like in the future?

Questions are constructed with a lead-in that sets context for the question. A backward question uses experiences to connect emotionally to the history and find circumstances that contributed to the situation. The second inward question attempts to derive lessons from the high-point experiences to discover what contributed, what was learned that is relevant to the current situation. The third forward-looking question is aspirational and encourages formulation of a vision of what is possible.[10] The city of Longmont took the "art of the question" to this new level by using AI. The procurement office then built on that training and used the approach to improve its operations.

Appreciative Inquiry in the City of Longmont

In 2005, the city of Longmont, Colorado, embarked on a "whole system initiative" to address city planning challenges caused by growth on the Rocky Mountain Front Range. Longmont had expected significant growth in the area north of Denver, but it far exceeded expectations.

With the help of consultants who trained the participants in the use of Appreciative Inquiry, the city engaged the whole community to address the challenges.[11] The city's team first interviewed key civic stakeholders in leadership positions who were particularly influential through their networks. Later they scaled out the interviews for a whole system engagement as trained facilitators went to community events and conducted appreciative facilitation in groups.

As a result of the AI process, the city developed a set of performance measures, its report card, to help it assess progress in executing its strategy. The city's goals and objectives included promoting a healthy business climate, revitalizing the downtown, enhancing the natural environment, supporting education, and improving the sense of community and cultural inclusion.

Danielle Hinz, the city's Procurement and Contracts Manager, was trained in the appreciative inquiry process even though the procurement function was not being addressed in the initiative. While the city's AI initiative tackled growth challenges, city reorganization was also underway, and Procurement was one of the business areas being examined. With the help of another department manager trained in AI, Danielle assembled fifty city stakeholders, organized into five different groups and conducted appreciative dialogues on about twenty-five procurement topics.

They eventually chose to focus on five "appreciative topics": contracts, procurement cards and training, solicitations, the procurement code, and construction. The teams asked, "What works well?" and "What from that experience can we learn about the procurement system today?" They then asked, "What would the procurement system be like if it were perfect?" The participants explored ideas in areas such as purchasing policies; contract renewals; purchasing card processes; the bid and request for proposal processes; construction contract closeout; and purchasing forms.

Danielle weeded out some ideas based on federal/state legal constraints and began modernizing the city's procurement code. She spearheaded the heavy lifting in getting the code completed. She

(continued on next page)

Appreciative Inquiry in the City of Longmont, cont'd.

coordinated the drafts with the stakeholder group, explaining why things were in the code and why some topics were not. On April 26, 2011, the Longmont city council unanimously approved the procurement code that AI had spawned.

Danielle was sold on the AI process. "There probably was some reluctance to go and find out what fifty people thought of procurement. So we used the AI approach internally on our own staff, to see how the questions were structured. They really got more comfortable. It's a motivating approach to change. We're believers."

To hear Danielle Hinz tell the story, there was some unexpected learning. They were surprised to learn that customers understood the need for internal controls. They also received unexpected, positive feedback from stakeholders about things that the procurement staff did well.

That positive energy is an outgrowth of the underlying theory behind appreciative inquiry. AI uses positive questions to forecast a possible, desirable future. It leverages good experiences in the past to inform the present and create a better future. The process is heavily imbued with inquiry and questioning. And the mere asking of the question begins the process of change.

Summarize Opportunities

One of the techniques teams may find helpful is the *opportunity summary*. Most projects and continuous improvement initiatives require a collaborative effort by a team. People have competing demands on their time, however. Sometimes some threshold work needs to be done to convince prospective team members that the initiative is worthy of their effort.

The summary should be simple and short, not adding too much structure too early. On the one hand, team members want to be involved in a project that is expected to achieve something, and some threshold planning helps alleviate that concern. On the other hand, team members do not want to feel that there is no room for contribution, that the work is already done. Still, some preliminary thinking about the issue can portray the merit of the activity and help motivate team members to get involved. The fact that there is some—just enough—structure may be attractive. It also can start the process of jointly creating an inspiring purpose for the team.

To create an opportunity summary, take a one-page piece of paper and divide it into sections. First, summarize in a short paragraph what the opportunity is. Also, include a short description of the origins of the opportunity with sufficient clarity to help potential team members understand the context. Is it a policy problem or a problem with processes? Was the opportunity uncovered in data from existing measurement systems? Was leadership involved in finding the opportunity? Or was there a customer service problem that warranted the initiative? Frame the possible benefits or value of the opportunity and what is known so far about barriers. Consider adding a preliminary list of potential stakeholders to the summary.

In 2011, the state of Colorado was undertaking a cooperative e-procurement system acquisition on behalf of the Western States Contracting Alliance (WSCA), a 15-state consortium that cooperatively procured goods and services.[12] One of the purposes of the initiative was to use technology to improve the availability of statewide price agreements to state and local governments. The system was expected to provide various other value-added features to state agencies, like ease of ordering. But the value of these systems for procurement does not end there. When state government orders are added to local government and higher education volume, the end result can be discounted pricing on state price agreements, which benefits everyone.

Achieving this strategic vision, however, required that all government entities be able to order from the e-procurement system. Colorado's state procurement office wanted to better understand other public entities' perspectives on e-procurement. The office wanted the views of higher education institutions, local governments and school districts. To assist in this effort, a local government focus group was established, and that group used an opportunity summary in its formative stages.

Colorado's Local Government Focus Group

In 2011, the state of Colorado and the Western States Contracting Alliance (WSCA) launched an e-procurement project intended to be used by state agencies, higher education institutions, and local governments. Participating states, their local governments and institutions of higher education were to use the system to order from WSCA contracts and price agreements. Colorado expected the system to provide enhanced electronic ordering, sourcing, and payment for all Colorado government and higher education entities. The initiative was seen as a process improvement initiative that promised to improve collaboration and efficiencies in procurement across multiple states.

John Utterback, the State Purchasing Director, used a focus group of local governments, school districts, and higher education institutions to understand the needs of the public entities regarding electronically enabled catalogs, sourcing, and payment systems. These lessons informed state decision-makers on selection and implementation of an e-procurement system that could be used effectively by Colorado governments.

A one-page opportunity summary was prepared for the first focus group meeting. It offered preliminary thoughts about the potential benefits and value if the initiative was successful. At the same time, the known factors supporting the change and any known barriers and constraints were summarized. One factor supporting conversion to a new system was the imminent retirement of the state's existing online bid-solicitation system. That system had to be replaced.

Moreover, all states and their local governments were facing economic challenges. Aggregated purchasing and better efficiencies are one way to save money. On the other hand, the variety of procurement laws and processes and overall resistance to change were known barriers. The focus group was considered an excellent way to get local government perspective on these issues.

The opportunity summary was used as a threshold document in the first meeting of the focus group. It helped orient the group and provided a sense of purpose to the group in the early meetings.

A simple opportunity summary can lead the way to later, more in-depth analysis by the team of the legal constraints and other environmental factors that might affect project performance. Use of an opportunity summary can be a precursor to better understanding who the stakeholders are, the nature of the political environment, and what key changes may be required that could face resistance. These considerations often are associated with organizational strategic planning,[13] but even in smaller projects threshold planning around an opportunity can demonstrate that there is thought and commitment behind the effort. It may help motivate engagement by others and serve as an initial compass providing direction during the early life of the team.

Figure 2-1 is an example of an opportunity summary. This summary was used by a NASPO workgroup looking at barriers to effective procurement. Note that the summary was styled as "preliminary." That characterization was used to ensure that the preliminary planning had not created the impression that there was no need for additional analysis and discussion. The opportunity summary was circulated in the online NASPO Network to find volunteers for the team, and individuals were recruited to get a broad perspective of senior officials. The summary framed the work of the group, was discussed in the initial virtual meeting, and led to certain group tasks. For example, the drafts were coordinated with other workgroups working on related papers, and the whitepaper was coordinated with the NASPO board of directors.

Note also that this summary did not address the substance of the whitepaper—the workgroup did that. The summary instead discussed the value, costs, supporting factors, and barriers associated with conducting the workgroup activity itself.

NASPO "Removing Procurement Barriers"
Preliminary Opportunity Summary

Opportunity
Can we collaboratively develop a short whitepaper for senior state executives and/or legislators that identifies procurement barriers to effective competition in state procurement? Is there a role for procurement professionals in the various states in identifying practices they have considered barriers? Can a product be developed that could be used by NASPO for direct communication or by state procurement officials in conjunction with their internal advocacy efforts? (This subcommittee would focus on procurement operations barriers, sharing information with the socioeconomic and preferences subcommittees.)

Origins of the Opportunity
The NASPO board has approved a project that aims to create short whitepapers on a range of topics important to NASPO that can be used for educating senior executives and legislators. The topics are: promoting procurement's value; socio-economic objectives and impact on procurement; how procurement can create jobs; the impact of preferences; and how barriers can be removed from the procurement process.

Measuring Success
Completion of a two-page whitepaper draft by July 2012 that is acceptable to NASPO and suitable for an audience consisting of senior state executives and state legislators.

Potential Benefits/Value
Serve as a resource for NASPO, State Procurement Officials and procurement professionals to adapt when briefing executive leadership, legislators, other agency procurement officials, local governments, and other associations.

Costs
Time from subcommittee members to conduct interviews/research and write whitepaper.

Apparent Factors Supporting Change	Known Barriers, Threats and Constraints
• Recent proliferation of proposed legislation • Misinformation about procurement operational practices, preferences, and socioeconomic policies • No recent in-depth analysis of impact from procurement practices commonly known as barriers, e.g. sourcing strategy practices, insurance and bonding practices, standard terms and conditions, use of flexibility that exists in procurement laws, perceptions that use of political leverage is viable • Availability of NASPO whitepapers, on-line community	• Variety of procurement practices among states • Need to coordinate to avoid duplication of this subcommittee and those looking at socioeconomic policies and preferences • Time/resource constraints and difficulty in collaborating virtually • Uncertainty about legislator/senior executive propensity to seek NASPO input • Need to coordinate the final whitepaper to get state procurement official consent to content before formal distribution

Recommendations for Initial Team
Use NASPO Community to generate interest in this subcommittee. Representatives from procurement offices who 1) have recent experience identifying impacts from ill-advised procurement practices or who have removed procurement barriers; or 2) would like to participate in the research and drafting of a whitepaper of this nature.

Figure 2-1. Opportunity Summary.

Context Shapes Opportunities: The Challenge of Project Management

Much of what procurement offices do is very project specific. Traditional procurement projects like requests for proposals do not necessarily lend themselves to systematic application of a rubric to find gaps in performance, assemble a team, conduct analysis and measurement, identify options, select a course of action, and implement. When a customer has a procurement requirement, any opportunity for improvement has to be aligned with the project's objective.

There are opportunities to improve procurement processes even in a project context. Before we tell the Idaho story, though, we will look a little closer at one of our stakeholders—professional project managers. This is a category of user that illustrates the different ways that clients sometimes see the world and how that perspective may shape opportunities for improvement. Just like familiarity with assumptions and values of clients guides the actions of consultants, as internal consultants, procurement professionals should have a basic familiarity with other professionals' values with whom they closely work.

Project management as a recognized discipline evolved from systems management in the 1940s to being practiced as project management in the late 1950s and 1960s, largely in the aerospace and defense industries. By the late 1960s, aerospace, defense, construction, engineering, and high tech companies had implemented project management methodologies.[14]

Project Managers (or PMs) are invaluable team members on many procurements. Construction projects have project managers. Information technology procurements often are managed by PMs. The Project Management Institute (PMI) and its flagship publication, *A Guide to the Project Management Body of Knowledge* (PMBOK®), frame the essential competencies in project management.

PMI has an accreditation program for project managers. The popularity of the Project Management Professional (PMP) accreditation has grown. The certification is based on an examination grounded in topics that appear in the PMBOK®.

The PMBOK® consists of various knowledge areas. The body of knowledge has fairly comprehensive coverage of the procurement process, because project managers traditionally either work for companies who are sellers, or they procure services and commodities (as buyers) in support of a project. The PMBOK® procurement knowledge area covers procurement planning, the development of statements of work, the solicitation of proposals, evaluation of proposals, contract types, pricing and estimating, and contract management.

Project management professions are also taught about the availability of sole source procurements, but perhaps not with the ease in governments that noted expert Dr. Harold Kerzner (2009) suggests projects may need. This is an example of where the project management body of knowledge designed for generality (for both public and commercial project management) may cause some confusion if stakeholders are not assembled early on to understand constraints imposed by law and policy.

The body of knowledge also covers quality management systems. Kerzner (2009) describes the history of quality management, from the growth of the discipline in Japan after World War II, to the writings of W. Edwards Deming and Joseph Juran. Kerzner also discusses the various iterations of quality management systems: Total Quality Management (TQM), ISO 9001,[15] Six Sigma, and Lean principles largely derived from Japanese manufacturing processes. IT project management books describe another approach to quality: process capability. The Capability Maturity Model Integrated (CMMI) is an assessment model widely used by the Department of Defense in software and derived from a model developed at Carnegie Mellon University.

Others may disagree, but what is striking to me about some project management textbooks is the linear nature of their description of the project management process. While quality management systems employ a variety of thought expansion (divergence) and focusing (convergence) tools and techniques—some of which we cover in this book—the project management literature in some respects is thin on its treatment of collaborative tools.

Instead, schedule appears to be a central focus of professional project management. Kerzner (2009) comprehensively discusses scheduling and use of various techniques to control a project: use of network diagrams, identification of dependencies, definition of slack time, estimating project and activity duration, PERT, and critical path planning.

Kerzner's book does not explain how to use the collaborative tools, however. Indeed, Kerzner counsels in his planning chapter that more than 60 minutes devoted to brainstorming may generate ideas that are "science fiction."[16] While brainstorming is mentioned in various parts of Kerzner's textbook, his treatment may signal a predisposition of some PMs about the utility of some of these tools. Varying perspectives may require adjustments in thinking by procurement professionals about approaches to continuous improvement that touch PM offices.

Project managers may use questions differently also. While opportunities to improve involve asking questions broadly addressing customer needs, project management tools use more targeted questions oriented around objectives, schedules, and task dependencies. What is the scope and is it realistic? Who are the stakeholders and how will they be involved? Can the project be finished within the desired timeframe? What resources are required? What are the risks? And have there been similar projects that we can learn from?[17] What results will you produce? What constraints must you satisfy? What assumptions are you making? What can go wrong?[18] These are all critical questions in project planning and execution. But they may involve perspectives slightly different from those of a procurement professional embarking on an initiative to improve the procurement process.

The best advice may be to get familiar with the likely project management delivery techniques for the industry involved in your procurements. Some information technology publications describe newer project management approaches to software development—Extreme and Agile programming are examples. Agile and Extreme Programming are iterative software development methods used in projects having less certainty about requirements and solutions. They are used where there is likelihood of change requiring application of more tacit knowledge and learning (with the client) during the project. Some of those publications explicitly say that scope is sacrificed for schedule. "Building a product the right way still sounds like a laudable goal, but—let's face it—what really matters today is building it fast."[19] Agile and Extreme Programming are iterative development approaches requiring close involvement of customers as requirements are clarified. The PM approaches reflect the fluidity of requirements development and place schedule at the forefront.

PM professionals often work for using agencies that procurement supports. This summary admittedly thin-slices the literature and borders on engaging in overgeneralization. But it illustrates how some professionals and clients may see continuous improvement of processes somewhat differently. Obviously, the identification of opportunities must account for these client perspectives. How does a team reconcile the differences? Open a dialogue. Perhaps show this part of the chapter to the team's project management members and discuss it with them. Are there really differences in perspectives? It is important to trade perspectives. Neither can succeed without the other.

The PMBOK® notes that procurement is relevant to several project management phases. There is a shared interest in improvement of processes, but be prepared for resistance when working on process improvements that may implicate schedule. Moreover, some PMs may have a predilection in favor of tasks and away from the behavioral elements of collaboration like taking time for team development.

Consultants are taught to balance approaches using behavioral science and those that emphasize objective data (like a schedule).[20] Procurement professionals can borrow from those suggestions. They find common ground with PMs in terms of improving processes, but procurement professionals must remain sensitive to differences in perspectives.

Still, there are opportunities. The state of Idaho tackled an improvement initiative that went to the core of the procurement process: It also faced some resistance from information technology professionals. Idaho fundamentally changed the RFP process in procurement of services.

Idaho Tackles Its Request for Proposals Process

"We realized that something was wrong here and we wanted to do something different." Mark Little, Idaho State procurement manager.

In 2008, the Idaho Division of Purchasing began asking questions to improve the success rate and decrease the risks associated with service procurements. With these procurements approaching approximately 80 percent of the state's strategic spend, there was increasing risk from not selecting the right experts (contractors) to get acceptable service over the contract life. Evaluators with far less expertise and experience than the vendors were spending more and more time in proposal evaluations.

The solution came from an unexpected place. Arizona State University's Performance-Based Studies Research Group (PBSRG) had developed a best value "Performance Information Procurement System" (PIPS) that had proved to be extremely successful in construction projects. PIPS identifies the vendor and vendor personnel best suited for the project (the experts) while providing an environment that permits them to be efficient and succeed without increasing costs. Mark had seen a presentation describing the new approach and thought PIPS had potential for use in applications other than construction.

The overall process is performance-based and permits the state to concisely define goals and let suppliers apply their expertise in fashioning a specific approach to the work. Service contract metrics and milestones are tracked over the life of the contract.

Two primary hurdles arose: 1) could the state of Idaho overlay this process on top of state statutes and make it work in the non-construction public arena, and 2) could the state engage the new process throughout the state and with the vendor community? The Attorney General's office helped answer the first question. PIPS could be implemented consistent with state law.

Mark has been candid about challenges in using the process. PIPS is a major process change and has met with some resistance from agency users and contract managers because of the perceived risk. The purchasing staff and agency evaluators had to be trained in the new process. In the IT area, project managers had to surrender some of the control they traditionally exercised in projects. Nevertheless, Idaho has used the PIPS system for several large procurements: a statewide university student health insurance system, inmate medical care, a major food services program, an asset management program, a child-support receipting provider, and an automated motor vehicles business management system.

Despite expected challenges in implementing a new procurement model, Bill Burns, the administrator of the Purchasing Office, is sold on PIPS. In his words: "This may be the most significant process improvement that I have seen in state government."

Just Get Started!

The examples in this chapter are different in scale and context, but they involve the same basic principles. They use artful questions and customer engagement to identify opportunities.

The best tool for finding opportunities for continuous improvement—even incremental improvement in procurement projects— is the question. Most of the time, a collaborative effort will be required to address the issues. To start the process, summarize the opportunity and what is known about its origins, the potential benefits and value, the costs, and supporting and blocking forces. Opportunity summaries can also help begin the process of team coalescence, focus, and collaborative participation. Most important, though, is to just get started.

Questions, along with purpose, are the core integrating concepts for continuous improvement and successful project management. They play a central role in molding the team, performing analyses, making decisions, managing change, learning, and leading laterally. "The seeds of change are implicit in the first questions we ask."

3   **Learn from the Stars**

This book is full of stars! Purchasing stars can provide an experienced view of the tools of continuous improvement. They may have defined best practices, developed relevant benchmarks, or solved the same problems that a team is tackling today.

——◆——

I just had a feeling. When I walked into the purchasing office in the city of Thornton, Colorado, I felt taken care of. Inside the door, there was a statement of values displayed in a prominent location: the city's guiding values. There were two people there to greet me for my meeting with the purchasing manager. They invited me to have a seat in the waiting area that was outfitted with a chair and a table. The second floor was full of places to network, to sit and wait. It was difficult to describe just the way I felt, but the place seemed put together well. The city of Thornton held the Outstanding Agency Accreditation Achievement Award (OA4), the performance excellence accreditation of NIGP—The Institute for Public Procurement. And it showed.

Susan White, the city's purchasing manager, had worked for the city of Thornton for over 20 years. She completed the last NIGP OA4 application. According to Susan, the OA4 award helped affirm the city's purchasing office as an organization recognized by its peers. "We all suffer criticism from internal customers. OA4 helps establish stature among our peers," Susan told me. For other professionals, Susan's city and organizations like hers give us clues about what excellence means.

According to Tina Borger, NIGP's Executive Director of Finance & Administration, 15 accreditations were issued in 1999, the first year that NIGP awarded the OA4. The city of Thornton, Colorado, was one of only four who had maintained a continuous accreditation since then. Do you think you might get some good ideas from them?

I use the telescope as the visual metaphor for remembering to look for best practices. Think about it. Telescopes are used for looking far away. To me, the telescope is a visual metaphor for looking far away at the practices and experiences in other organizations and finding the "stars."

The essence of this chapter is to ask, "Has anyone else encountered this opportunity or solved this problem before? What can I learn from their experience?" Throughout, this book uses stories to illustrate the power of learning from success stories. Some of these stories may provide ideas about how to improve your team or organization. In your own organizations, find someone who just seems to have the capacity to get things done in the face of resistance. Take them to lunch and learn from them. What best practices did they use and why? Did they use benchmarks?

The accreditation and awards programs of NIGP, the National Association of State Procurement Officials (NASPO) and the National Procurement Institute (NPI) are good sources for finding success stories. The awards and accreditation recipients can provide insight into how you might improve.

NIGP, NPI, and NASPO Awards and Accreditation

The NIGP Outstanding Agency Accreditation Achievement Award (OA4) program establishes a body of standards and an accreditation program that exemplify a solid purchasing program.

The OA4 criteria place heavy emphasis on strategic planning: the role of the procurement officer and the use of measurable outcomes in the organization's strategic planning. The OA4 criteria also look at continuity of operations, the chief procurement officer's role in emergency operations, organization structure—whether the chief procurement officer is strategically placed in the organization—delegation and training programs and the separation of functions commonly associated with sound internal controls. Other criteria include use of standards and specifications, professional development, use of best practices, participation in cooperative procurement, and the use of technology. Agencies must satisfy 100 out of 132 criteria to receive the OA4.

The crème de la crème of process excellence is NIGP's Pareto award, given to an OA4-accredited agency that undergoes a rigorous program of self-evaluation and validation by an independent, on-site peer review in the areas of leadership, strategic planning, customer focus, process management, technology and IT management, and performance improvement. Given only eight times in the last decade, Central Puget Sound Regional Transit Authority (Sound Transit) was the 2012 Pareto Award winner. [1]

The National Procurement Institute (NPI), the public procurement affiliate of the Institute for Supply Management, has similar criteria in its award program. AEP award recipients are evaluated on their procurement practices, ethical guidelines, and information provided to companies about doing business with their entity. The criteria also look at whether the entity has a continuous improvement program consisting of certain elements: recent focus group meetings with stakeholders, customer service surveys, and use of formal vendor-training workshops.

Like NIGP's OA4 program, the Achievement of Excellence in Procurement (AEP) award promotes centralization of procurement authority, an effective organizational structure, and use of automation and e-procurement. The AEP further promotes effectiveness through use of cooperative purchasing and procurement cards, as well as socially responsible, environmentally sensitive procurement. AEP also has specific award standards that relate to professional certification and training. Both NASPO and NIGP also have annual awards for procurement excellence and innovation. NASPO's George Cronin Award criteria, for example, include innovation, transferability to other states, reductions in cost and improvements in efficiency, and improvement of customer service. Many of the stories in this book were discovered from those awards.

The "stars" can guide you through use of the tools of organizational improvement. Some of the tools discussed in this book are sophisticated and best learned from someone who has used them. Discussions with those who are known for excellence or have successfully improved their organizations help you navigate through some of the complexity and develop an overall approach to a project or continuous improvement initiative.

You learn on two dimensions from stars who have succeeded. For those looking to streamline their payables process, Punta Gorda, Florida, achieved deep smarts about procurement cards that could be invaluable. But you also can learn about how to run a great project, assemble and achieve with an extraordinary team, and crack the code of successful change management and implementation. Punta Gorda learned not only about procurement card solutions, they showed they could run a continuous improvement project.

This book highlights ways to identify other offices or people who have had similar opportunities and challenges. No solution or project can be ported over "as is" though. This chapter looks at best practices and its cousin, benchmarking, considerations in their use, and some ideas about how to use them in tackling your own problems or realizing your own opportunities.

Find and Learn from Best Practices

In social research, one of the scientific terms used to identify vital behaviors critical to change is *positive deviance*. Positive deviants are practices that are outliers in the sense that they succeeded where others failed. By studying their vital behaviors, and recovery behaviors when things do not go so well, behaviors can be identified that set them apart.[2] Then practices can be piloted in a mini-test to see if the ideas are valid. Thomas Linley's Ohio multifunctional-copier project is an example. By studying his and other stories in this book, one can learn what they do that works, how they get ideas and results to stick, in short, how they succeed.

Thomas Linley and the other exceptional people in this book are "stars." No doubt you know others. Some of the stars in this book were found using the accreditations and awards by NIGP, NASPO, and NPI.

In other cases, the online NIGP Nsite discussion forum and NASPO Community Network contained discussions that created leads to finding stars. Those discussion groups are both great resources. The Punta Gorda story in chapter 1 was discovered from an NIGP online discussion about process maps that Marian Pace responded to. The chapter 9 story about Oklahoma's brown-bag training was found using the NASPO network.

Looking for Best Practices in Public Procurement Online Communities

In October 2011, a procurement professional posted on the "Purchissues" discussion list (now changed to Nsite, NIGP's online discussion community) the following inquiry, "I was wondering what type of performance measures your purchasing department may use to provide various information and statistics to the finance director, city manager, etc."

The responses identified the person's contact information so there could be further follow-up. Among the ideas shared were a reluctance to "count widgets" as a performance measure and the importance of refocusing on activities that are easy to identify as having real value to the government.

Examples of measures were provided by community members: savings resulting from the formal bidding process and the method of computing savings; numbers of vendors registered online; numbers of requisitions; numbers of solicitations; numbers of purchase orders; numbers of contracts; numbers of blanket purchase agreements and orders; total credit card expenditures; number of credit card transactions, which demonstrates efficiencies from reduced purchase order processing; average transaction value of procurement card purchases; and revenue from surplus property sales.

These kinds of discussion lists provide evidence of practices that might warrant further investigation.

Teams can find best practices by looking in places they might not expect. For example, information technology is a discipline that often intersects with procurement in public entities. Project management professionals share concerns about project cost, project scope, and schedule. In complex information technology projects, project managers often define requirements, help procurement professionals run the procurement, and then manage the resulting contract. In recent years, as systems have gotten more complex, there has been more and more attention to management of these projects.

The California Office of Systems Integration has teams that manage a variety of large information technology systems. The next story takes place outside of traditional procurement offices but touches procurement in significant ways.

The California Office of Systems Integration

Looking for best practices? There's a web site for that!

The California Office of Systems Integration (OSI), an office within the California Health and Human Services Agency, maintains a best practices website that has won national acclaim.[3] The office consists of teams of personnel who manage large information technology implementations. Their mission is to procure, manage, and deliver technology systems that support delivery of health and human services to Californians. OSI information technology projects include an Unemployment Insurance Modernization (UIMOD) project, Case Management, Information and Payrolling System (CMIPS II) project, Electronic Benefit Transfer (EBT) project, the state's Statewide Automated Welfare System (SAWS) project, Statewide Fingerprint Imaging System, and the Child Welfare Services/Case Management System (CWS/CMS).

The Center for Digital Government (CDG) and the National Association of Chief Information Officers (NASCIO) have both recognized OSI for developing a unique web-based best-practices framework for project management and acquisition services. The CDG awarded OSI the nationally recognized Digital Government Achievement Award for its management of large IT projects in the government-to-government category. NASCIO announced OSI as a finalist in the "Enterprise IT Management Initiatives" category for deployment and use of its own unique brand of project management tools and processes.

On OSI's best practices webpage, other governments can find a host of best practices including:

- Visual depictions and descriptions of the project management lifecycle—initiating, planning, executing, and closing—as well as the system development lifecycle from requirements definition through system decommission;
- A model project charter with instructions;
- Model governance structures with roles defined for various project teams and personnel: executive steering committee, project sponsor, project director, project manager, acquisition specialist, procurement team, contract manager, organization change manager, and independent project oversight and independent verification and validation (IV&V) contractors;
- Visual depictions and descriptions of the acquisition life cycle—acquisition planning, contracting, product acceptance—including templates (with instructions) for IT procurement, evaluation planning, and templates for quality management, deliverable management, and overall contract management;
- Measurements and metrics for assessing project management and contract performance;
- A contract-management plan used to manage contractors on projects that describes how deliverables are approved, contract deficiencies are addressed, and contract amendments are processed;
- A lessons-learned template for performing project assessment;
- A risk-management template with instructions;
- A knowledge-management data item description for use in solicitations that requires the contractor to develop a knowledge transfer and training plan having prescribed elements; and
- A variety of other documents useful in IT projects.

Kim Heartley-Humphrey is the Chief of OSI's Acquisitions & Contracting Services Division. When you drill deep into a world-class organization like OSI, you'll strike it rich in creativity.

Kim had a challenge. It came from OSI's Director and Chief Deputy Director. They knew that some state agencies were asking vendors to conduct pilot demonstrations of information technology systems, often the only way to get a true picture of industry capabilities. The directors wanted to use demonstrations in OSI. However, demonstrations tend to be a touchy issue among procurement professionals—they can give unfair advantages to some companies. Still, Kim agreed to explore the issue.

In a prior department, Kim had conducted requests for information (RFI) and had vendors perform demonstrations. But she also had one bad experience where a company filed a request under California's public records law to get access to information a competitor had provided in connection with a demonstration. In addition, the programs supported by OSI are federally funded, and the federal department with oversight responsibility had strong feelings about transparency and competitive processes even in the market research phase before issuance of competitive procurements.

(continued on next page)

The California Office of Systems Integration, cont'd.

A federal grant to the department gave Kim an opportunity. They received a $1.5 million grant from the federal Administration for Children and Families for a study of interoperability, or the feasibility of "horizontal integration" of data. State departments within Kim's agency have information in silos, largely the result of years of evolution of IT systems starting with older legacy systems that did not permit much sharing of data between separate state systems. A grant of $1.5 million would only scratch the surface in terms of eventual functionality that could take upwards of hundreds of millions of dollars. But demonstrating proof of concept is important. The key question: Does the state of current technology permit the department's system achieve horizontal integration of data?

Kim designed an approach, what she calls a "request for demonstration" (RFD).[4] The RFD essentially is a competitive solicitation that gives companies the opportunity to be selected to showcase their solutions and prove that the concept works. The RFD process mirrors a competitive procurement with discussions, description of the basis for award, and disclosure of the evaluation factors and their weighting.

Kim incorporated learning from her previous experience with similar demonstrations. She included explicit language that permitted responding companies to designate selected portions of their responses as proprietary and confidential under the California public records law. Otherwise, companies would only provide vanilla responses with little useful information.

The RFD also expressly stated that companies participating in the no-cost demonstration would not be precluded from future solicitations and/or contracts that may address the issue of interoperability. This provision solved the concerns by companies that those selected to provide demonstrations might be deemed to have an organizational conflict of interest, precluding involvement in a later project. That exclusion wouldn't be good for the state.

The RFD is a true win-win. Apart from some travel expenses, there is no cost to the state for the demonstrations. And OSI will have rich information that can be applied if a full-scale interoperability project is ever funded. The potential benefit to the country is huge if the concept of data sharing and interoperability can be shown to be achievable. Families and state staffs will not suffer through duplicative data entry. IT companies potentially win also. They could be one of a handful of vendors who are selected to present the proof of concept at a national symposium on data sharing and interoperability—selected by the state of California, no less.

Kim is sold on the RFD process. "We are trying to encourage vendor dialogue. We want their participation. But there needs to be structure and trust." OSI's request for demonstration promises to do just that.

Once a "star" like Kim Heartley-Humphrey is identified as one whose lessons may be relevant to an opportunity or problem, the context has to be understood. Organizations may be operating in an overarching culture that is significantly different. Laws and regulations vary. There is an unfortunate tendency to draw conclusions about reasons (or causes) from a complex situation without accounting for differing circumstances. When there are multiple dimensions to a problem, teams have to account for the fact that outcomes often depend on the circumstances.[5]

The stories in this book attempt to find overarching lessons of general relevance. One often-cited business theorist and Harvard professor, Chris Argyris, coined the term *double-loop learning* to describe two dimensions of learning. Many professionals are good at problem solving and task completion—single-loop learning. Single-loop learning focuses on the substance or task, monitoring the progress of a project to see what is learned as it proceeds and making adjustments periodically. Responding to vendor questions, revising terms and conditions in solicitations, aligning an evaluation spreadsheet with revisions to solicitations, and modification of a sourcing strategy are all task-based and associated with the process of single-loop learning.

This book is about double-loop learning. It goes behind the substantive project lessons and culls the broader lessons: making the team more effective, planning for change, and learning from the missteps, among others. These lessons are transferable: find the back-story for why the project succeeded and determine how it is relevant to your project.

Benchmarking against the "Best in Class" and Yourself

Benchmarking is a related issue. Benchmarking is defined by NIGP as "[t]he act of measuring a process, service, or product against the characteristics of the recognized leaders in the given area of review; a study, review, or process whereby a procurement organization identifies world-class organizations with which to compare its practices, policies and performance outcomes. An organization's performance is judged against selected criteria from other organizations deemed 'best in class.'"[6]

Sound Transit, for example—who operates the buses, light rail and commuter trains in the Seattle metropolitan area—is "best in class." Sound Transit won NIGP's ultimate award, the Pareto Award, given to only to eight government entities in the past ten years.

Xerox is credited with first using benchmarking in the early 1980s as a pillar of its quality management program. The American Society of Quality characterizes benchmarking as a quality management system on the same par as TQM, Six Sigma, ISO 9000, and Lean. Quality professionals define benchmarking as "a structured process for comparing your organization's work practices to the best similar practices you can identify in other organizations and then incorporating these best ideas into your own processes."[7]

A benchmarking study is a formal process that requires significant effort and commitment of resources. A benchmarking initiative requires a purpose and defined scope of the effort, assembly of cross-functional teams, and study of the processes under investigation. With regard to collection and analysis of information relevant to benchmarking, the team would:

- Identify other organizations that may have best practices.
- Collect information directly from those organizations, information that both describes and measures processes where available. This may require interviews and even site visits.
- Compare the team's data, both descriptive and quantitative, to the organization used as a benchmark.

- Determine gaps between the team's performance measurements and those of the "best in class" organizations studied.
- Determine the differences in practices that caused the gaps.[8] McCue and Pitzer (2005) noted that at the time their book was published there was no agreement on benchmarks for public procurement.[9] The common definition of "benchmark" does not just mean the use of precise metrics though. NIGP is moving toward development of principles and practice standards that will serve as benchmarks for "best in class" organizations.[10] They include practice standards for, among other things, performance-based contracting, cooperative procurement, ethics, performance measurement and metrics, spend analysis, and sustainable procurement practices. These standards are peer reviewed and can point the way for a procurement organization.

In many respects, criteria for the NIGP, NPI, and NASPO accreditations and awards also serve as practice benchmarks of "best in class" procurement organizations. Best practices can be investigated by digging into the way organizations have met the criteria of accreditation programs. Agencies do not have to satisfy all criteria—there are over 100 in both programs—so some preliminary research is needed with similar agencies to see which of the criteria they met. Many of the applications are digitally recorded in ways that make sharing easier.

The Denver School District's OA4 application is an example. It included an outsourcing study of its waste management program. The district ultimately decided to use an intergovernmental agreement with the city and county of Denver to handle its recycling program. This project was a "star," but not all accreditation applications would have outsourcing examples.

Formal benchmarking studies ultimately lead to the analysis of the gaps between organizational measurements. One complicating factor in procurement offices, for example, could be the effect of differing legal structures, varying approaches to centralization and small purchase thresholds, and the absence of good data. Yet, even though quantitative comparisons are challenging, there still is significant value in looking at the practices of excellent organizations.

Benchmarks can also be internal to an organization, even though benchmarks traditionally have been thought to mean the comparison of an organization's performance to measurements from an external source. Often though, in the early development of performance management systems, the organization's own historical performance is used as a "baseline" from which to evaluate future performance or targets against which an organization measures improvement.[11]

The Colorado Division of Finance and Procurement used internal benchmarking. From 2002 to 2005, the division consisted of the Office of the State Controller, State Purchasing Office, Office of the State Architect, and Central Collections Services (who collected on a portfolio of over $500 million in debts owed to the state). Some clients were frustrated with the length of time required to route and approve contracts. A number of initiatives were undertaken—e.g., adjusting central approval thresholds and pre-approving contract forms—to reduce the volume and improve performance. The statutory structure requiring contract approval by the Colorado State Controller was rather unique compared to other states, so comparing performance to them would not have been meaningful. However, a prior fiscal year's performance in Colorado served as a useful baseline against which to measure later performance and progress towards improvement.

The benchmarking of time to complete requests for proposals (RFP) and invitations for bids is another case in point, much like the Colorado contract example. On NIGP's discussion community, a purchasing agent posted a topic. "I am looking for benchmark survey data on the average amount of time it takes your agency to award a formal bid or RFP (request for proposals) in terms of the number of (business) days to award from the time you receive specifications/scope of services in Purchasing to award by your governing board." An agency responded that its historical time to process invitations for bids was 60–90 days. Requests for proposals took 90–120 days. There was a qualification in that response: "Depending on complexity, of course."

Indeed, another reason for variations in answers to this question might have been the legal requirement relating to publication of solicitations. The time required by law to formally advertise varies among jurisdictions and will directly affect the number of days between publication of the solicitation and award. However, an agency's tracking its own time for average completion in each category still provides useful information. It can serve as a baseline from which to measure the improvement in performance over time.

In the literature, one encounters a fair amount of skepticism about putting too many resources into large benchmarking studies. The conditions in one organization, the way that measurements are done, and the nature of the process in that organization may be entirely different. Transaction cycle times in an organization with large proportions of small, simple transactions may have a different strategic importance compared to other organizations where customer intimacy is more important to its strategy. There, fewer, more complex transactions may be the norm. Transaction processing time may be less important.

Do not latch onto benchmark numbers without analysis. Remember also that the metrics are not the point. The practices are the focal point. Adopt best practices that lead to great results.

Use the Stars to Help Illuminate Systems Thinking

A telescope has two ends. The traditional way to gaze at the stars is to look though the small end. But there is value to reversing the perspective by looking through the large end as well. You see the world differently. I use the wrong end of the telescope as my visual metaphor for keeping an eye on overall system performance.

The "stars" featured in this book in many respects are big picture thinkers. Peter Senge in his classic *The Fifth Discipline* (1990, 2006) popularized systems thinking. Ronald Heifetz (2009), the Harvard professor credited with developing the theory of adaptive leadership, also emphasizes the importance of systems thinking. Heifetz uses "go to the balcony" as his metaphor for keeping diagnostic when solving problems, keeping perspective "above the dance floor" while in the throes of problem solving.

Exceptional managers often have rich intuitions about complex systems that they cannot explain.[12] They may sense the dangers of eroding goals or loss of purpose, or may have dealt with the overemphasis on performance measurement at the expense of deeper problems. Big picture thinkers have vision and an ability to see the whole.

In Chapter 1, we saw the central role of purpose and how it helps orient the team. Keeping an eye on the purpose includes systems thinking. One of the technical terms used when a process is made perfect at the expense of other objectives in an organization is "sub-optimization." In Senge's world of systems thinking, his name for the concept is "compensating feedback."[13] So, for example, a procurement card program could establish a set of perfect controls with purchasing approvals required from three separate supervisors. Those reviews may achieve perfection in the internal controls, but unintended consequences can arise. Other work may suffer because of the time needed for complying with the policy. Or the existence of multiple approvers over time can encourage loafing if each reviewer believes another will catch errors. The adverse effects of unintended consequences often have a delayed effect; they are not be known until long after the practice that causes them.

Star performers can help you anticipate these types of patterns. If the patterns about unintended consequences are known, they can be avoided with proper project strategy. Lessons about systems often involve application of tacit knowledge not found in any book, and having experienced team members helps avoid unwanted consequences for the system as a whole. The lessons are heavily dependent on context; it often takes experience to learn the lessons. While you are learning lessons from these and other stars around you, find out what they learned about the system performance.

For example, were there concerns in Punta Gorda about enabling procurement cards for small purchases but sacrificing potential cost savings that might have been achieved by aggregating purchases from a single vendor? In some instances, the greater autonomy and efficiency that is granted by procurement cards to users can conflict with objectives of reducing pricing through aggregation. This could be an example of Senge's "shifting the burden," as when one solution to a problem can eventually place greater burdens on other aspects of the system. Other systems patterns—what Senge calls archetypes—include the relationship between process and delay, unbalanced commitment of resources, focus on short-term fixes at the expense of long-term solutions, and the "tragedy of the commons" caused by mismanagement of common resources shared by the members of an enterprise.[14]

Call me wrong, but people who are good at leading successful projects often have an innate sense of systems impact. The possible systems impact illuminates who the stakeholders will be that must be involved. System impacts also are key to identifying potential project risks and forecasting where the resistance to change may come from. Find out from the stars how they looked at the system in their projects.

What to Ask the Stars

Learn from others who have tackled similar kinds of challenges. Find the common themes in others' experiences with continuous improvement. Go read the OA4 and AEP applications of procurement offices near you. Call recipients of innovation awards to learn from them. Talk with leaders in those offices and teams about the context for their success and what they might see as differences in your projects.

And don't forget others in your own organization. Other offices and professionals have dealt with centralization/decentralization issues. Finance offices long have struggled with the balance between internal controls and operational efficiency. Human resource professionals constantly face challenges from the aging workforce and other knowledge-transfer issues caused by employee transition. While they may not have the task knowledge necessary for procurement projects, they often have insight into change challenges relevant to your team's efforts.

Several years ago, when I was in the Colorado Division of Finance and Procurement, we wanted to do some division-wide strategic planning. I had never led such a session, nor had others in the division. But in the Division of Central Services, which had the statewide fleet and document management programs, there was an employee who was exceptional at leading group facilitation and brainstorming. He had been used by the department's executive director for senior leadership planning sessions. Needless to say, we enlisted him as well, and we all learned from him. You may have stars like that in other parts of your organization.

It's unlikely that you can graft someone else's solution wholesale onto your opportunity or problem. Moreover, be wary of the *halo effect*, that is, the tendency to use positive outcomes in organizations as evidence for certain propositions advocated as timeless truths without sufficient research or accounting for the role of luck.[15] Still, even critics of overeager acceptance of best practices find value in studying the decision processes of those who have encountered similar problems in complex systems.

Organizations, teams, and their projects are different. Here are some questions you can ask a star that can help get to the deeper lessons in any continuous improvement project.

- When was the time right for the opportunity? Was there anything in the organizational culture that either promoted or hindered moving forward on the project?
- Did they learn valuable lessons from anyone else? What one or two considerations of context influenced the execution of their project? How did the particular circumstances affect the expected outcomes, perhaps in ways that were unexpected?
- How did they decide who was on the team? Who was not on the team but should have been? How did they overcome resistance by critical but busy members to join the team?
- Did they use any particular project management approach? Was a formal charter used? What did they wish they had done that they hadn't done? How did they assign and control completion of tasks?
- What worked and what didn't in terms of project communications? Can you have copies of the project communication documents that were used?
- Did they identify the right stakeholders and have them involved in the appropriate way?
- How did the team reach decisions, both for its routine team activities and the ultimate decision?

- What types of expansion (divergence) or focusing (convergence) tools or techniques were used that were particularly effective to create, study, and select ideas? What were tried but not useful? Why or why not?

- What did they measure, why did they use the measure, and how effective was it?

- What did they see as the primary risks to the project? Did they become realities? What approaches did they find valuable for mitigating, controlling, or transferring risk?

- What stakeholders were the primary sources of resistance? How do they think their project might differ from your project in that regard? What did they do to help stakeholders understand, forecast, and exercise some amount of autonomy over change?

- Were there unintended consequences that they hadn't forecasted, perhaps impacts on other aspects of the system that were not anticipated? How did they respond to those surprises?

- Did they conduct an after-action review? What were the main things they learned in terms of what worked and what could have been done better?

- What other tools or practices were used to make ideas sticky and promote continual learning in the team and about its products?

- What one thing should you do first to start your project?

Talk to the Stars

Well-developed questions can yield a deeper understanding gleaned from purchasing stars' experience with and tacit knowledge about the tools of continuous improvement. Purchasing stars may have solved similar problems, developed relevant benchmarks, or defined best practices. Stars can be found throughout this book, and they are often the recipients of awards from national, state, and local procurement organizations. However, stars can also be found in almost every workplace: they are the ones who always manage to get things done.

4 Step to Their Side Often: Help Mold and Promote the Team

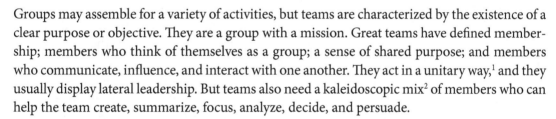

*"Creativity is a lot like looking at the world through a kaleidoscope.
You look at a set of elements, the same ones everyone else sees, but then
reassemble those floating bits and pieces into an enticing new possibility."*

—Rosabeth Moss Kanter

Groups may assemble for a variety of activities, but teams are characterized by the existence of a clear purpose or objective. They are a group with a mission. Great teams have defined membership; members who think of themselves as a group; a sense of shared purpose; and members who communicate, influence, and interact with one another. They act in a unitary way,[1] and they usually display lateral leadership. But teams also need a kaleidoscopic mix[2] of members who can help the team create, summarize, focus, analyze, decide, and persuade.

Teams can have indirect value apart from achievement of specific tasks, however. Where change-management challenges exist, for example, problem solving by a group increases the chances of acceptance of the outcome because the group develops a sense of ownership and belonging.[3]

The title of this chapter is derived from one of my favorite authors, William Ury. William Ury was one of the original authors of the classic negotiation book, *Getting to Yes*. In his subsequent book about difficult negotiations, *Getting Past No*, Ury counseled, "Step to Their Side." It was a reminder of the importance of empathy, putting oneself in the shoes of another to get their perspective. Empathy essentially means considering the feelings and emotions of others when decisions are made and actions taken. It is central to leadership and effective teams, and the admonition to "step to their side often" is a reminder to be an empathetic, facilitative leader.

In 1965, Bruce Tuckman identified phases in the life cycle of teams: forming, storming, norming, and performing. Adjourning was later added to recognize that team endings and transitions also have to be accounted for. Other authors have used team life cycles as a useful way of looking at effective team behaviors, characteristics, and conditions.[4] A team's beginning, middle, and end serve as a good perspective from which to look at effective teams.

The Right Composition

Research has shown that there are optimum sizes for teams. Teams are most effective when size is limited to between four and seven members, with significant degradation of performance when team size moves into double digits. Potential gains can be offset by process efficiency losses in larger groups.[5]

Group size, however, often is not purely dictated by team process effectiveness. Some groups are chosen to get a number of representative perspectives and have a size that may exceed the optimal size of teams. In other kinds of groups, the need for information exchange among constituents (like between different departments) can lead to large team sizes. In major change initiatives, successful change depends on buy-in from stakeholders, and having members representing the various constituencies may be important. Subgroups and interlocking teams can be used to accomplish tasks and bring the necessary perspective, with team members fulfilling the role of communicator or collaborator between the groups.

Teams need contribution by technical experts, like user or other functional expertise in a procurement team. But teams also need members who are strong on the interpersonal skills required to facilitate and draw out constructive conflict in team discussions. Teams need members who can effectively use questions to expand the range of ideas and promote group discussion. And some teams need people especially adept at negotiation and persuasion, especially where there are change management considerations or expected challenges dealing with other leaders in an organization. Teams commonly do not suffer from insufficient technical skills. The interpersonal and soft skills more often are the missing ingredients.

So consider both the substantive content and team process needs when recruiting team members. Teams need members who can foster collaboration and build a network to other teams. They also need members strong in planning, following-up, and meeting management. While designated team leaders may fulfill these roles, typically teams need other contributors who can assist with team management activities.

Oregon's WSCA Lodging Services Team: Overcoming Obstacles

Travel-lodging services present unique challenges for state and local governments. While the General Services Administration has favorable pricing, those rates cover only federal employees. Identifying hotels that offer discounted pricing for state employees, however, was manual and time intensive. Moreover, travel was very decentralized with extremely limited cost data; there was little information from which to evaluate state expenditures strategically. To help alleviate this problem, the state of Oregon led a WSCA cooperative effort resulting in the first ever multi-state lodging program. The program provides states with preferential pricing and terms and conditions via a website database that permits travelers to search for lodging by travel destination. In September 2011, Oregon received the George Cronin Gold Award for Procurement Excellence from the National Association of State Procurement Officials for the project.

Tim Hay, a founding member of the State Travel Managers Alliance, was Oregon's project lead for the WSCA lodging project. Tim knew the importance of adding travel experts along with procurement experts on the team. For example, Lenora Kingston, manager of Colorado's travel program, had special expertise in environmentally friendly practices in hotels, a benchmark that permits hotels to be identified as "green" on the database. In addition, the special involvement of members of the travel industry was critical to finding solutions. They helped get the codes necessary to integrate lodging reservations with the global travel system and identified franchisees who would participate in the program.

The team unexpectedly encountered a condition in the hotel industry that required a change in procurement strategy and a mid-course correction during the solicitation. They found that the traditional solicitation methodology requesting that large vendors commit to multi-state pricing was not going to work.

At the pre-proposal conference, the team learned that hotel chains could not commit individual properties to standard contract terms because the hotel industry was so heavily franchised; the properties are independently owned. The team was disappointed, but they immediately started looking for solutions. They realized that hotel booking did not require use of the traditional competitive process; the value of lodging was under the small purchase threshold.

The state of Oregon had "special procurement" authority to accommodate a change in procurement strategy to a Request for Qualification process, a less constraining procurement method.

A team approach often permits more creative outlooks about solutions to problems. This team exemplified the agility that comes with great teams. They had the benefit of having worked together on a prior rental vehicle cooperative procurement. That previous procurement had fewer industry players, which gave the team a way to develop a working approach in a more limited scope procurement.

When Oregon received its Cronin Award, its WSCA lodging website had over 10,000 properties. Qualification requirements placed limits on certain terms like cancellation fees and early departure fees. The hotel industry liked the initiative also; it made working with states much easier. In the words of an industry official, "This was awesome . . . a giant step in the right direction!"

Having teams with virtual collaboration expertise is helpful as well. Many meetings are conducted using Web collaboration tools. When teams move into the post-award phase after the completion of national WSCA-NASPO cooperative procurements, they hold webinars to promote the use of the cooperative contracts. While team members can be added later to assist with the webinars, having someone familiar with the project from its beginning makes the process of contract promotion easier.

One team-performance strategy that should be considered is the use of subgroups when teams are large. The 15-state consortium known as the Western States Contracting Alliance (WSCA) works together to find cooperative procurement opportunities to achieve better value or reduced costs. WSCA eventually grew into its own limited liability company, the WSCA-NASPO Cooperative Purchasing Organization, a subsidiary of the NASPO. WSCA-NASPO state procurement directors approve cooperative purchasing opportunities identified by state sourcing teams. Lead states are selected to conduct the procurement and sourcing teams identified to help the lead state. Other states nationally can "participate" in the procurement.

The 2010–2012 WSCA/Colorado cooperative e-procurement project was initiated by WSCA to acquire an online platform for ordering from WSCA contracts. The e-market part of the procurement was expected to permit ordering by state agencies, institutions of higher education, school districts and local governments. They all used WSCA contracts, but the process of ordering from and managing the contracts largely was manual. The procurement was designed to make other e-procurement capabilities available to states who wanted them, such as electronic bidding. When WSCA launched the project led by the state of Colorado, there were a variety of stakeholders, and the evaluation was complicated.

The core evaluation committee included representatives from a small number of lead and participating states. The evaluation committee size was kept manageably small in order to provide continuity and consistency in the evaluation. Nonvoting advisors were used to gain other perspectives.

For example, John Utterback, the Colorado State Purchasing Director considered local government input very important. A separate focus group was assembled to help WSCA better understand the needs of local governments regarding electronic ordering and sourcing systems. Local governments of various types, locations and sizes met to discuss the utility of these systems. Representatives from the focus group served as nonvoting evaluation-committee members to add the local government perspective to discussions with vendors about electronic catalogs and sourcing systems.

Ideally, team membership is stable,[6] at least in a core group. Reasonably stable teams perform better. They develop a pool of knowledge. They learn how to work among themselves effectively. In the WSCA e-procurement evaluation, nonvoting advisors provided stakeholder perspective while avoiding growth in size of the formal evaluation committee. That way the committee did not have to deal with the challenges of committee member illness or other unavailability that can compromise an evaluation.

In Oregon's WSCA lodging project, the team had continuity. In fact, Tim Hay cited continuity as a strength of his team. They had worked together before on a smaller-scale project and knew each other well.

Despite the value of team stability, teams that have worked together for a long time can align too much in terms of group norms and perspectives. They may be more insular and resistant to innovation. *Groupthink* is a term used to refer to this effect. Team leaders should consider bringing in new members and strive for diversity in perspective using periodic infusion of new talent into a team.

Pay Special Attention to Early Meetings

The early stages of team development are especially important. In some instances, members may already know each other and may have worked together before. However, teams must be sensitive to the needs of new members who haven't gotten to know the other team members.

Pay particular attention to the first meeting.[7] Get a team off on the right step by exposing the team to meeting approaches that are different from the tiresome meetings that everyone has come to expect. Create a realization that the meeting and team can satisfy some of the personal objectives of individual members. Being part of a bonded group having a consequential purpose that only can be achieved by collective action.

Ideally, use face-to-face opportunities to get to know one another. There is a natural shyness in initial meetings among team members, and informal face-to-face gatherings are useful ways to develop the informal relationships necessary for team cohesion. In the WSCA e-procurement project led by Colorado, a special effort was made to assemble evaluation team members from across the United States for an off-site dinner. Sometimes face-to-face meetings are not possible, and teams may use conference calls or virtual tools to hold team meetings. Some online collaboration tools permit uploading photos of meeting participants, one way to make an otherwise impersonal virtual meeting just a little more personal.

Use an icebreaker, even on a virtual team meeting, when there are new members. One effective tool after introductions is a round-robin discussion of a relevant question, such as, "What's a great team experience I've been involved in?" Another might be, "What do I personally hope to get out of this team experience?" Because new members may be reluctant initially to participate, team leaders can break the ice by starting the discussion. Other members can follow to make it safe to share personal experiences and expectations. Even with established groups, use short, informal icebreakers. One way to continue the personal bonding of a group is using a "check in." Everyone is asked to share the one most pressing thing that they are leaving at the "door" of the meeting in order to focus on this particular meeting.

If you are a team leader, model the way in the first meeting. Use open-ended questions such as agenda items to promote engagement. Permit members to express expectations and concerns. Don't inject too much structure early by over-specifying the work or tasks. Define only the ends (not the means) in order to promote creative solutions. And if you happen to be the leader, be cautious about your role. Most team leaders having expertise err on side of trying to influence team performance too much at the expense of facilitated creativity and collaborative engagement.

In general, the first meeting is the time to allow team members to get to know one another, assess the value of the group to them personally, and explore their possible contributions and role. The first meeting ideally uses a "go slow" approach with little risk and an introduction of the opportunities presented to the team. The use of the opportunity summary described in chapter 2, with threshold topics like origins of the opportunity, potential benefits, known costs, supporting factors and apparent barriers—are amenable to an expansive, low-threat discussion in an early meeting. This approach gently introduces a little substance to the group and helps collaboration and joint learning start early.

Early team meetings tend to be different from the recurring information exchange meetings that we are all accustomed to. Meetings for information exchange are built for efficiency. They have agenda items with constrained times for information presentation and discussion. On the other hand, an initial team meeting would have fewer agenda items, meeting objectives that include team familiarization and bonding, and proposed questions as agenda topics. If you lead this kind of meeting, expect more preparation. The best way to characterize the team leader's role in early meetings is "facilitative."

Facilitation and Team Leadership

Facilitation is helping a group advance a discussion in a meaningful way without necessarily contributing to the content of the discussion. Facilitators actively listen. They avoid interruption, remain alert, seek areas of agreement, and demonstrate patience.[8] A facilitator can pose a question, ask for an opinion, clarify and paraphrase to summarize ideas, and bridge among ideas to show their relationship to one another. Facilitators provide positive reinforcement, e.g., "That's a good point," or "Let's make a note of that," and can ask for more specifics. Independent facilitators can be valuable, especially when team leaders are substantive experts and may be at risk of dominating discussions. Every meeting or discussion requires some amount of facilitative leadership.

Teams need leaders who can stay attuned to reading the group, its enthusiasm, attentiveness, interest, and the degree of agreement or satisfaction. These indicators often manifest themselves through nonverbal behaviors as well as in what is said, another advantage to face-to-face meetings. If everyone is interested and involved, then a meeting probably is going well. But boredom, apathy, or low energy may signal a need for a change in process, use of smaller groups, or a shift to a different topic or activity.

If you are leading a team meeting and the group seems stuck, consider using a facilitation tool known as mirroring. Make an observation, e.g., "We seemed to have lost the energy. What do we need to do now?" Or consider asking, "What's happening right now for people?" or "There's a lot of energy, but we seem to have lost productivity and focus. What can we do to get it back?"

One common mistake in facilitation is moving too quickly to fill in silence. Give team members time to consider questions and formulate possible responses. According to Rees (2001), it is not uncommon for seven to ten seconds to go by in groups without anyone responding, but eventually someone will speak up. Facilitators should avoid the temptation to answer their own questions.[9]

Team leaders often move back and forth between this facilitative role and a more directive role where the team expects a leader's intervention. Leaders may have to step out of a facilitative role when dealing with recurring non-constructive conflict between individual members, making some decisions for the team, taking ownership of potential risk in certain actions, or taking the lead in carrying difficult messages to senior leadership.

Tuckman's "storming" phase, the early part of a team's life, is less a discrete period than a characterization of certain team behavior in the early stages of a team's life cycle. In the storming phase, the team exchanges ideas regarding team goals and priorities and whether the team can reach its goals. The team begins to experiment with and develop an effective working approach. The storming phase moves the team towards norming: team leadership and decision making, team roles, and a working approach to conflict.

Nudge Towards Development of Team Norms

Daniel Fisher, of *Getting to Yes* negotiation fame, and his co-author Alan Sharp wrote *Lateral Leadership* (1998, 2009), a book aimed at persons who are not in charge of a team but working with others to get things done. To them, lateral leadership means choosing to help the team by asking relevant questions, offering ideas, and acting in ways that promote team success. Teams need lateral leaders who keep purpose in mind, organize thinking, help the team learn, promote full engagement by everyone, and encourage feedback.

Even though teams may have designated leaders, leadership in this context is largely character-ized as facilitative: moving a team towards achievement of a team purpose while promoting full engagement of team members and integration of their ideas and opinions. Still, team members sometimes look to specific individuals to assume more directive roles in things like steering the team in the right direction, getting stuck teams unstuck, connecting to other parts of the orga-nization, or taking the lead on difficult decisions. The challenge for team leaders is striking the right balance between drawing out everyone's perspective—stepping to the back—and knowing when to move back to the front in assuming a more directive role when appropriate. In fact, this role of the leader is an appropriate topic for a team discussion early in a team's life.

Team leaders cannot guarantee success. But they can help establish the right supportive struc-tures, often spending most of their time in the formative stages establishing the conditions that promote success. Team leaders help the team develop and use constructive norms for working together, scan the environment periodically to assess the need for adjustment, get expertise for the team when needed, revisit the team's method of performing, and otherwise coach the team through its life cycle.[10]

Research has shown that groups can have too little structure in order to be successful.[11] In other cases, two much structure can impede creativity, promote social loafing, and adversely affect intrinsic motivation. The key is finding the right balance.

Using Just Enough Structure: The Colorado Public P-Card Group

"Just enough structure"—but not too much. Like a "soft touch" of leadership, it's another characteristic of a great group.

In 2007, Terri Brustad, the procurement card (P-Card) administrator for the city of Arvada, Colorado, had a problem. In fact, she was encountering a variety of challenges in building and managing the city's P-Card program, but she knew others were facing similar issues. So, Terri sent an email inquiry to Colorado P-Card administrators to assess interest in getting together. Terri learned they were very interested, and the Colorado Public P-Card Group (CPPG) was born.

Terri created a first meeting agenda that everyone could relate to. The city had recently developed a Microsoft Access auditing database to track cardholder audits. Terri asked the audit database administrator to speak at the meeting. The topic was well received, and the CPPG meetings continued. Now, CPPG meets quarterly and features presentations about best practices. In recent CPPG meetings, attendees compared

(continued on next page)

Using Just Enough Structure, cont'd.

incentive rebate structures (offered by the banks) among entities. CPPG also invited the Colorado banks offering procurement card services to give presentations to their members.

The CPPG is an excellent example of how the leaders of great groups find just the right organizational structure. The membership has grown to over 60 entities across Colorado. Terri has remained chair of the CPPG, but she has gotten lots of help. Groups need people who fill the role of "contributors," and Terri found an invaluable partner in Carol Wills, the procurement card administrator/contract specialist from the Academy School District in Colorado Springs.

"Carol was a godsend. She was there at the first meeting and has helped with agenda development and prepared the minutes since the beginning. She and I set the agendas for our meetings."

While Terri and Carol share leadership roles in structuring meetings, they haven't added unnecessary organization. Terri explains, "We don't have bylaws. We don't have a formal leadership structure. We just get together. And people are willing to contribute."

Terri and Carol surveyed CPPG membership in February 2013 to assess topics, revisit meeting logistics given the economic challenges everyone faced, and solicit ideas about meeting frequency. Their five-minute survey asked among other things whether the group wanted to reduce meetings to three times per year as opposed to meeting quarterly. As a testament to CPPG's value to the procurement card administrator community, the majority still wanted quarterly meetings. What's more, they received lots of ideas for future meeting topics, and 11 agencies offered meeting space!

CPPG as a group has thrived. Carol explains, "We still learn something at every meeting. We share ideas, procedures, forms, and we feed from each other." Carol credits Terri's leadership for CPPG's success; Terri credits Carol for her contribution. For my money, they both are lateral leaders who agree, "If it wasn't for the agencies' participation and interest, our group would have stopped meeting a long time ago."

The Colorado Public P-Card Group is not organized in the classic sense, but they do great work. No formal governance structure: just two committed individuals who use just enough structure to contribute to their professional community.

Teams should acknowledge and support team member behaviors that encourage creativity. The creative phase in a team's work gives way eventually to a focusing or narrowing phase where priorities are set and decisions are made. But teams shouldn't move too quickly into narrowing phases while the team works toward establishing its norms for working together.

Work norms are established in various ways. Some teams that are well established can move quickly to the performing stage by applying their historical method of working together. Norms sometimes are imported from other groups where participants have been members.[12] Norms are good agenda items for meetings, so team members can actively discuss these kinds of behavioral expectations.

Norms often are not written down. More often, they are either discussed or exemplified in the historical way in which the team works, evolving norms implicitly as they work together. One way explicitly to raise the issue of norms is a team member's taking the initiative to write a brief list of bullet points about how he or she personally likes to operate in a team. The list is shared with other team members, and they discuss how others' perspectives may be different.

The sharing of work is an especially important norm for a team. If you have a team leadership opportunity, have open discussions about the nature of the contributions that the team needs. Discuss how to divide the work so everyone has a meaningful, manageable contribution. Strive to have all members contribute to the completion of "real work" between meetings. Make shared leadership and coaching an expectation of every team member. In the Oregon disaster preparedness workgroup, Marscy Stone made a point of having all team members lead meetings at various times.

The team also must adopt an approach to decisions. This norm refers not just to the approach to substantive decisions: procurement evaluation and vendor selection, for example. The team also must move beyond substantive decisions and define decision norms for the work of the team. How are meeting dates set? Who has the final say on substantive decisions like what terms and conditions to include in a request for proposals? Who decides how assignments are allocated among team members?

Team Decisions

Typically, there are three decision models used by teams. A designated leader can make the decision after consultation with team members. Sometimes teams make decisions by unanimous consensus, although care should be taken not to rely on unanimity too often. In another model, a democratic one, the team votes with the majority representing the team decision, even though all members may not necessarily agree. The overall objective is to achieve reasonable consensus on actions or decisions that the members of the team can support.

Teams often make decisions on priorities, or even on preferences among competing alternatives. Two popular methods of formally setting priorities or making choices are the impact-effort chart and multi-voting. While they are useful tools, they probably should not be used for routine team decisions.

In the two-dimensional impact-effort chart, alternatives are defined. Then they are discussed and assessed against two criteria: the positive (or negative) impact and the ease of implementation. These are sometimes called four-quadrant matrices, where the various alternatives are ranked in four quadrants from most to least favorable: easy-high impact, difficult-high impact, easy-low impact, and difficult-low impact. The technique is most effective when teams can visually see the two dimensional chart, but it also is simple enough to be reasonably useful during virtual meetings. Figure 8-1 shows a two-dimensional matrix used for assessing risks to a project; the same approach can be used for other team decisions.

Multi-voting, on the other hand, is a voting technique where members individually assign rankings or vote on identified alternatives. In one version, members assign ordinal ratings to alternatives in order of preference, e.g., using the whole numbers 1 through 5, with the lowest ordinal total representing collectively the most preferred alternative. In a variation, members are given a total number of votes that they can cast for any combination of alternatives, in any amount. This method permits members to express the magnitude of their preference by casting multiple votes for a single preference or spreading their votes among several. The highest vote wins. In either case, the team can discuss voting preferences, vote, and then decide whether it wants to vote again after discussion.

(Mock) Lobbying Against Procurement Barriers

Spend your money wisely!

Committees can use multi-voting to focus issues. In 2012, NASPO's President Ron Bell established workgroups to study and write whitepapers on special topics of interest to the profession. One workgroup studied legislative and policy barriers to effective procurement. The 15-member workgroup polled NASPO members nationally to get ideas on the structural issues that stood in the way of world-class procurement. Figure 2-1 is the opportunity summary used by the workgroup.

After polling and research, the team ended up with over 25 potential barriers that included among others: proliferation of inconsistent regulations; absence of centralized procurement authority with adequate discretion; inadequate staffing; widely varying approaches to common contract issues like limitation of liability and protection of confidential information; use of procurement laws to enforce socioeconomic policies; and laws that do not permit the use of best value procurement methods (instead of "low bid").

The workgroup's task was to write a whitepaper that was no longer than three pages. The number of good ideas made that goal impossible, so the workgroup needed a way to select the most important.

The workgroup devised a mock lobbying campaign to have a little fun. It was a disguised multi-voting tool. The instructions said:

1. You are a lobbyist for the Public Procurement Profession, trying to promote effective procurement practices. You are lobbying legislators/state executives on how to eliminate obstacles to effective procurement.

2. You have a limited budget! You have only $100 you can spend. Allocate your budget to the lobbying themes (described in the spreadsheet) anyway you like, e.g., all $100 in one, none in others, splits among some.

3. The spreadsheet has places where you can add other lobbying objectives in addition to the themes already identified. Please state the objective as if you were talking to a legislator/executive about what they should do. Remember to budget for it!

4. Vote on the specific advocacy ideas by spending your money. Spend it wisely!

The votes were collected and tabulated. Some team members had spread their votes evenly among four or five ideas. Others put a sizeable chuck of the $100 in votes on a single procurement barrier.

The votes and tabulations were entered into an Excel spreadsheet and conditional formatting used (more about conditional formatting in chapter 6) to highlight with colors the range of individual preferences and the consolidated preferences when votes were combined. The results were distributed and a conference call scheduled to discuss them.

In the end, the workgroup used the votes to shape the content of the NASPO briefing paper, *Meeting the Challenges of World-Class Procurement*.[13] The workgroup decided to change the focus from *barriers* to the more positive *meeting the challenges*. The paper breaks down the issues into five key points for achieving world-class procurement: simplify, clarify, and modernize procurement laws; leverage competition (and cooperation) in the acquisition of goods and services; increase public confidence in public procurement; promote a system of integrity; and engage the senior procurement official early in the legislative process.

Decision norms fall into three categories. In some cases, the team decides using consensus. In other types of decision, the team permits the majority to "rule" and supports the collective decision, whether by multi-voting or another voting method. In some cases, like meeting dates and other process issues, the team may defer to designated team leaders who confer with the team before making the decision. Team decisions are particularly important norms that the team should discuss and develop together.

Support the Team during Performance

The performance phase is the stage when the real work is done, when the team plans, communicates, and follows-up on tasks during implementation. Most of the work occurs between meetings. Meetings become central to following up, checking progress, and adjusting plans where necessary.

One way to get varying perspectives about team performance is to share leadership of meetings. Effective teams track project status in visible ways and rotate meeting briefings about project status. Try to have every team member contribute during project meetings.

Meetings are the circulatory system of teams. If you lead team meetings, mix up the meeting design. Plan which meeting type to use, informational versus problem solving. State a clear purpose, use objective-oriented agendas, have a variety of activities and leaders, arrange the room to encourage participation, and try to get everyone contributing. Be wary of routinely recycling agendas; they can deflate enthusiasm. Change up agendas periodically, especially the order in which topics are discussed.

What's an Effective Meeting?

Meetings are the lifeblood of any project. Teams should assign the meeting facilitator role in advance. Meeting leaders must determine the purpose of the meeting and the desired outcomes. If you lead team meetings, provide advance notice of any pre-meeting work. And begin and end on time! Evaluate attendance at meetings, and invite only those who are essential to the meetings outcome.[14]

While effective meetings require a certain amount of structure, meetings have different purposes. Those that are intended to be expansive in generating ideas and mining for various participants' perspectives are hindered by too much structure. On the other hand, meetings that are informational in nature can tolerate more rigid adherence to set guidelines.

(continued on next page)

What's an Effective Meeting, cont'd.

While not all of the following considerations may be relevant to every meeting, keep the following in mind when planning meetings:

- Build just enough—but not too much—structure into your meetings. Use questions to promote participation.
- Especially in recurring meetings, get ideas from meeting participants for future meeting design and agendas. How have your meeting "should be's" compared to their "as is"?
- Invite meeting participants with diverse perspectives, including the "voice of the customer."
- Balance the need for just enough structure with questions that promote exchange of ideas.
- Know the purpose of the meeting and have the agenda reflect it. Is the meeting used for informational exchange between members of working groups? Is the purpose expansion and focusing of ideas for a team?
- Use books and other resources to get ideas on various meeting designs, e.g., Patrick Lencioni's *Death by Meeting.*
- Use agenda topics to define an issue, invite possible solutions, and then look deeply at issues. Have you used questions on agendas?
- Consider using a relevant icebreaker to begin the meeting and get everyone briefly talking about themselves.
- Share roles for leading discussions. Mix up the order of agenda topics on recurring meetings. Know who will take minutes regarding key topics and discussions. Distribute agendas and key documents in advance.
- Keep minutes brief and record only key topics. Distribute them quickly. Use the minutes distribution as a way to promote thinking about future meeting design and topics. Are lessons learned and core learning captured?
- Plan for things that can go wrong. What if you lose internet on a virtual meeting? What if your projector lamp burns out in a meeting involving presentations?
- Plan also for common problems in meeting participation. Plan open-ended questions to use if you can't get anyone to talk. What if someone talks too much?
- Use a light touch as a meeting facilitator. Keep a running sense of how much talking you are doing.
- Don't shy away from constructive conflict in meetings. Good debate leverages the value of diverse perspectives.
- At the right time, when the team is ready, start summarizing the next actions and identify team members who will perform them. Record follow-up actions in the minutes.

Make the final agenda item an assessment of the meeting and discuss possible ways to improve it. Ask someone to lead the discussion about meeting assessment. If you have historically led the meetings and need an infusion of new ideas, step out of the meeting during the assessment.[15]

If you are a team leader, keep leading with a light touch. According to Hackman (2002, 2011), peer coaching at the midpoint of team performance is consultative in nature and focused on performance strategy and helping the team overcome obstacles and cement commitment to group goals. The team should occasionally revisit its performance. Mid-point corrections are not uncommon. The team might want to reflect on questions like, "What isn't working?" or "What do we wish we had done?" or "What should we do going forward?"

Periodic environmental scans should be part of the team's practices. Other performance strategies may be needed to carry out the team's work.[16] A team's use of subgroups to divide the work might have to be considered. A crisis situation may make consensus decisions impractical. Significant change management issues could require larger group engagement in order to achieve stakeholder engagement. Like other norms, discuss these practices as a team.

Sometimes groups get stuck and fall into old behaviors. What does a stuck team look like? Teams may start having attendance problems. Important decisions languish and are not made. Meetings or conference calls seem characterized by apathy, and people do not talk or otherwise seem tuned in. There may be conflicts that are allowed to fester and are not dealt with. One symptom is absence of open discussion of issues having obvious differences of opinion. Or deadlines pass without actions being completed.

When teams appear stuck, develop multiple, possible explanations. Underlying causes of poor team performance can be an ambiguous purpose, poor team composition, or inequitable approaches to work assignment, for example. It often is best to diagnose and treat the problems in the context of the task at hand rather than using generic exercises aimed at team dynamics like interpersonal skills or conflict resolution.

Sometimes a change in environment can help promote constructive dialogue. Brown-bag lunches, for example, or other informal gatherings can take people out of their usual roles and make it safer to candidly discuss issues.[17] Stuck teams sometimes can get unstuck by focusing on a small, tangible performance challenge. Or they can return to a critical team characteristic by putting a question on the agenda relating to team purpose. Working through a performance challenge—no matter how small—can be a unifying experience for a team that helps solidify effective working practices.

Revisiting team norms may be another way to get the team unstuck as a group. Focus on the norm, not an individual member's manifestation of behavior. Adding to an agenda, "Lencioni's notion of team commitment," may be less threatening than "Joe's not showing up for meetings."

Patrick Lencioni describes a practical approach a team can use to keep from getting stuck: "cascading messaging."[18] A "cascaded message" is the public statement of team progress or project status that a team uses to communicate to other stakeholders in the organization. The team works together on a statement for the rest of the organization (communicated up, down or sideways) about the status of the project or progress of the team. This is a collaborative activity that helps build collective accountability.

An effective, self-managed team shares responsibility. At meetings, they jointly keep the team on track if they wander. Effective teams also share responsibility for facilitating input by all members. They openly question the team processes, listen and build on the discussion, and ask the team's permission to change the subject when it looks like a different direction is needed.[19]

Reinforcing constructive behavior by members of the team can help a team fine tune its norms. Rewards are an essential element of the supporting context of a team. The team succeeds or fails as a team, but there are opportunities to recognize individual contribution to team success. Public recognition should be reserved for those who truly contribute to team success. Team members can show lateral leadership by acknowledging the special contributions of team members and celebrating the achievement of significant milestones. When a team leader sees constructive team behaviors, timely, specific praise provides visible, positive reinforcement.[20]

One final caveat: be on the lookout for "groupthink." Teams who have worked together for a long time, in particular, can fall into habits over time that merit reexamination. Parker (2008) identifies various roles that teams need to have filled: collaborator, communicator, contributor, and challenger. Members who fill the challenger role effectively raise uncomfortable issues constructively and should be encouraged publicly for their contribution. They are dissenters, and they must be protected.[21] Moreover, teams should bring in new team participants occasionally. Advisors or outsiders can be brought into a team and encouraged to ask questions. If certain team members have historically organized meetings, teams should consider rotating meeting leadership to get new perspectives.

Pay Attention to Endings and Transitions

In 1997, "adjourning" was added as the fifth stage to Tuckman's model. Teams need to think about the process used during the final phase of a team's performance, independent of the substantive tasks like record-keeping and, later, contract administration. Moreover, transition of teams though change of membership or movement into a different phase, implementation for example, may require self-reexamination by the team.

Team member transitions, especially changes in team leadership, should be treated in some sense as an "ending" with steps taken to revisit the group's purpose and norms. With a change in membership, team leaders should consider revisiting the team's purpose, perhaps by including a summary of the project history on a meeting agenda. The team can reassess whether it needs to reuse collaboration tools that were used in earlier phases of its life cycle. Members may need to discuss the evolution of group norms and the team's way of working together. For example, a team focused on contract management might have different purposes, goals, and roles for members than the team that conducted the procurement. The method of working together may change even when the team members stay the same.

The Colorado Field Accounting Services Team (FAST) is a special kind of team that illustrates one way to handle transitions.

Team Transitions: Colorado's FAST Self-Directed Work Team

"At first I was skeptical," says Roger Cusworth, "but then I became a strong supporter. Those five or six years that I was on FAST represented the best professional relationships I ever had."

Roger was an inaugural member of the Field Accounting Services Team (FAST) in the Colorado Office of the State Controller. This team of accountants has operated as a self-directed work team for 20 years. Team members are assigned agencies in state government, and they support the agencies' controllers. They also maintain the annual instructions for preparing the financial reports and implement the various appropriation statutes with the agencies. FAST is the primary means the State Controller has to analyze and implement various legislative changes and policy initiatives related to the office's mission.

The FAST developed written guidelines regarding how they would work together, adopted from the book *Skill Building for Self-Directed Team Members,* by Ann and Bob Harper (1993). The team had expectations regarding conflict, for example. If one FAST member had an issue with another, the team expected the matter first to be addressed individually. If it could not be resolved, then it was taken to the team. Roger remembered, "While we may not have used our *Skill Building* book as much in later years, whenever there was conflict, we got out the book." The book permitted the team to focus on the issues and revitalize the essential elements of effective teambuilding without personalizing conflicts.

The team controlled the hiring process. They prepared the position descriptions and the advertising. They also conducted the interviews, integrating questions relating to effective teaming. When FAST made a hiring decision, they made a recommendation to the State Controller; the recommendation was never rejected.

The performance-evaluation process was especially interesting. Each FAST member did an individual self-evaluation and a rating of every other member. One member was assigned as lead to prepare the evaluation for another member based on input from the group. FAST would assemble to discuss the self/individual evaluations without the subject member in the room. After they reached consensus on a team rating, they scheduled the FAST member for individual feedback. The State Controller sat in on the team feedback sessions.

The self-directed type of a team may not work for everyone. According to Roger, "We essentially had the same type of work, with different agencies assigned. While we all had unique strengths and expertise, we all were supporting agencies basically the same. Even where this alignment in mission exists, it takes a special kind of individual. We had our share of candid discussions in the FAST meetings."

How has this team sustained itself for so long? In the early years of FAST, they went through each chapter's training exercises as a team, reserving time away from the normal daily meetings that the team held. Later, as the team concept became more familiar, perhaps not every exercise was completed when a new member came to FAST. But the team's norms included jointly completing key exercises from the book.

When asked what she thought was most important to success of a team like FAST, Linda Bradley—another inaugural member of FAST—didn't hesitate. "It takes the commitment of everyone on the team," Linda emphasized. "In some professions like accounting, you don't really learn team skills," Linda said. "And if you don't have the support of management, it won't work."

As Roger Cusworth reminds us, self-directed teams require a special environment. It takes a special kind of individual also. "Team atmosphere is critical, and there has to be a commitment to honesty and straight-forward communication," Roger says.

When a team's goal finally has been reached, teams can use after-action reviews to help a team capture and solidify its learning. The team discusses what was supposed to happen and contrasts what actually happened in the team's performance. Team members ask, "What was the reason the actual performance differed from what we planned?" They don't just focus on the team task, though. The team evaluates how the team's direction, composition and boundaries, structure, supportive context, and peer coaching[22] contributed to success or could be improved.

Effective teams use "endings" to celebrate their achievements. They personally acknowledge contributions. Simple things like use of certificates sent to team members' superiors and public recognition before coworkers can be effective in acknowledging the contributions of team members.

Choose to Contribute Your Time and Attention

Effective teams have leaders who are empathetic and facilitative. They "step to their side" often to help members work together to achieve tangible results. They support learning, help members find fulfillment, and facilitate better performance over time.[23] Bellman and Ryan (2009) identified the litmus test for great teams: compelling purpose, shared leadership, just enough structure, full engagement, diversity, unexpected learning, strengthened relationships, and great results. A true team feels mutual accountability, trusts one another, has committed members, displays lateral leadership, and is able to use conflict constructively.

Teams keep purpose in mind. They pay special attention to early meeting design while the team is bonding. They learn and practice the effective use of questions to promote contributions from everyone. Teams find just enough structure and stay attuned to practices that may stifle creativity. Members depend on each other and find roles in which they can help the team succeed.

PART II

FOCUS THE TEAM'S ATTENTION

5 Use Just Enough Structure: Plan, Communicate, Follow-Up

The hallmark of any team activity is achievement, and project management is critical to that success. Indeed, some experts distinguish teams from other groups based on the existence of tangible objectives that teams must attain.[1] Other experts attribute success in great teams to their ability to band together and solve tangible problems. Every project requires management: scoping, planning, follow-up, monitoring, control, adjustment of plans, and project closure.

A radarscope metaphor applies well to project management. The radar screen allows the operator to see the targets; sometimes weather, sometimes other airplanes, sometimes bombing targets. Often the electronics in radar permits tagging targets so important ones are highlighted. The screen refreshes often and provides an image of the external environment. This permits aircrews to adapt to changing conditions.

When I started finding stories for this book, I was on the lookout for the formal project management tools that procurement professionals used. What I discovered was that procurement professionals were puzzled by the question!

In fact, when I went for the back-story of the neighborhood-stabilization project in Port St. Lucie, Florida, Cheryl Shanaberger was mildly taken aback by questions about the project management skills and tools used to manage the project. "We do this all the time," Cheryl told me. Same with Marian Pace, whose Punta Gorda, Florida, implementation of Lean Six Sigma was featured in NIGP's *Government Procurement* magazine. She thought the tools were useful but did not see why I valued the achievement so much. To Marian, her team continuously looked for ways to improve; they just happened to be using Lean Six Sigma tools this time. This chapter highlights some examples and tools used to manage projects perhaps a little better.

A team needs to know when to move into the disciplined structure that project management affords. One author on project management has noted the tension between creativity and project management structure. Price (2005) says that some critics of project management claim that its use impedes creativity and innovation. Price disagrees, but he calls for a proper balance in project management between process and openness to change and improvement.

The evolution of a project from creativity towards management means turning the corner from the expansive (divergent) stage of team activity to more convergent or focusing stages. Choices are made about execution strategies. Actions are chosen and priorities set. Schedules are developed, progress monitored, and corrections in project strategy made as the project gets underway.

A team has to be at the correct phase of its life cycle, with established norms for working together, when they start planning and move to execution. Chapter 4 had a mild caution about starting too early on team tasks. But once norms regarding teamwork are reasonably established, the team is ready to take the steps necessary to accomplish its purpose.

Planning is the touchstone of effective project management. It lays the foundation for successful execution. And teams are essential to planning of the project. The Colorado Field Accounting Services Team (FAST) is a special kind of team that, because of its self-directed nature and the variety of issues it encounters, places a special emphasis on planning and managing projects.

Colorado FAST Team Planning

The self-directed FAST team described in the last chapter is the eyes and ears of the Colorado State Controller, serving as the interface with state departments on a variety of statewide issues. FAST uses disciplined project management techniques, developing project plans for every task. Later, as they gained more experience with project planning and execution, they were selective about which projects to do formal plans on. However, even when formal written plans were not used, project planning still included an understanding of project scope descriptions and objectives, the expected time for the project, and the resources required.

According to Linda Bradley, a charter member of FAST, the team emphasized project discipline. "The team tackled projects by breaking down activities, designating the project lead, identifying timelines, establishing goals and objectives, assigning tasks, and deciding how to evaluate success," Linda said. "Even team training was a project, with someone assigned to lead the training effort with new FAST members and—as the FAST approach matured—to select the exercises that the team would use. We used the weekly FAST meetings with the State Controller to meet the management needs for timely information about priorities and project status."

The FAST story illustrates how sound project management is important even in functions not traditionally associated with delivery of end products. California's Office of Systems Integration (OSI) is a project management office that develops and uses project management tools in software development and integration projects. FAST, by contrast, serves as liaison with state agencies during preparation of the financial statements. FAST also manages special projects assigned by the State Controller related to state financial management. While OSI and FAST have widely different missions, both teams need sound project management skills.

Clarify the Identity and Needs of Stakeholders

The Project Management Body of Knowledge (PMBOK®) is widely regarded as the definitive guide in the United States for project management. It sets out the essential knowledge for the certification of project managers. PMBOK® identifies phases of project management—project initiation, project planning, project execution, and project closure.

The PMBOK® model is closely followed in traditional construction project management. As we discussed in chapter 2, information technology has adapted iterative software development strategies that involve the same considerations as the PMBOK® model but are more suited to information technology projects that encounter rapid changes in the industry and technology.

Project initiation is the first phase in project management. Projects start with a fundamental purpose. What are the business needs of the organization? What decisions will have to be made? The team's direct customers and other stakeholders affected by a project help frame the overarching objectives. They often are the key to helping design strategies and measures that make a project successful. Achieving a shared vision among the project team, the customers, and the other stakeholders is critical to success.

Among the first activities in the initiation phase is stakeholder analysis. Many project management strategies revolve around relationships with the stakeholders. Planning a project requires clarity about the various stakeholders and what their interests are. In many projects—especially those spanning organizational units and broadly touching established habits and practices—project management involves changing the behavior of entire groups. Communication planning requires in-depth knowledge of stakeholders' information requirements so they can understand, anticipate, and exercise some amount of control. Change management strategies largely are tailored to the concerns of individual stakeholders in order to effectively involve them in creating solutions. The development of a project team's purpose and threshold framing of the opportunity begins the process, but stakeholder analysis is performed early in the project to clarify the identity and interests of the stakeholders that help sharpen the team's objectives.

Price (2005) identifies essential questions for looking at stakeholder interests. Who are the stakeholders and will they be on the project team? While stakeholders hold the key to identifying solutions and strategies that are success, are there stakeholders whose interests might understandably lead to resistance? What strategies can be adopted to meet the concerns? More important, can their expertise be used by the team to fashion a project approach that can work?[2]

In information technology implementations, the procurement office will be a stakeholder. The information technology department often will lead, integrating project objectives with overall strategy of the enterprise, managing the change that comes from large implementation across the organization, and ensuring compliance with appropriate security and other technical requirements.

Price identifies two other stakeholders: the project sponsor and the customer (or client). But there are others. In an e-procurement project, for example, the finance department will have a stake in the payment processes. Vendors who will be using the system to maintain catalogs or submit bids also are stakeholders. Other governance organizations may have approval responsibilities and an interest in being at the table when requirements are defined. The solicitation and contract terms and conditions set the stage for effective communication with contractors and overall management of a project.

From stakeholder analysis, various requirements are identified. A change management strategy may have to be developed that addresses stakeholders' interests. In smaller-scale projects, mere communication of the project objectives and progress may be sufficient. In other cases, a project's success hinges on stakeholder commitment to the project approach. The analysis considers which stakeholders hold the key to designing a solution that meets their business needs.

Stakeholders must participate in planning of enterprise-wide information technology projects, for example. IT professionals know that stakeholders know their processes and requirements. So they have to be involved throughout a project for it to succeed. While some change-management strategies may look at stakeholders solely in terms of "buy-in," that perspective is misplaced. They have to help design successful projects that will meet their business needs.

Of course, there will be categories of stakeholders affected less by a project. So stakeholders will have different communication needs. Some stakeholders have specific responsibilities that require access to the schedule as it unfolds. Other stakeholders may have to be trained, requiring communication of training needs in sufficient time to establish training schedules. Occasional users of information technology systems may require training in later stages. In e-procurement implementations, close coordination among information technology, procurement, and financial professionals is needed if financial system integration is contemplated.

The content of communication, of course, is important but the direction is also. While organizations have become flatter and interconnected, there still are hierarchical elements. Project communication strategies need to address "cascading," the communications that need to be moving "down" the organization. Other communication needs to go up to executives. In information technology implementations, for example, steering committees need access to essential information related to project status. They also may be the circulatory system for cascading communications down other organizational hierarchies. The nature of the communication strategy is an important early element of planning, and a key part of a project charter. Stakeholder analysis is a bedrock element.

The Port St. Lucie neighborhood-stabilization project showed excellent use of stakeholder analysis. The building department, legal department, and vendors all were intimately involved in the project. Likewise, Oregon's disaster preparedness project had the right stakeholders involved in planning. So they would not miss important participants, the team used brainstorming to identify stakeholders beyond the initial group that was assembled.

Project management models almost all refer to a project charter and project management plan in the initiation phase.[3] These are written documents that define the scope of the project, costs, required resources, schedule, and deliverables. The charter also identifies stakeholders. Oregon's two-page disaster-preparedness workgroup charter (partially shown at figure 1-1) included the purpose and several other elements:

- The groups who would be participating in the workgroup;

- Expectations regarding participation, such as engaging subject matter experts as needed and fostering effective communication with stakeholders;
- The approach to recommendations and decisions, including identifying pros and cons of any recommendations made to the governing disaster preparedness council;
- The use of subgroups to develop or research specific issues;
- The identity and role of the facilitator who developed agendas, coordinated meeting dates, distributed information, and facilitated workgroup discussions;
- The method of modifying the charter;
- The key objectives for the next year; and
- The signature of representatives from each of the member agencies.

The signatures on a charter serve an important purpose. Coordinating with those affected by a project can be among the most difficult aspects of a complex project. A charter helps identify who owns the policies related to a project implementation. For example, in states that have looked at strategic sourcing initiatives, identifying the policy owners is essential. An example? A plan to look at telecommunications expenditures, with a view towards rationalizing the vendor base by reducing the number of vendors and standardizing requirements, will fail if the officials setting telecommunications policy are not an integral part of the project. The signatures on a charter vividly portray the collaboration and help solidify a commitment to the project's strategy.

The charter is a written document that identifies these considerations, illuminates the stakeholders, and serves as a "lightning rod" to ensure that the project has been well thought out. By circulating the project charter for signature, key stakeholders can help sharpen the strategy to make it more successful.

A formal project charter was not used in many of the projects featured in this book. The elements of effective project management were incorporated, however, during the team's activities. In procurements, for example, there may be sufficient clarity about the roles of cross-functional team members and planning steps so that execution of a formal project charter is not necessary. The published policies and procedures, meeting agendas, procurement file requirements, and prior methods of working together may serve the same role if the practices are imbedded in the team's norms.

Depending on the nature of the project, a cross-functional team should assess during procurement planning whether it has the right members to fulfill roles needed for the project to succeed. If not, they should involve other stakeholders having an interest in project success.

Procurement-Planning Checklists

Procurement-planning checklists are a good way to identify essential steps and considerations required for a successful procurement. They are tailored for the type of commodity or service involved. In some cases, procurement professionals and sourcing teams have enough recent experience with a requirement that formal pre-solicitation team meetings are not required.

But using a checklist is a good way to manage planning. Consider these considerations that could be included in a pre-solicitation planning meeting with stakeholders:

- Identify responsibilities. Clearly define the responsibilities for arranging a business strategy meeting, specification drafting, solicitation development, evaluation team selection and management, preparation of a quality management plan (or portions of the solicitation dealing with quality control), inspection and acceptance, and post-award contract administration.

- An approach to market research. Agree on the nature of market research needed. Who will conduct informal vendor one-on-one meetings with known industry leaders, and what are the constraints on those meetings? Do the open records/freedom of information laws permit requests for information that invite confidential information, improving the chances of getting useful information? Will a draft request for proposal be used?

- The expected solicitation strategy. Will a request for proposal (RFP) be used? If so, what are threshold views regarding the factors that will be evaluated: technical, management, past experience/demonstrated capability, cost? What will be the timing for development of a more detailed-evaluation/source-selection plan, and who is responsible for leading its creation?

- Budget and contingency. Discuss the pros and cons of disclosing at least a rough-order-of-magnitude estimate regarding availability of funds. Should a portion of the appropriated/ allocated amount be set aside as a reserve for changes that may be needed?

- Contract type, e.g., firm, fixed price. What price or costing information, e.g., labor hours and labor rates, should be requested?

- Key milestones. Will progress payments be used? At what stages? How will progress be measured or assessed?

- A quality management approach. Key performance or compliance metrics must be in the solicitation document and contract if they will be used for acceptance or computing payments tied to performance. What metrics are used to assess program performance now? Should those be disclosed to vendors? Will vendors be asked to propose contract performance metrics that are aligned with the business unit's measurements (such as service level agreements in IT procurements) that can be used for acceptance of deliverables or other performance? How will those measures factor into the proposal evaluation? Can and should incentives (e.g., payment incentives) be used that are tied to performance that significantly exceeds minimum standards?

- Risk management. Is a formal risk management plan required? Have at least the important risks been identified, assessed, and handled in the solicitation and proposed contract?

- Key constraints on the project. Discuss assumptions regarding constraints during planning meetings. These can include such things as schedule, agency resources, financing options, and legal requirements imposed by law.

- Contractual governance structure. If there will be a governance body used during contract performance, like an information technology steering committee, who will be members? What will be disclosed in the solicitation regarding the governing body's responsibilities during contract administration? Should any commitments be made in terms of times for review and approval of changes, for example?

- Major areas of proposal, schedule, and contract risk. Address, at least generally, the likely expectations of the vendor in terms of their risk and change management challenges. This topic often is a subject for market research meetings before solicitation development.

- Expected issues in key terms and conditions, e.g., intellectual property ownership/licensing and liability limitation/allocation.

- Issue escalation. In complex projects, would it be helpful to define an issue escalation process (a meet-and-confer process short of formal disputes clauses) that permits either party to elevate an issue above the project team to a project sponsor or contractor executive?

- The solicitation/contract approval requirements. Invite key reviewers to solicitation-planning meetings. For example, legal counsel may want to be invited so she can build her own knowledge base about the procurement, making her better able to perform a timely legal review of the solicitation and awarded contract.

The use of a procurement-planning checklist can help identify agenda items for procurement team meetings. Having stakeholders involved early in the procurement-planning meetings helps a team understand their needs. Stakeholder analysis and planning help identify requirements that can impact the project schedule. In a procurement project, for example, the decision about the sourcing strategy—invitation for bids versus request for proposals—is an early schedule driver.

Many of the traditional project management tools focus on the schedule, particularly its monitoring and adjustment. The schedule is developed by working backward from the objective.

Work Backward From the Objective

In continuous improvement projects, definition of the problem occupies the chair at the head of the table. In more traditional projects—requests for proposals are an example—objectives are the compass that guides the effort. In continuous improvement projects taking aim at problems, understanding and clearly defining the problem is a key early focus. Sometimes, the mere act of clarifying the problem definition will suggest solutions or lead the team in more productive directions than were initially thought. And the way to define the problem in these kinds of projects is to write it down.

Typically, a project will start with a cross-functional team that includes key stakeholders. Questions are used to identify the contours of the project. What is the objective? (In a continuous improvement project dealing with a problem, has the problem been written down so it is adequately defined?) What is the project scope and is it realistic? Can the project be finished within the desired timeframe? What resources are required? What are the risks? And have there been similar projects that the team can learn from?[4]

At some point, requirements need to be coordinated and collected. In procurements, specifications are drafted, solicitation language developed, evaluation plans prepared, and the solicitation published and managed. In continuous-improvement projects, once the opportunity is defined, the team moves forward defining the nature of customer outreach, analysis, and possible solutions to identified problems. All of these actions have to be identified, responsibility assigned, and monitored. Essentially, this is project management.

While complex projects like major construction and IT implementations use more sophisticated models, these are the initial steps in project management:

1. Have the team members brainstorm the list of everything that must be done. A useful tool is a tree diagram, where overall objectives are listed and branches progressively developed to get to more discrete objectives.

2. Expand the tree until tasks are broken down into appropriately sized tasks that can be done by or effectively managed by individuals. Self-stick notes are useful tools used by teams to define and collect requirements at the appropriate level.

3. Consider numbering the tasks for ease of discussion where there are many. Statements of work use work breakdown structures (WBS) having numbered paragraphs (e.g., 3.1.1) to identify progressively more detailed descriptions of subtasks.

4. Determine how much time each task takes. Include the duration of tasks on the self-stick notes.

5. Armed with the tasks and schedule requirements, move to the next phase: finding schedule dependences.

Identify the Dependencies between Activities

With tasks and their duration identified, the dependencies that exist between tasks must be identified. The development of a solicitation-evaluation plan is a good example of how dependencies between tasks affect schedule.

An evaluation plan is used to instruct evaluation committee members about the evaluation process. Some planning must occur first, however. The request for proposals must be completed because it identifies the relative order of importance of evaluation factors that go into an evaluation plan. The request for proposals also identifies the requirements for the submission of proposals. The content of those instructions, as well as related instructions like proposal length limitations, may affect the timeframes in the plan for evaluation activity. As a result, the development of the evaluation plan is dependent on completion of the RFP.

The evaluation plan also may be tied to other events. Agencies commonly strive to complete evaluation planning before proposals are received. So on a timeline, the order of dependencies could be, "Issue request for proposals—complete evaluation plan—receive proposals."

Outreach events like vendor reverse trade shows and other similar events also are projects, complex ones often. The McKenna Long & Aldridge Procurement Update in Denver, Colorado, illustrates how these events are projects that need to be managed like any other.

Learning from Lawyers! McKenna Long & Aldridge LLP's Procurement Update

Events need project management, too! McKenna Long & Aldridge LLP is known internationally for its expertise in government contract law. In 2006, the firm decided to begin hosting an event in its Denver, Colorado, office that was designed around state and local government procurement.

The first step in planning an event like this is to determine the objectives. In this case, the firm's Colorado procurement law update was intended to create an event where industry could learn about recent developments in state and local government procurement and could meet public procurement leaders and ask them questions.

Fundamental decisions were made early. Often people cannot commit to a full day, so the firm settled on a half-day seminar. Downtown Denver was selected as the location most convenient for the firm's event planners, probable attendees, and the public procurement leaders who likely could participate.

Planning: Event minus four months

Lisa King, a legal secretary at McKenna Long, had an uncanny ability to keep the lawyers on track! Every year during early summer, Lisa would initiate plans for the fall event. To the extent that this event had a formal project manager, Lisa was her!

Including state and local procurement leaders makes these events more informative, and tying the event to recent developments encourages their participation. An event like this often serves their interest, too, by getting the word out to industry about new laws and practices. During the summer, informal contacts were made with potential speakers and panelists to assess their interest in participating and whether they had ideas for topics.

Events of this nature are largely driven by availability of venues, speaker schedules, and the nature of the expected audience. Lisa steered away from dates when Colorado state and local government procurement leaders participate in annual national association conferences, and she helped the firm forecast competing commitments and avoid them. These considerations steered the event toward October or early November.

Armed with some idea of speaker interest and possible dates, Lisa's next step was to find a location and a date. Normally the event venue would "pencil in" the date and then identify a date by which a deposit was due to hold the reservation. The firm informally cleared the date at least with the featured speakers so they could pencil-in the event on their schedules. Lisa coordinated with her colleagues so they could avoid scheduling other events on the same day.

At about the 60–90 day point, the program director started conferring with key speakers to identify other panelists. He prepared drafts of panel descriptions for the flyer used to promote the event. The flyer became the centerpiece of the event planning. Lisa added panelist and moderator names to the flyer as commitments become reasonably firm. As materials were developed for possible distribution, they were shared with potential panelists. Involving potential participants in the planning not only enriches the event, but it also helps solidify commitment.

(continued on next page)

Learning from Lawyers, cont'd.

Moving Toward Execution: Event minus 30 days

By one month prior to the event, the flyer was essentially complete and promotional emails were sent to interested companies. The firm scheduled a working lunch to discuss the program. Speakers, panelists, and moderators attended. The primary objective of the planning meeting was to discuss the contours of the presentations and eliminate significant overlap. Sometimes it was the first time that panelists met each other and panel moderators.

At the planning meeting, the participants discussed useful documents for the program folders. This was also the meeting when deadlines were established for PowerPoint slides and other written materials.

Executing, Monitoring, and Controlling: Event minus three days

For Lisa, the heavy lifting started again about three business days before the event. She had to firm up head counts for the continental breakfast. She also had to prepare the nametags for the attendees. Luckily, she got help with preparation of the attendee packages.

"McKenna has terrific office operations support," Lisa told me. "The other legal secretaries help put together the attendee packages. There usually were 80–100 packages and lots of stuffing of folders. We all support each other with these events."

Assemble the Schedule with Assigned Responsibilities

With tasks, dependencies, and durations, a schedule can be developed. The schedule identifies what needs to be accomplished, by whom, and when.

One of the simplest tools used to manage a schedule is a task list. Microsoft Outlook has a task function that permits reminders to be set for actions due on specific days. Figure 5-1 is an example of how a task list can be used for an event like the one conducted by McKenna Long & Aldridge. The comments section can be used to record upcoming milestones; the most immediate is carried on the subject line of the task list so it is prominently displayed. As tasks are completed, additional tasks are carried forward from the comments section to the subject line, and priorities are assigned.

Figure 5-1. Microsoft Outlook Tasks.

The advent of "cloud computing" has made sophisticated project management software applications available to even the infrequent project manager. Network schedules, also known as program evaluation and review technique (PERT), are a type of schedule that graphically depicts events, their relationships, and durations. Often there are parallel activities occurring on a project, each with its own dependencies in terms of completion.

On complex projects like construction, contractors use a network-scheduling tool that permits them to identify the *critical path*. Activities (an operation or task requiring a resource and having duration) on the path can start immediately after a predecessor activity. Sometimes activities involve a time lag or lead between predecessor or successor activities on a schedule. The pouring of concrete foundations is an example; framing cannot begin until some period of time after concrete has been poured and has cured.

The critical path is the sequence of production activities that takes the longest time from start to finish.[5] "Critical path" is a common term in construction for the path taken through the project schedule with the longest duration to achieve the required completion date.

When there is a complex schedule, some activities may have completion dates that do not drive the critical path. This slack in the schedule, permitting schedule flexibility for some activities, is known as the "float" on construction projects.

In project management software, these activities and the dependencies (including time between them) are loaded in the software. The software graphically displays the schedule, identifies the critical path, and calculates the float. If you have complex schedules, you may need a more sophisticated software package to manage the schedule.

In procurement offices, PERT and critical path schedules may not be required. Gantt charts are useful here, though. They are graphic scheduling devices that display the tasks to be performed on the vertical axis and the time required for each task on the horizontal axis. A Gantt chart has a modest ability to show linear schedule dependencies. For example, one activity on the chart may require completion before the time scheduled for the next activity. The chart can be modified to show dependencies between activities, e.g., one activity must be finished before another starts, or the beginning of an activity lags the start of another activity.

Gantt charts are the simplest of the various charting techniques for planning and controlling major projects.[6] Figure 5-2 is a Gantt chart created from a free software application, GanttProject, in about one hour. It shows the tasks, sequencing, and dependencies for the McKenna Long & Aldridge LLP procurement update. This application also permits development of PERT schedules and display of the critical path.

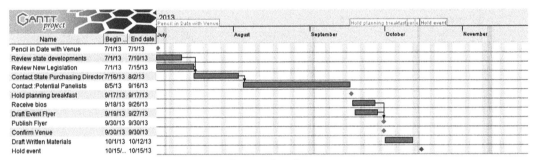

Figure 5-2. Gantt Chart

By this time in a project, the lists of tasks must have clearly assigned responsibilities for completion. Whatever scheduling system is used, the person responsible for completing the scheduled activity must be identified. This is particularly important in team efforts like procurement where everyone shares responsibility for various activities.

In procurement, typically the purchasing agent provides the solicitation and contract templates and assists in revising the solicitation language to reflect decisions made during the planning process. The user or project manager normally leads development of specifications and the statement of work. Moreover, while the procurement office has templates for the evaluation plan, the user usually is in the best position to develop the evaluation criteria and weighting. Evaluation committees are briefed about the process of evaluation and cautions regarding information exchange with the offerors. Team members must assign responsibility for these actions during pre-procurement-planning meetings.

Schedule development generally ends the planning phase of a project. The plan is published, however informally, so team members and other stakeholders know what is required and when. The next phase is project execution—when the work is done.

Think Ahead: Communicate, Monitor, and Follow-Up

Projects are not static. Plans map out a forecasted future and often need adjustment. Some even say that the plan is out of date the minute it is published. After the planning phase of a project, there are essential steps required to make a project successful. Thinking forward is one of them.

When I was an aviator, we used to call this "staying ahead of the airplane." We flight-planned, but once the aircraft took off, there were a myriad of things to keep up with. We had emergencies and encountered severe weather that required rerouting. The best of plans fell by the wayside. We sometimes filed amended flight plans in-flight with the Federal Aviation Administration. But whether the flight was proceeding as planned, or we were dealing with unanticipated developments like weather or equipment failures, the mantra was, "stay ahead of the airplane." How does one stay ahead of a project?

A procurement project requires continual monitoring. Communication with stakeholders is an essential ingredient in monitoring progress. Projects managed by formal project management methodologies use both project charters and communication plans. Even in less formal projects, some means of communicating project status with external stakeholders and managers is essential.

Many times, an important objective of communication is to portray the value of the project. Sometimes called an "elevator speech," Price (2005) calls the value proposition his Unique Value Perception (UVP). To Price, UVP is a succinct statement that summarizes the reason the project exists, who it serves, its value and the return on investment.

Communication plans vary in formality, but certain choices must be made. Passive communication methods, like static web pages, may be sufficient for providing project status information. Where more stakeholder involvement and commitment is needed, actively sending information to them is preferable. Well-designed status or review meetings are good tools. In some cases, personal briefings by project managers of key executive staff may be preferable.

Also, consider the informal hierarchy of communications. Personal conversations are the most informal but in some cases more effective for getting feedback. Emails may be next in formality, and attachment of a written, succinct report probably next in terms of effectiveness. Combining a succinct report with a meeting with senior executives may have the most impact; it promotes cascading communication in other stakeholder departments where commitment may be needed.

The communication strategy must identify frequency along with the tangible deliverable used to communicate. In the Colorado/Utah e-procurement contract, weekly status reports were provided (figure 5-3). The one-page report visually showed the schedule status, a 30-day "look ahead" schedule with key activities and deliverables, working issues, and briefing and marketing opportunities designed to help other governments and stakeholders anticipate the change.

E-Procurement Implementation Update
August 28, 2001

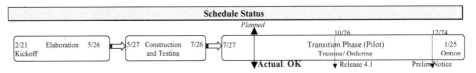

Schedule Status

These dates show the amended pilot period dates. This will give the State more time for evaluation and pilot familiarization than was available in the original schedule. Release 4.1 on 10/26 will include bid solicitation, comprehensive workflow, advanced reporting, and pilot COFRS integration. CU and CDOT western region will be joining in the pilot in late October, early November.

Schedule 30-Day Look Ahead

Date	Activity/Deliverable	Expected Resources
8/29	DOLE Administration Set-up	Austin and DOLE team
8/30, 1:00	Critical Design Review (CDR) in Bids Solicitation and Phase II Workflow at 1525 Sherman, B070. Planned 2-3 hours	Project Team, Pilot Agency reps, Super Users, and political subdivisions reps invited.
9/6	CIO Forum Briefing	Austin and Pennington

Last Week's High Points

8/22-23   Bid Solicitation and Advance Workflow Demo to Project Teams
8/24   Pennington meets with Greenbrier and Russel re: catalog maintenance
8/24   GSS User Training
8/27   System goes live for pilot ordering
8/27   Gap Analysis Discussion and priorities set; emphasis placed on improvements for suppliers

Working Issues

☐ Draft contract amendment, extending contract period to January 26, 2002, has been exchanged with final draft sent to NIC.
☐ NICC assembling team for COFRS integration. Colorado has provided comments on potential consultants. NICC is trying to find on-the-ground consultants here in Colorado that are familiar with our AMS implementation.
☐ Change management system being implemented, along with Excel system for tracing software bugs. 43 "bugs" notices have been identified, one critical that relates to system enforcement of ordering limitation parameters against the system roles. NIC has said it will be fixed for 4.01 8/27 release.
☐ Preparing conceptual paper for how to add political subdivisions and other States
☐ Preparing user and vendor feedback survey instruments for evaluating pilot performance.
☐ Preparing concept paper on piloting of bid solicitation module by State pilot agencies/institutions.
☐ Preparing joint Utah/Colorado press release.

Planned Marketing/Briefing Opportunities

9/17   Pennington/Richins at Annual Conference of National Association of State Procurement Officials (NASPO)
10/2   Briefing to MAPO/CEPC
10/25   Colorado Procurement Advisory Council (PAC) Meeting with Demo
10/31   Government, Business, and Education Expo in Los Angeles (working)

Richard Pennington/303-866-4414/August 28, 2001

Figure 5-3. Project Status Report.

Getting feedback during project execution is vitally important, meaning that some sort of monitoring mechanism is needed. Formal project reporting generates useful feedback. Formal surveys can be designed in continuous improvement initiatives, but informal means are useful also. Go to the stakeholders. Invite stakeholders to project status meetings. Send them periodic reports by email. Call them occasionally. And listen to what they say. Follow-up on any feedback that is a "so-so" response. Don't promise perfection, but promise to listen.

During execution, projects require religious monitoring of the schedule, following up with persons who are responsible for tasks. Project adjustments may have to be made, the due dates for deliverables may have to change. Training plans may be delayed. Other priorities may be levied on the organization. Without a communication, monitoring, and feedback loop, one quickly loses touch about where a project is in relation to the plan and competing demands for resources.

The space between the project plan and actual project conditions is often where problems arise and where adjustments need to be made to the project performance. This space or gap triggers another reality in projects—there is a close relationship between schedule, scope, and cost in changes to project strategy.

The Triple Constraints and Change

The contours of change require special attention. Project management professionals may see revisions to the project management plan, and the use of the governance mechanisms, as key components in change. To procurement professionals, on the other hand, changes may implicate specific contractual modification mechanisms. A contractor may be entitled to schedule or even price adjustments for some changes.

Change has less impact on a project schedule when change is managed early. Denver International Airport's completion was delayed by two years when the baggage handling system was redesigned late in the project completion. In software development, as well, changes late in the project ripple in terms of schedule throughout the project and are magnified.

Perspectives about "change" may be different among team members in a project. Software programmers may focus on customer satisfaction, and some books describing software development methodologies downplay the significance of change to the contractual business relationship between the program and the contractor. To account for all the potential effects, cross-functional teams are useful to assess the effect of "changes."

Project management and procurement professionals certainly agree on one thing in particular: the central role-played by scope, schedule, and cost. These are sometimes called the *triple constraints*.[7] These constraints and their relationships are widely recognized in projects.

When planning, there are trade-offs between constraints. Increasing scope in a statement of work may add both cost and time to a schedule. In later stages of a project, when reacting to unexpected financial conditions, there may be pressure to reduce project cost. That usually means a reduction in project scope, maybe even a change in schedule.

"Favor Scope Changes When Possible."[8]

This statement illustrates biases that may exist in various project management contexts. It appears as a subsection in a book by Mike Cohn (2010) about Agile software development, a variation of its cousin, Extreme Programming.

In the case of Agile, development and testing cycles are very short, sometimes as short as a week. Cohn (2010) discusses the triple constraints—schedule, cost, and scope—and concludes that scope is the easiest to change. However, he offers little discussion of the contractual implications of this philosophy in his book.

Admittedly, Agile and Extreme programming are software development approaches. Many of the information systems projects that teams encounter in public procurement involve little development. They more often integrate off-the-shelf software. Still, there sometimes is customization, making familiarity with software development and project management approaches important. We raise these project management concepts because some treatments of information technology project management seem different than the more traditional project management approaches (like major construction).

The public procurement professional needs to be attuned to the effect of change on the contract with the vendor. The best way to deal with varying perspectives about change and its implications is to openly discuss these issues with project managers.

Lengthening a schedule may appear to permit savings, but often that is not the case. Demobilization and remobilization of work force may come with increased costs. Having to keep people on a project longer usually means costs increase unless labor can perform other work. In software development, there is even a "law" for this principle. Brooks' Law[9] says that adding manpower to a late project will only delay it further.

When conducting procurements, ask offerors to squarely address how they will address change. Are they building in contingencies that increase proposal price to manage anticipated change? Some IT projects, for example, use management schedule reserves or scope "banks" as techniques to manage the possibility of anticipated change, often with client involvement.[10] More traditional construction approaches and associated contract terms and conditions use reserves and changes clauses (and other contractual provisions) to deal with unknown conditions (e.g., unusual site conditions). Events and contingencies covered by these clauses may lead to entitlement to schedule and price adjustments. You should clearly understand on your project how these triple constraints trade-offs could occur and what contract mechanisms are available for managing them.

The trade-off of schedule, price, and scope is at the heart of project planning and execution. The triple constraints also are at the core of the procurement-planning process.

Don't Forget the Closing Phase of Projects!

The project closure phase has its own set of requirements. In procurements, there are record keeping requirements related to the solicitation and award. After award and contract execution, the project moves into contract administration, a phase with its own requirements.

Even with the documentation requirements satisfied, an often-overlooked step is the celebration! An after-action review also is useful to capture lessons learned: what went well, what didn't, the reasons, and how the project could be improved.

At the end of the McKenna Long & Aldridge LLP event, Lisa King made a habit of getting pictures of the participants. The firm used them to showcase the event and acknowledge the contributions of those who made the event a success. The firm sent out thank you letters to speakers, acknowledging notable parts of each presentation. (In this day and age, written letters have become more powerful than emails.) Lisa also sent copies of handouts to those who responded with an RSVP but were unable to attend the event.

Lisa also performed what formally is known as an after-action review. Along with artifacts (like the handouts and letters), Lisa included lessons learned in a folder that she used for the next year's event.

Keep an Eye on the Scope

This chapter offers an abbreviated look at project management, emphasizing tools that public procurement professionals can use. It provides a planning model that is at the heart of more sophisticated project management planning: work backward from the objective when planning. Then think ahead during project execution.

The essential elements of effective project management are well established: clarify the needs of stakeholders, plan, communicate, and monitor the project.

As figure 5-4 illustrates, the radarscope visually displays the priority of projects. This particular radarscope was used by the Colorado Division of Finance and Procurement. The division maintained a public SCOPE website where clients could see the progress. Perhaps more important, completed projects were moved to the missions accomplished section, sort of a digital celebration of achievement.

Figure 5-4. DFP RadarSCOPE.

Project management is critical to team success. Every project requires organization: scoping, planning, follow-up, monitoring, control, adjustment, and closure. A project plan can be developed by working backward from the objectives. However, plans often require adjustments. Therefore, good communication plans and practices are essential to effectively manage the scope, schedule, and cost—the "triple constraints"—on all projects.

6   Use Meaningful Measures of Merit

"If it's not measured, it won't get done." It's a common mantra, but many have become cynical about measurement, feeling that it is less about seeing reality and more about driving accountability from the top down.

Measurement is a quantitative reduction in uncertainty based on one or more observations. It is often controversial because it sometimes focuses on measures that have little or no value. To ensure that measurement is meaningful: clarify the purpose, engage stakeholders in defining the measures, and develop a reliable method or approach to measurement.

Dr. W. Edwards Deming, widely considered the father of Total Quality Management (he reputedly did not want his name associated with the TQM movement of the late 1980s), had a surprising outlook on measurement. Famous for his 14 principles, Dr. Deming espoused one particularly relevant here: numerical goals should be eliminated as a basis for managing people. Dr. Deming believed that systems, not people, ultimately were responsible for defects in performance. His outlook on measurement: it is a way to evaluate the capabilities of the system.

Over the past twenty years, measurement and metrics have occupied an increasingly central role in organizational management. Industry has developed measures of purchasing performance. The National Association of State Procurement Officials has published guidance about measuring savings that can be used to evaluate procurement value.[1] NIGP has a strategic partnership with a company who has developed a tool for measuring savings from the procurement function and in strategic sourcing. Balanced scorecard is being used by governments and has transformed measurement with its emphasis on using performance measures other than financial ones.

Those measures are meaningful. I admit to having used meaningless measures of merit. Years ago, I managed the Air Force Commercial Litigation Division. We assisted the United States Department of Justice in defending government contract cases. We tracked a metric that the generals loved: the ratio of the dollar amount of judgments against the Air Force divided by the amount claimed by plaintiffs in lawsuits. The metric was meaningless, however, as a measure of our division's value. The plaintiffs often wildly inflated the amount they claimed in their complaints. When a single $1 billon patent infringement claim was filed against the Air Force, the entire metric was skewed. In short, the number had no utility for measuring the quality of our work or any relevance to decisions that needed to be made. But because the senior stakeholders liked the measure, it persisted, precise but meaningless.[2]

This chapter will look at recent examples of exemplary use of measurement by the procurement profession. The chapter is organized around a proposed structure for looking at measurement: find the purpose of measurement, use a balanced approach to measurement, and engage stakeholders in developing measures. In some ways, this chapter is a precursor to the next chapter on analysis and decision making.

The Purpose of Measurement: Inputs, Outputs, and Outcomes

Measurement is defined as "the act or process of ascertaining the extent, dimensions, or quantity of something," a "quantitatively expressed reduction in uncertainty based on one or more observations."[3] When functional experts express their preferences numerically during proposal evaluation, they have reduced uncertainty regarding selection of the best vendor to some extent. Often the characterization of subjectivity of a consideration—that it is incapable of measurement—is reached before analyzing whether measurements may exist that help with a decision.[4] Data does not make decisions, though.[5]

A measurement is useful if it reduces uncertainty in decision making.[6] Organizing information may itself reduce uncertainty because it improves the process of decision making. A sound decision process includes clear understanding of how a decision will use the data and how it reduces uncertainty.[7] Moreover, sometimes asking pointed questions about the relevance of data may lead to clarification of the problem in a way that obviates the need for data.[8] Most importantly, do not shy away from measurement simply because it is imprecise.

Absolute accuracy in management data can seldom be achieved, but information that is available in management systems can be useful for better seeing the reality of processes objectively. A measure that improves the confidence in a decision using the data is generally considered preferable to not having a measure at all.[9]

A common characteristic that differentiates types of data is when and what it measures along a process. For example, in a procurement environment, the number of requisitions that an office receives and turns into purchase orders or solicitations would be an example of an input measure. The data may be useful for measuring efficiency of operations, but it says nothing about the effectiveness (quality) of the work performed by the office. Yet, tracking the number of requisitions can help assess workloads of an office. Historical knowledge of seasonal workloads of a procurement office can be useful when planning staff vacations, for example.

A related output measure can be the number of purchase orders and solicitations. These are useful process measures because they represent productive work done by an office after the input of the requisitions. Again, these kinds of measures address the workload and perhaps efficiency of an organization, not quality.

The time taken between the input and output—time for completing solicitations and purchase orders, for example—can be a measure of efficiency. Efficiency is generally the ability to get the most in terms of results with the least amount of resources. Process time often is used as an efficiency measure.

The term "outcome measure" is typically associated with the effectiveness or quality of a process. Some offices use customer satisfaction surveys to assess one element of quality of performance, the value in the eyes of stakeholders like agencies or departments that use central procurement services. A few offices use "successful protests" as one measure—some question its validity—of the effectiveness of the procurement process. The underlying idea is that a successful protest by a vendor represents a deficiency in the procurement process.[10]

The use of management information data in continuous improvement initiatives is common. The state of Colorado contracting reengineering project story we tell next is an example of the use of input, output, and outcome measures in a procurement reform initiative.

Colorado Contracting Reengineering

"Where's my contract?!" It was a common lament. Clearly, the execution and approval of state contracts in Colorado took too long.

The Colorado State Controller is statutorily required to review and approve all commitment documents, which includes contracts. In addition, the Controller's fiscal rules required Attorney General review of all bilateral contracts prior to approval by the State Controller. Adding reviews required by other offices, the approval times for contracts stretched to weeks, sometimes longer.

Progress came in baby steps. By using waivers for certain contract formats and using less formal contract modification tools that did not require legal review, the number of contracts reviewed by the Attorney General decreased 50% from over 5,000 in the late 1980s to about 2,500 in 2003. Still, though, the number of contracts sent by agencies through the central approval process was sizable, and the review times overall were not acceptable.

By 2005, more progress had been made through the preapproval of contract formats, but that process was not widely used because of the difficulty in generalizing contracts for varying requirements. In addition, small purchase thresholds were raised, which allowed purchase orders, commonly used in the acquisition of commodities, to be used without formal State Controller approval (or legal review) to purchase services up to $100,000. Still, agencies were dissatisfied with the centralized contract review and approval process.

There was little data about the quality of state contracts overall. The financial system had codes showing the reasons contracts were "rejected" by the central approvers, and this data indicated that the rejections in some agencies were in excess of 20% of the number of contracts reviewed. But virtually no other information existed regarding the quality of the contracts submitted for approval, and some felt that perhaps the rejection rate did not accurately reflect the quality of the contracts.

(continued on next page)

Colorado Contracting Reengineering, con'td.

In 2006, the State Controller's office reached a "tipping point" in its approach to review and approval. The State Controller decided to consider an approval process based on the idea that contract legal reviews, the part of the process that appeared to be adding the most time, might not be required in all instances. The new process would allow agencies to perform a risk assessment to determine whether or not contracts could be approved by a State Controller delegate in the agency, without being reviewed for legal sufficiency. Even the "high risk" contracts sent for State Controller approval would receive legal review only when requested by the State Controller. We'll finish the story in chapter 8, but essentially the risk-based approach represented reengineering of the contract approval process and got contracts out of the system that did not need more comprehensive review.

Harry McCabe, the contract manager for the Department of Human Services, was really sold on the improvement process used by the State Controller. "I believe in the continuous improvement model that Dr. Deming taught," Harry maintains. "This was an exceptional example of application of those principles."

The Colorado initiative illustrated the use of various kinds of measures. The number of contracts submitted for review was an input measure. The number of contracts approved, as well as the number of contracts rejected, represented output measures that also could be used to measure efficiency of the process.

The process efficiency, the amount of wait time (in queue waiting for review) compared to the average time taken to review a contract is an efficiency measure that shows the relationship between value-added and non-value-added activity. For example, when I performed legal reviews of contracts, I bragged that my review time average was only two business days. What customers didn't know was that the average time I spent reviewing my 2,000 contracts/year was only about 30 minutes. The process efficiency (30 minutes divided by an average of 16 hours in queue) was 3%: service processes should be above 50% to be considered lean.

The visual display in figure 6-1 was a useful way to compare visually the time taken by various central approvers to review the contracts.

Contract Cycle Time and Errors

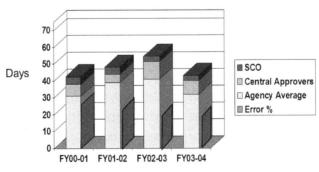

Figure 6-1. Contract Review Times.

Careful analysis of figure 6-1 reveals an interesting fact. The time taken internally in agencies to complete the contract on average was about a month. Still, some of that time was caused by rework after contracts were returned from the central approvers, and the significance of the "rejection" errors remained a subject of debate.

The analysis of rejection reasons—the error percentage in the chart—was a questionable measure. It purported to measure outcomes in terms of contract quality, but admittedly, the measure suffered from ambiguity in the rejection coding on the financial system about the severity of the defect. While the data was fairly good for looking at process efficiency and workload, its ability to measure quality was more suspect.

Measures also can be leading or lagging. Ideally, both kinds are used. Lagging indicators tend to focus on historical performance. Leading indicators are chosen to predict future performance.[11] Leading indicators often are drivers of lagging measures; a relationship between the two is assumed to exist. Timeliness of contract reviews and approvals might be a leading indicator to a lagging measure of customer service, for example. People who have to wait a long time for contract review are not very happy about the process.

Colorado's contracting improvement initiative illustrated the value in distinguishing between the kinds of measures and their relevance to assessing efficiency and effectiveness. The initiative also demonstrated the relevance of existing data, in this case, contracting routing data in the financial system for assessing process performance.

There generally is more data available in today's information systems than expected. Relevant new data may be more accessible than the team expects.[12] While the original intent behind Colorado's contract approval tracking system was to permit users to monitor the progress of a contract through the approval process, the data entered into the system over time (and thousands of contracts) also permitted a more objective view of the contract system performance as a whole.

The state of Ohio's office-machine initiative described in chapter 2 introduced the growing use of measures to evaluate procurement savings more strategically. Thomas Linley's project used existing data about contract prices to evaluate the anticipated savings. He used a limited experimental pilot to validate conclusions, and the data provided the impetus needed to persuade agencies to change to multifunction machines.

Measurement tools are growing in importance. NIGP's *Observatory* and *Measure* tools, provided by NIGP's strategic partner, the Spikes Cavell Company, assist in developing procurement savings and cost avoidance measures. They help identify expenditures by commodity and service category, assisting in agency initiatives to better manage expenditures through strategic sourcing. They also provide a structured method of calculating the value of procurement activities like competitive sourcing processes and negotiation.

A variety of input, output, process, and outcome measures can be relevant to decisions. When establishing measurement systems—as teams often are called to do—an equally important consideration is achieving balance in measurements. The balance of process and outcome measures is one consideration, but there are others.

Use a Balanced Approach to Measurement

Historically, financial measures have occupied a central role in measuring performance. In a publicly traded company, investors focus on annual reports or even quarterly company webcasts about revenue and profit expectations. In governments, public procurement professionals are familiar with the annual budgets that measure financial performance and trends in expenses. The budget process is useful for forecasting future resource needs.

In 1996, a Harvard Business Review press book introduced the concept of balanced scorecard.[13] The central theme of *The Balanced Scorecard* was that financial measures do not portray the entire performance picture. Especially for internal service organizations like procurement offices, budget performance shows nothing about how performance objectives relate to strategic sourcing effectiveness, client agency support, and the like. Financial measures tell little about effectiveness.

Balanced scorecard approaches connect an organization's strategy to performance measures. The scorecard popularized by Kaplan and Norton differed from traditional approaches by adding measurement perspectives other than financial: customers, employee learning, and internal processes.

The use of perspectives beyond financial ones better defines the entire value proposition of organizational performance. Under the balanced scorecard approach, the customer perspective provides a definition of value in the eyes of the ultimate user. The internal process perspective— and public procurement is an example—evaluates the quality of the organization processes that are essential to success. The third performance perspective is the employee learning and growth perspective.[14] This completes a triad of additional perspectives that supplement the financial considerations used to assess organizational performance.

Still, financial systems often have data relevant to the other measurements. In procurement, for example, financial systems may record purchases using the NIGP commodity codes that categorize expenditures among various commodities and services. This data is critically important for the analysis of government expenditures necessary for strategic sourcing initiatives. And as we saw in the Colorado contracting reengineering story, the financial system time-stamped the review and approval events, providing insight into the performance of the contracting process.

Organizations may have a few upper level measures that frame the strategic priorities of the entire organization. Subunits of organizations that own the internal processes also contribute to organization success, of course. Strategic objectives are cascaded down to those subunits, and they often have their own scorecard measures.

The use of balanced measures is important. For example, an emphasis on purchasing costs without paying attention to quality can hurt an organization's performance overall. Similarly, blind adherence to short-term goals can sacrifice long-term effectiveness. Internal control functions like accounting and procurement illuminate the tension that sometimes exists between operational efficiency and effectiveness and the constraints of control systems.[15] And in classical hierarchical organizations, one department's performance measure targets may be reached at the expense of those of another department or the entire organization.[16]

The advent of balanced scorecard represented an explicit acknowledgement that measures need to embrace more than financial measures. They need to be vertically and horizontally coordinated so the entire system is achieving desired performance. As the Dallas Area Rapid Transit story below illustrates, government procurement offices can use balanced scorecards to get a more complete performance picture.

Dallas Area Rapid Transit's Dashboard

"The department just wanted to see what the customers thought about our performance." According to Connie Arrington, a contract analyst in the Procurement Department, there was no particular event that spurred the initiative, but the Dallas Area Rapid Transit (DART) decided to create a performance dashboard to measure customer satisfaction with the department's performance.

The survey was designed to obtain both open-ended responses and responses that could be quantified into the dashboard analysis. Open-ended questions included how respondents thought the procurement process could be improved, and how Procurement could further streamline the procurement process and make it more efficient.

The closed-end survey questions permitted three responses: very satisfied; somewhat satisfied, and dissatisfied. The questions included customer satisfaction feedback about the Procurement Department: time to process purchase requisitions, ability to clearly communicate during the procurement process, timeliness of response regarding contract related issues, and ability to meet the customers' objectives on the procurements. The questions were divided between contracts and purchase orders, effectively stratifying the survey because the department's procurement work groups were organized between contracts and purchase orders.

DART's information technology department played a key role in designing the survey system; the online feature helped encourage responses. The department typically received 30–50 responses to each survey. Jason Edds, the department's procurement information systems analyst, also derived data for the dashboard from existing IT systems using reporting tools.

On its one-page dashboard summary, a chart displayed the overall customer satisfaction ratings of the department's customers over the prior three years. In addition to this outcome measure, the dashboard contained both workload and process measures. The dashboard reported total number purchase orders, orders from stock (inventory), the number of open purchase orders, and total numbers and dollar amounts of contract awards. The report included average processing times in a variety of categories, and numbers of invitations for bids and requests for proposal broken down between commodities, services, construction and professional services.

The customer satisfaction chart showed satisfaction using four categories: no response, dissatisfied, somewhat satisfied, and very satisfied. This data was derived using a 12-question survey that was collected online, with responses recorded directly into a database. A single dashboard presentation of "customer satisfaction" was calculated by averaging the responses. There were plans to improve the dashboard by adding a chart showing solicitation development times and better automating the process of data collection.

(continued on next page)

Dallas Area Rapid Transit's Dashboard, cont'd.

Both Connie and Jason reflected on the process. Connie advised, "People take the time to fill out the surveys, and they want to know the results. Share the results!" Jason offered an equally wise perspective, "You have to be honest about how you present the data; the truth must be told."

DART's dashboard uses various kinds of measures. For procurement offices, customer satisfaction is an outcome measure. As an input measure, the dashboard tracked the number of purchasing requests the office received. The number of contracts awarded is an output measure. Processing times in days is a process measure. This type of reporting provides a much more complete picture of performance than the typical financial picture in traditional expenditure and budget reports.

The 2012 NIGP Pareto Award winner, Sound Transit, uses a scorecard also. Sound Transit's Procurement and Contracting Office supports the agency's mission of planning, building, and operating express bus, light rail, and commuter train services in the Seattle metropolitan area. Their experience with the scorecard reinforces the importance of organizational alignment and the learning nature of scorecards.

Their scorecard is briefed quarterly to the Chief Executive Officer at a meeting attended by executive directors. The procurement office has used scorecards since 2009, and the 2010 Procurement and Contracts Scorecard is available on NIGP's Resource Library.

The measures include measures in four categories, what Sound Transit calls "themes": project delivery, service delivery, system expansion, and stewardship of resources. The procurement office aligns with overall agency goals. For example, the overall agency strategy includes a goal of environmental responsibility. The division aligns with Sound Transit's goals using initiatives that comply with its environmental and sustainability objectives. One goal is that 100% of solicitations contain provisions requiring use of environmentally friendly practices and materials.

But even Sound Transit's performance measures are continually evaluated. Some targets for timeliness of purchase orders are always met, suggesting that the annual 80% timeliness target needs to be reevaluated. A more recent cost savings measure is being revisited. The team found that users sometimes took the first offers or quotes, when a simple phone call had been shown to lead to price reductions as high as 15%. The team sees the value of measuring the cost savings from procurement professional intervention, but it is not satisfied with the formula for measuring the amount of savings achieved. The office wants to get the measure correct.

A customer focus is part of the balanced scorecard. Perhaps one of the most powerful and challenging measures is the survey. Surveys are especially valuable because they are a direct measure of at least one aspect of performance: customer satisfaction. Surveys are widely used in internal service organizations like procurement offices.

A Note about Surveys

Surveys are an important tool for assessing effectiveness in governments and public procurement offices. Most publications about survey design contain guidance about sampling that may not be relevant to procurement teams developing or using customer satisfaction surveys. Why? Because sampling approaches start from the assumption that the universe of data is so large only a portion can be sampled to assess the characteristics of the larger population. Procurement teams typically are surveying fewer numbers of agencies and users, however, so the teams normally strive to obtain input from them all.

Still, there can be errors. Most surveys are voluntary, and self-selection causes errors. I never have seen survey-adjustment approaches that account for the fact that self-selected response rates are never 100 percent. In an audit I encountered while I was a manager, the auditor indicated that I needed a response size of at least thirty to make my results valid. I learned later that this number was related to the central limit theorem, a statistical concept. The theorem says that in a universe of data where there is no standard distribution, the means of random samples taken from that data population will be distributed normally around the mean for the entire population. The theorem is powerful because it permits central tendencies and distribution to be analyzed in large populations of data.

For the central-limit theorem to hold true, though, statisticians say that the sample sizes must be at least thirty. In our division surveys, we were attempting to derive customer-satisfaction results for all of our using agencies; we were not taking random samples from agencies. So I always wondered whether this particular statistical principle was a valid basis for criticism. (Not one to be headstrong, though, from then on I tried to get thirty responses.)

Still, the failure to get all surveys returned—self-selection error—can interject some error. Intuitively, our division teams thought that we likely were going to get responses from those customers who were really happy and those who were not. So the distributions might have been skewed at both ends of the spectrum. Yet, with four different offices using similar survey constructs, over the course of three years, the patterns of the survey results appeared to paint a reasonable picture of how our office was doing. The measures were included in our department's strategic plan that accompanied the performance-based budget submission to the governor's office.

One way we improved survey response rates was to offer anonymity with online survey completion. When the surveys first were used, responses were mailed, faxed, or emailed back to the originating office being surveyed. Survey respondents were known in most cases. Later, online survey tools permitted anonymous completion of surveys and automatic submission to email addresses not in the office being surveyed. The survey instructions notified survey recipients that we were consolidating and analyzing survey results in an office other than those being surveyed. Response rates significantly improved.

We used a consistent method of surveying over a three-year period, with customer satisfaction questions aligned between the controller, procurement, state architect's office, and central debt collections. While there were program-specific questions in each office, general customer satisfaction questions were essentially the same. The comparison of the individual office ratings revealed patterns that helped validate the survey question design.

Widely available spreadsheets have statistical functions that assist in survey analysis. The correlation function permits internal analysis of survey questions to assess whether logically related questions have responses that appear to be correlated in the way one would expect.

The use of correlation can be a source of error in decision making, though, as when conclusions about causation are drawn from the fact that two sets of data have a certain statistical level of correlation. Generally, correlation does not suggest causation unless one phenomenon comes before the second, there is a functional relationship between the two, and no third factor exists that causes both of the other two.[17] For example, when analyzing contract approval processes, one might find a correlation between low customer-satisfaction rating in the procurement office and the contract approval unit in the accounting office. It would be impossible to conclude based on that correlation that one office's performance caused adverse perceptions regarding the other, when the common factor between both might be an unacceptable total delay in contract processing from solicitation through contract execution.

But analysis of survey results can use correlation between factors without establishing a causal connection. So, for example, in our division survey, each office had a question about timeliness of support. When survey responses to individually tailored questions about program support were compared to the overall customer satisfaction rating, one would expect there to be some correlation between the two. A wide variation might have pointed to an issue with survey question design. Our division did not use the results necessarily to establish which factor (timeliness or satisfaction) was a cause of the other rating, even though we had a strong suspicion.

Survey Design

A common survey format for customer satisfaction is the Likert survey. The Likert design uses declarative statements and responses like strongly disagree, disagree, agree, strongly agree, and the like. These are easily converted into numbers for analysis using basic statistical functions like mean, variation (e.g., standard deviation), and correlation.

For example, in the Colorado Division of Finance and Procurement surveys, the four offices (State Controller, State Purchasing, State Architect, and Central Debt Collections) used an identical numerical scale for the survey. The five-point rating scale was five- excellent (model performance that consistently exceeds expectations); four- commendable (frequently exceeds expectations); three- proficient (meets expectations); two- needs improvement; and one- poor. The ratings permitted use of basic spreadsheet functions to analyze means, distribution, and correlation. They were used over three years in performance-based budgeting and permitted analysis of trends.

A survey should be designed so it can be completed in no more than 15 minutes. Lengthy surveys get fewer responses.

One possible surveying error is "response bias," or errors caused because the design of the survey unintentionally affects answers so that true attitudes are not reflected in the responses. To avoid response bias, some approaches to developing questions include:

- Keep questions precise and short so that only one dimension is measured in any one question.

- Avoid compound questions.
- Avoid terms that are emotionally charged, imprecise, or ambiguous.
- Avoid leading questions that suggest the answer.

Be careful about using reverse-bias questions, where the polarity of the ratings is reversed, meaning for example that the high number is the favorable response except for one reverse-bias question. Unexpected responses to reverse-bias questions—those that do not correlate with other similar questions—may be an indication that a survey response was not thoughtfully completed. But a high number of surprising reverse-bias responses might be caused by poor question design. Because single-bias design is so prevalent, though, use clear cautions in the instructions about the importance of reading questions carefully.

One way to avoid survey design errors is to test the survey with a small number of customers or stakeholders. Do they validate the survey design? Does the survey permit anonymity? What are their views on how survey response rates can be improved?

I admit that I violated some of these general guidelines on our Division of Finance and Procurement surveys, because we also wanted to establish expectations. Some questions that combined the evaluation with our view of expectations for our office included:

"Although the State Purchasing Office (SPO) may not always give you the answers you want, we attempt to base our decisions on the statutes and regulations, and we seek to help you understand the reason for our positions. How are we doing?

SPO tries to identify issues affecting the state procurement environment (like laws and regulations) by obtaining agency ideas and input. How are we doing?

The State Purchasing Office seeks input from other purchasing agents in the field, as well as people in various job areas in other departments, to assist us in formulating strategies, changes, and procedures for solicitations and price agreements. Do you feel you have an acceptable level of opportunity for involvement regarding these issues?

We hope our overall customer satisfaction is tied to our giving you responsive, practical, useful help that meets your needs. Overall, how are we doing?"

Our survey received some subsequent criticism among survey professionals for measuring multiple dimensions in single questions. However, our questions prompted reflection and we got thoughtful responses. We also had senior executive buy-in over a three-year period; the measures were part of the division performance-based budget and strategic plan.

One other caveat about surveys: take a close look at patterns that arise. We all get fixated on the mean, or average, when we compute ratings. But look at other measures of central tendency. The median is the point at which half of the values are below and half above. A wide difference between a median and mean may signify the existence of an outlier value that is skewing the results.

The mode also can be a useful measure for looking at patterns in data. The mode is the value that appears most often in a set of data and can help explain surprising distributions of data.

Moreover, the mode is useful when non-numeric data is collected. For example, mode can be used to look at patterns in evaluations that use descriptive works like excellent and fair rather than numerical ratings.

Consider the data distribution as well as the mean. Figure 6-2 shows hypothetical customer satisfaction ratings for a single office for three consecutive years.

Customer Satisfaction

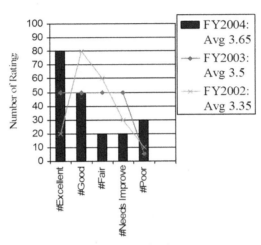

Figure 6-2. Customer Satisfaction.

With normal distributions, statistical functions like standard deviations can show the amount of distribution, whether values are spread out widely or concentrated near the mean. Sometimes, though, a visual display of data shows patterns better. In figure 6-2, the customer satisfaction surveys all have about the same mean, probably about the same median, but the FY2004 distribution is surprising. Was the office giving great service only to those who were its best advocates? Look at the distribution of data.

Our division's three-year history of customer satisfaction ratings differentiated between offices in terms of customer perceptions. The variations in ratings among offices were consistent with how intuitively we thought clients felt about our division performance. One year, the ratings were successfully used to quantify the performance effect of declining staff and justify an additional hire.

More importantly, though, we thought the nature of the questions and the responses they invited promoted a constructive relationship and dialogue between the central procurement office and agency offices.

Get Stakeholder Buy-in to the Measures

We started this chapter by broadly defining the characteristics of effective measures. Measures are relevant if they reduce uncertainty in decision making. Consequently, one of the touchstones for meaningful measures is whether they are accepted by the other stakeholders who base decisions on them. The customer-satisfaction ratings used in the Colorado Division of Finance and Procurement, for example, were part of the department's strategic plan. The measures were reported annually to the governor's office as part of the performance-based budgeting process.

The issue of stakeholder buy-in is illustrated further by the experiences of two local governments—Miami Dade County, Florida, and Rockland County, New York—in tracking cost savings and cost avoidance. These kinds of measures go the heart of the value of the procurement function. Other kinds of input, output, and outcome measures can be used to manage and improve the procurement office processes. How much money the procurement office saves is an underreported part of the profession.

There is significant work involved in tracking procurement value in terms of cost avoidance and cost savings. So one wants to ensure that the resources devoted to tracking the measure can be justified by the value the measure has to decision makers.

NIGP—The Institute for Public Procurement—defines cost avoidance as "those costs, direct and indirect, that will be avoided if certain action is taken by the government."[18] In 2007, the National Association of State Procurement Officials (NASPO) published a comprehensive whitepaper on the topic of measuring procurement cost savings.[19]

The distinction between cost avoidance and savings is important. Some procurement operations, formal bidding methods for example, avoid higher contract costs in the future. Other activities, contract renewal negotiation for example, can reduce costs measurably when compared to historical costs of agencies. Cost avoidance tends to have a forward-looking focus on what costs were avoided by a particular activity. Cost savings measures look at reductions in costs that have been incurred historically.

Miami-Dade County, Florida, and Rockland County, New York, have used this kind of reporting to their leadership. Their stories show how important stakeholder involvement was to the development of their measures.

Measuring Cost Savings in Miami-Dade County and Rockland County, NY

Miami-Dade County, Florida, and Rockland County, New York, track procurement cost savings. This story examines how cost savings and avoidance can be measured and illustrates the role of stakeholder involvement in developing the measurements.

Miami-Dade County, Florida

Procurement is a self-supporting business in Miami-Dade County. In fact, Procurement contributes revenue to the general fund to support other county business operations. So, needless to say, the mayor and county manager of Miami-Dade County value the business/financial results of the procurement organization, and they publicize procurement cost savings through press releases.

The procurement measures are defined in the Department of Procurement Management Business Plan. Miriam Singer, the county's procurement director, has an overall guiding principle on measurements: keep them credible by keeping them conservative. The savings from contract negotiations, for example, are one of a number of measures that are a source of pride for the organization, its staff, and the community.

(continued on next page)

Measuring Cost Savings, cont'd.

The business plan presents negotiation savings in three ways: current contract versus new contract price, proposed price versus negotiated price, and current contract price versus renegotiated contract price. Miami-Dade's procurement team conducts the analysis of savings collaboratively. Collaborative development enhances the staff's negotiation skills, and looking at cost savings also helps motivate them when they see the results of their effort.

Miami-Dade uses a spreadsheet to compute savings. The spreadsheet defines three fundamental savings computation models for measuring "capture of negotiated savings." Where there is an existing contract (with substantially the same specifications), the department managers and buyers compare the current contract price to the new contract price. When vendors having term contracts request price adjustments at the time of option exercise, the department may achieve a reduction in the price increase through negotiation. Occasionally, as in strategic sourcing initiatives for specifically targeted commodities, negotiation during the term of a contract is initiated to achieve more favorable pricing and can lead to quantified cost savings for the county.

The Microsoft Excel spreadsheet used to track savings is updated as sourcing events occur. The cost savings entries identify the specific contract number and how the savings were computed. The savings are tracked separately for the various units in the department: bids and contracts, construction, information technology, and requests for proposals. While the office keeps a running tally of contracts, not all are approved for cost savings reporting. The spreadsheet is reviewed collaboratively by unit managers in the department, and the savings that they agree to report are reviewed and accepted by management.

With the current budget challenges, the contract-renegotiation measurement model is being used more frequently. Many contracts involve option exercises for renewal, and some of those may include index-price-increase clauses, such as the consumer price index (CPI) or other relevant indices. Six months before contract expiration, the department conducts market research. Prices may have actually gone down in some industries. The department may decide to competitively procure a requirement rather than exercise a priced option or may negotiate to have a vendor forgo a CPI index increase or reduce pricing to reflect market conditions. Done right, these kinds of negotiations are time intensive but can be very valuable. As an example, the department was able to achieve sizeable savings by renegotiating numerous software-as-a-service (SaaS) "cloud computing" contracts.

Sometimes adjustments must be made in the basic formulas to account for peculiarities in the sourcing contexts. According to Miriam, "We used a slightly different approach to measurement in a fuel bid. In the previous contract, we pre-qualified vendors for a spot market solicitation. We have now changed the approach to aggregate quantities for all of our gas and diesel spend to award to a single vendor. We have achieved excellent pricing even when compared to what other jurisdictions around the state are paying—the state's purchasing organization was looking at the option of riding our contract."

In requests for proposals, where factors other than price are considered in the award, more analysis is done. Miriam explains, "We conduct market research, look at cost drivers, price indices that are relevant, and prices in other jurisdictions and those available from other consortia contracts. To negotiate savings, we compare our contracted award with a conservative price arrived at after market research to negotiate savings."

In another instance, negotiations with vendors permitted a substitution of an open architecture countywide radio system, saving an estimated $75 million. Likewise, negotiated extensions to warranty provisions created savings for the county.

Miami-Dade savings analysis is not applied in a cookie cutter fashion. There is collaborative analysis of the procurements by professional buyers and managers. The "value added" by the Procurement Department, as well as the method of cost savings computation, is shown on the spreadsheet. The document is available to anyone wanting to audit the method of computation. The Miami-Dade model is part of the reason the county has retained the NIGP Outstanding Agency Accreditation Achievement Award and was the first county in North America to receive NIGP's Pareto Award of Excellence in Public Procurement.

Rockland County, New York

Paul Brennan, the Director of the Purchasing Division, characterizes the procurement measurement system of Rockland County, New York, as a focus on efficiency. Paul developed the model in 2007 to track the value that the Purchasing Division brought to the county's procurement process. The project won Rockland County the 2009 NIGP Innovation Award.

Cost savings and avoidance are only a part of the county's overall procurement measurement system. The county integrates revenue growth and other elements of value that can be quantified from procurement operations. According to NIGP's website, Rockland County's model was a basis for the Spikes Cavell MEASURE system.

The county uses a Cost Containment and Revenue Generation Activities report to identify the savings and revenue realized. The goal is to demonstrate cost savings and revenues that at least equal the operational costs of the division on an annual basis. The cost-saving and cost-containment activities are broader than commonly used by other governments for measurement. For example, obtaining more value for the same cost—e.g., by negotiating extended warranties, additional spares, etc.—can lead to quantifiable savings. Audit savings can be realized by reviewing county payment vouchers to ensure that vendors are charging the proper bid/contact prices, and the savings from refunds can be measured. Utility and telecommunication invoices are often complex and can be fruitful places to find savings from overpayments.

In some cases, savings can be achieved in a requisition request by researching and developing innovative ideas or developing a source for an equivalent product or service at a reduced cost. Negotiation of improved or new incentive or rebate payments by vendors can lead to tangible increases in revenue. These are all examples of interventions by procurement professionals that can add value in measurable ways.

Using the data, the division produces an annual profit & loss statement that details all costs associated with operating the Purchasing Division, cost savings realized from procurement activities, and revenue produced as a result of procurement activities. The division prepares a comprehensive annual report that integrates all of the financial and performance metrics. The report identifies the "net profit" per professional buyer, demonstrating how each buyer returns more in savings to the county than the cost of the position itself. Notably, the report also describes other aspects of the Purchasing Division that show quality and value: awards and other recognition; organization mission, vision, and values; staffing levels; professional certifications; participation in professional associations; major projects and initiatives;

(continued on next page)

Measuring Cost Savings, cont'd.

and purchasing goals. The annual report's discussion of projects and initiatives highlights many of the cost savings achievements. Examples in recent reports have included reduction in operational expenses through restructuring a transportation contract; reduction in costs of pharmaceuticals; and savings from a copy paper cooperative procurement led by the county.

According to Paul, "Getting buy-in from management is a key to the success of performance measurement—and cost-savings measures in particular." The profit-loss calculated using the model—Paul's operations also receive revenue—has been publicly reported annually by the county.

Note, in both of these stories, the importance of stakeholder buy-in.

The cost savings reporting by Miami-Dade County and Rockland County are meaningful in that they satisfy their governments' objectives. Rockland County's measures were developed in consultation with county finance officials. Miami-Dade's measures are audited by, among others, the county's internal and external auditors.

Achieving buy-in from stakeholders on use of measures may require some initial, limited testing. Thomas Linley's office-machine consolidation project involved a test program among a few Ohio agencies to demonstrate the validity of the cost savings measures. Success on the initial pilot was leveraged in making the case to other agencies to convert to multifunction machines.

In balanced scorecard implementations, organizations are advised to limit deployment to a portion of the organization first.[20] This can be an effective "laboratory" for learning about cascading of measures and alignment with organizational strategies, before broader deployment throughout the organization. Especially where there may be resistance, a pilot can demonstrate success and stimulate needed change.

We often think of measurement as being a precise yardstick with accurate scales. In many ways, the time and financial measures described in this chapter represent traditional uses of measurement. They are relatively precise, and their accuracy can be assessed.

But another kind of measurement that procurement offices commonly use involves more subjectivity. In evaluations, there is considerable judgment applied in selecting among alternatives. While the cost or price aspects of proposals fit the more common characterization of measurement—they are precise, for example—the evaluation of technical merit, management capability, and past experience is much closer to qualitative or subjective evaluation. This topic crosses over into decision-making theory that will be discussed in the next chapter. Because evaluation methods often are numerical and use statistical functions (however basic), and are considered objective, this chapter introduces some considerations to make these measures more meaningful.

Evaluation and Measuring Preferences

This chapter ends with an introduction to decision making in the context of measurement. Many decisions are a collaborative activity by a variety of people. Whether a team is selecting organizational award winners, or procurement teams are evaluating proposals and choosing the one most advantageous to the government entity, the process involves resolving varying preferences and estimates about future project success. While these evaluation methods often are assisted with numerical evaluation methods, they are inherently subjective.

Douglas Hubbard (2010), a noted expert in decision research, believes that anything can be measured, although sometimes the value of measurement may be offset by the costs to measure effectively. Experts can express opinions about the desirability or probability of future courses of action. With training, they can be "calibrated," so there is a reasonable degree of certainty in their projections and consistency with other experts.[21] In large measure, this approach to measuring desirability is what evaluation committees do in evaluating competing proposals.

The organization of data so it is consistently presented can improve evaluation.[22] Even though matrix evaluation techniques sometimes are criticized,[23] the criticism often stems from evaluation criteria that are arbitrary. All measurements have to be clearly defined in order to be valid. This is known in metrology as an *operational definition*. The operational definition of a measure is designed to achieve consistency.[24] A team may have to test the application of a definition before engaging in data collection, for example. In an evaluation context, in order for numerical systems to achieve generally acceptable results, there are certain components widely considered necessary.

One is the existence of criteria. Use of written factors and standards helps mitigate the effect of an error: the emerging preference error. It has been shown that people will adjust their internal criteria for evaluation to justify their preferences. Written criteria are one way to reduce the possibility of this error.[25] Criteria should go beyond simple one-word descriptions like "excellent" or "satisfactory." Instead, criteria should use descriptors that include a target or goal of the feature. For example, the term "excellent" has no target goal or feature. An evaluation plan could instead include a descriptor saying that, in the case of the project personnel, "excellent" means that "offeror and its personnel are well qualified and have recent, extensive, directly relevant experience with projects substantially equivalent in scope to this project." That descriptor adds a goal or target of the "feature," in this case experience of project personnel.

Criteria must also be weighted in terms of importance to the decision.[26] In procurement, assigning weights or importance to criteria usually is done through evaluation factor and sub-factor weights, as illustrated below.

Visualization of evaluations is one way to facilitate the decision-making process. Some people are good at deriving meaning from columns and rows of numbers. Other people are better at processing information visually. Ullman's book, *Making Robust Decisions* (2006), describes how computer decision-support software can visually display evaluation differences and relative satisfaction with alternatives. Standard Microsoft Excel tools do not have those sophisticated decision support features built-in, but Excel does have a visualization feature that can be useful in team decision making—conditional formatting.

Use of Conditional Formatting in Microsoft Excel

One especially valuable tool to assist in measuring preferences is conditional formatting in Microsoft Excel. This spreadsheet tool is used most effectively in procurement evaluations if it includes a written definition of the factors and numerical ratings used by evaluators in evaluating proposals.

Conditional formatting assigns colors based on the values of cells. So the spreadsheet can display a blue for outstanding scores and red for poor scores, for example.

To use conditional formatting with a numerical rating system, start by agreeing on a numerical scale. Five-point scales provide enough granularity for evaluators who may be asked to judge a proposal using descriptive words like no response, poor, fair, good, excellent, and outstanding.

Write generic word descriptions for the various ratings. Ideally, the generic descriptions are relevant across the range of factors, although in procurements the definition of standards for technical/management and experience aspects of proposals may be separate. The goals for some factors (such as ease of use of a computer system) typically are defined in the RFP. One example of a criteria description for a technical factor might be, "4- excellent (proposed an excellent approach that meets all requirements and exceeds many; requires no clarifications; good understanding of project, recognizing non-obvious dependencies that demonstrate more than surface understanding; low risk of unacceptable or late performance; agency involvement not likely to exceed normal contract administration)."[27]

Evaluators perform individual evaluations using the criteria. They enter their evaluation scores, e.g., the ordinal numbers 1 through 5, and the spreadsheet does appropriate conversions into the overall ratings. The spreadsheet assigns the evaluation factor weights according to their importance as described in the request for proposals.

Excel permits the spreadsheet cells to be formatted by colors or other formatting according to value in the cells. Red, yellow, green, and blue can be used to portray ratings in the poor, marginal, good, and outstanding categories. Excel RANK, QUARTILE, and MAX functions can be included in conditional formatting formulas and are especially useful for highlighting the range of desirability among evaluators and in the overall ratings.

Typically, once the spreadsheet is completed after the initial evaluation, it is distributed and a meeting held so evaluators can discuss differences in perspectives. As is shown in the top portion of figure 6-3 comparing the ordinal ratings (ordered rankings), the cell formatting easily identifies significant differences between evaluations. Some procurement team evaluators saw things very differently. Procure7 had a strong preference for the third vendor. Procure8 strongly favored the second proposal. Ideally, evaluators discuss significant differences. After the discussions, adjustments can be made to individual evaluator ratings.

The process is repeated after oral presentations and receipt of best and final offers/proposal revisions, if any, before the final evaluation. An example of a final evaluation spreadsheet is shown in the bottom portion of figure 6-3. It shows factor weights and composite evaluations for a major information system technology procurement. Of course, the factors and sub-factors have to align with the criteria and weighting as stated in the request for proposal.

Tech1	3.9	1.6	2.0	3.4	2.4
Tech2	3.7	3.4	2.1	3.4	2.8
Tech3	3.3	1.0	3.1	2.3	2.0
Tech4	3.9	2.7	3.1	1.7	2.3
Tech5	3.9	2.3	3.4	2.0	2.3
Tech6	3.6	2.6	2.1	1.3	3.3
Tech7	3.8	1.8	3.0	1.3	1.8
Tech8	3.6	2.8	3.6	1.8	1.4
Procure1	2.5	2.2	2.6	1.4	2.3
Procure2	2.2	1.3	3.3	2.3	2.3
Procure4	3.1	2.1	3.5	2.2	3.2
Procure5	2.7	1.5	2.4	2.0	2.5
Procure6	2.3	1.4	3.0	2.0	2.7
Procure7	2.1	1.5	1.4	1.8	2.1
Procure8	2.7	1.5	3.2	2.3	2.7
Procure10	1.4	1.1	1.6	1.7	2.3
Cost1	3.5	3.8	3.3	2.3	2.0
Cost2	4.0	3.0	3.8	1.8	1.8
Cost3	4.3	3.3	3.5	1.5	2.0
Cost4	4.3	3.5	2.0	2.5	1.8
Cost5	4.0	3.0	3.3	1.5	1.3
Cost6	4.0	3.5	2.8	1.5	1.5
Exper1	2.0	3.0	4.0	1.0	3.7
Exper3	3.3	3.0	4.3	1.3	1.7
Exper4	3.7	4.0	4.0	1.7	1.0
Exper5	1.7	3.3	4.7	1.0	2.7

Vendor Recaps	Weights	Vndr B	Vndr E	Vndr F	Vndr H	Vndr I
TECHNICAL SCORE	685	506.68	539.88	502.63	527.93	533.82
Technology Requirements	130	94.40	109.34	103.17	112.29	110.03
Hosting Model (4.3.1)	25	18.34	21.86	19.91	21.69	20.63
User Interface (4.3.2)	40	28.10	32.03	31.28	32.40	32.38
Security (4.3.3)	40	29.30	35.26	32.05	35.80	36.28
IT Platform, Performance, Reliability (4.3.4)	25	18.66	20.41	19.94	22.41	20.76
Functionality	500	375.99	383.91	366.17	378.97	380.85
Accounting Interface (COFRS/FINET) (4.4.2)	40	31.80	32.93	33.13	33.73	33.87
Product Catalog (4.4.3)	40	30.35	31.76	30.50	32.35	30.66
Inventory System (4.4.4)	5	2.64	2.28	1.46	2.36	2.05
Trading Community (4.4.5)	25	16.16	19.97	20.31	18.59	15.25
Electronic Invoicing (4.4.6)	25	15.96	19.79	20.18	15.63	16.18
Supplier Support (4.4.7)	40	28.85	30.40	28.35	29.95	29.50
Bidding Process/Quote Capability (4.4.8)	15					10.44
Full procurement solution	10					
Electronic Ordering (4.4.9)	40	32.05	30.46	29.80	31.25	32.20
Workflow (4.4.10)	40	32.21	32.24	33.07	33.39	31.33
Political Subdivisions Extendability (4.4.11)	40	31.20	32.05	31.06	32.05	31.00
Electronic Authorization (4.4.12)	40	32.64	31.96	32.13	34.16	33.89
Logging and Auditing (4.4.13)	25	19.87	21.02	20.62	20.97	20.53
Reporting (4.4.14)	25	18.98	20.53	20.18	19.83	19.06
Systems Integration (4.4.15)	40	32.40	34.46	30.69	34.11	32.97
Software Maintenance and Support (4.4.16)	25	20.80	21.71	17.32	21.60	21.57
Training and Documentation (4.4.17)	25	18.53	20.48	16.67	19.10	20.35
Other System Features	15					
Procurement Card Interface (4.5.1)	5	3.87	3.96	3.53	3.61	3.88
Procurement Card Program	10					
Implementation Strategy (4.6)	40	32.32	32.54	29.76	32.85	31.23
COST TO STATE/IMPACTS	500	314.79	335.63	383.33	373.33	410.63
Fee/Revenue Analysis	125	63.75	57.50	125.00	65.00	101.25
Impact from Vendor Fees/Revenue Model	125	76.04	89.58	87.50	98.96	101.04
State Infrastructure/Personnel Costs	125	86.46	88.54	80.21	102.08	104.17
Expected Efficiencies and Cost Savings	125	88.54	100.00	90.63	107.29	104.17
EXPERIENCE/DEMONSTRATED CAPABILITY	300	246.00	219.75	192.00	269.25	253.75
Past Experience Web-based Procurement/Catalogs	100	63.25	80.75	83.25	91.75	88.75
Past Experience Integration	100	80.00	52.50	46.25	88.50	80.00
Qualifications/Resumes	100	82.75	86.50	62.50	89.00	85.00
TOTAL POINTS	1485	1067	1095	1078	1171	1198

Figure 6-3. Conditional Formatting.

The measurement of preferences by experts comes with a set of biases.[28] *Anchoring* is a bias: simply thinking about a number can influence the value of subsequent judgments. Similarly, the *halo/horns effect* is a bias that stems from the inclination to be predisposed to an early observation that is either favorable or adverse. An evaluator can subconsciously let a preferable (or conversely an unattractive) alternative like a proposal create a predisposition that can affect later evaluations.

Evaluation instructions and training can remind evaluators to rate against the criteria and standards, not one proposal against another. One sometimes sees evaluation committees rotate the order of evaluations among individual evaluators. This may help mitigate the anchoring error or the halo/horns error.

Bandwagon bias refers to "group think," or the tendency of a group's persuasive power to interfere with an individual's evaluation. One recommended procurement practice in RFPs is individual evaluation of all proposals prior to the evaluation committee's meeting to discuss the ratings. This approach helps mitigate the effect of bandwagon bias.

Arbitrary application of standards can overemphasize the importance of factors where the scale is not understood and there is a subjective trade-off between factors in the evaluation.[29] Ordinal ranking of proposals in a request for proposal, for example, may not properly identify trade-offs between technical merit and price. For example, ranking three proposals first through third would numerically imply that the best proposal is 66% better than the third, even though point totals might have differed by as little as 5%. Having defined standards better shows the true, relative differences in proposals.

There are studies that validate the use of calibration techniques to improve the estimates of experts. Use of questions to test the extremes of reasoning may also help improve the quality of assessments.[30] Pre-evaluation meetings of evaluation committees can be used for calibration. Evaluators should at least meet to discuss the criteria and what they mean. Better yet, a previous proposal on a similar procurement (not one of the current competitors) could be used to apply evaluation standards. The evaluation committee could individually evaluate, then meet and discuss the application of criteria.

This section introduces the topic of complex decision making, in the context of one of the more complicated team activities: proposal evaluation. These kinds of evaluations still involve subjectivity even though math is used to manage the process. Many of the errors can be minimized by making the evaluations collaborative, and having evaluation teams discuss their evaluations in order to reach clear understandings about the meanings of criteria, the information relied on in the evaluation, and how that information satisfies or does not satisfy the criteria.

Make Measurement Meaningful

Measurement reduces uncertainty. Therefore, stakeholder confidence and agreement are critical to the process. In addition, balanced approaches that measure the customer perspective, internal processes, and employee growth increase the usefulness of measurement. A successful evaluation methodology requires techniques that reduce bias and increase confidence in the results. Meaningful measures support effective decision making.

7 First Ask How? Then Why? Then Decide

Decision making involves examining and selecting ideas and alternatives. Solid decisions require an understanding of the current process, a well-organized analysis, and, of course, stakeholder buy-in. Teams use a variety of tools to expand the pool of ideas, compare them, and select and eliminate options.

One key to an effective team project is knowing when the project and team have evolved sufficiently to begin the analysis phase. There often is time pressure to move quickly into team performance. Focusing too early on time and schedule, however, can get the team into solutions before there has been proper discovery and exploration.

The best place to start in analysis is a clear definition of the problem. The problem often is a result of something that is known to be unsatisfactory. The customer or client often is the best source for identifying problems.

An effective problem statement describes what is wrong without suggesting the solution. For example, "The procurement process needs to the streamlined" is not a good problem statement. On the other hand, "The vendors often cannot keep a proposed 'A-Team' on a project by the time the contract is awarded" describes a problem without suggesting the solution. This chapter is about getting to those root causes of problems.[1]

An effective problem statement is concise and specific. One way to develop a succinct problem statement is to think as a team about the what, where and when of the occurrence. What's affected? Where does the problem arise? When? What is the extent of the problem? How does what occurs compare to what should be occurring. Is there only one problem?[2]

Note that "Why?" is not included in the list of questions. That analysis comes later. But a clear definition of the problem begins the process of determining the root cause.

The title of this chapter highlights a common error: prematurely moving to the "why" and solutions before there is a clear understanding of either the problem or the process "as is." In many continuous improvement initiatives, a team looks at the value of steps in a process. The relative placement of "how" and "why" in the title is a reminder to first understand the process, the "as is" condition, before asking the "why" questions.

We've all encountered situations where leaders or other problem solvers had not taken the time to understand the process and why it exists. Take internal controls. Like financial approvals and even procurement rules, they exist for a reason. Among other things, controls protect against errors and malfeasance, assuring that financial reporting is accurate. No matter how wise a solution might ultimately be, leaders can lose the support of those who have lived with a process or system and, in many cases, have tried to improve it (often successfully). Those employees may be particularly proud of a process that they helped develop. Teams should have a firm handle on the "as is" before they tackle the underlying value propositions in a process. Otherwise, they risk triggering resistance no matter how good the solutions seem.

Divergent, Emergent, and Convergent Thinking

The thinking phases in problem solving generally are categorized into three types.[3] Divergent (expanding or opening) thinking expands the pool of ideas. Brainstorming is a way to generate ideas or alternatives. Tools like brainstorming leverage the power of teams by uncovering varying ideas or alternatives for any given problem or issue. The problem of using too much structure too early is that it cuts off creativity and inhibits the creation of ideas.

The exploratory or emergent phase is where various tools are used to look at, compare, and relate ideas to one another. This chapter explains process mapping, the use of the Ishikawa (or fishbone) diagrams, and other root-cause analysis techniques. They are traditional tools used by teams for exploring ideas. These tools, in fact, are considered part of the essential arsenal used by quality management professionals.

The follow-on to brainstorming that starts to categorize ideas—a tool known as an affinity diagram—begins to narrow or focus ideas as they are grouped into categories. Ideas not fitting into grouped categories sometimes move to a "parking lot" or other list used to manage ideas that do not seem to fit. This is a modest form of convergent thinking (closing) that begins the process of focusing the team on certain ideas.

The closing phase (or focusing or convergent phase) is when certain ideas or alternatives are selected and others eliminated. Priorities are set. Decision making, the ultimate closing, is discussed last in this chapter.

Understand the Process the Way It Is

But what comes first? The first step in problem solving is defining or clarifying the problem. Problem solving and continuous improvement initiatives often start with a perception that a gap exists between the "as is" state of a process and its "desired state." A team must have a clear understanding of the "as is" before moving towards solutions.

One of the tools used most often to analyze the "as is" is the process map. A process map (also known as a flowchart) improves understanding by creating a visual depiction of a process, its steps, decision points, and outputs. Punta Gorda, Florida, used this tool (along with other quality management tools) to look at its payables process.

Process Mapping and Root-cause Analysis in Punta Gorda, Florida

In chapter 1, we described Marian Pace's opportunity to improve the city's payables process. Marian, the Procurement Manager for the city of Punta Gorda, used an approach that the city had adopted: Lean Six Sigma, a process improvement model that was an outgrowth of Motorola's Six Sigma process used to improve manufacturing. Since the mid-1990s, Six Sigma has been integrated with Lean principles, the Japanese approach to process improvement. Lean Six Sigma has well-known tools, some of which were used by Marian's team. The steps in Lean Six Sigma are defined by the acronym DMAIC: define, measure, analyze, improve, and control.

Marian assembled a team that first defined the problem in writing. The project's purpose was to improve the city's payables process. Eventually the project led to implementation of a procurement card. As her team defined the problem, "The current process for ordering and payment of goods and services is not efficient or cost effective with the advancement of technology and current procurement best practices."

After defining the project scope and surveying vendors about their procurement card practices, Procurement dove deep into an analysis of its process for purchase orders costing less than $1,500, those not arising out of a formal solicitation process. Higher dollar purchase orders typically are more complex and do not generate the high transaction volumes that the project was intended to address.

The team used process maps (see, e.g., figure 7-1) to visually depict the payables process. The process map included times for each step derived either by physically measuring process steps or by sampling transactions identified through the financial system. Once the average times for processes were computed, the times were recorded on the process maps.

Color-coding was used on the process map to identify steps considered non-value-added and "bottlenecks." As Marian explains, "It was hard to hear that your hard work didn't add value. In some instances, however, steps were required for auditing. We all went through each step to identify if that step offered anything of value to our customers (i.e., would the customer be willing to pay for it). If we ended up disagreeing, we would take a vote from all team members and the majority ruled.

"For example, the process of returning a purchase order was considered non-value-added. The steps associated with correcting nonconforming goods after rejection were considered both a non-value-added step and a bottleneck. Likewise, much of the manual document handling (like printing and scanning) associated with receiving, acceptance, and payment was considered non-value-added and identified as bottlenecks."

As a part of the analysis phase, the team also used Ishikawa diagrams, sometimes known as the fishbone diagram, to get at the root causes of problems. (See, e.g., figure 7-2) Through brainstorming, the team identified the environmental, people, resources, documentation/materials, and process factors that might have been causes of the problems. The teams worked down through causes of problems. For example, a first-level root cause identified by the team was having "manual processes." The next level drilled down to the root causes of not having automated processes and the fear of change to current processes. In the purchase-order process, the team found root causes that included completion errors by users, such as incorrect account numbers. In receiving processes, there was insufficient attention paid to

(continued on next page)

Process Mapping and Root-cause Analysis, cont'd.

the city's receiving procedures. Processes generally were burdened by excessive manual paper handling throughout the receiving and payment processes.

The team then moved to identifying solutions. These steps required setting priorities among competing solutions (using a prioritization matrix, discussed later in this chapter), evaluating costs and benefits associated with solutions, the time for implementation, ease of use, and other change management considerations.

The team eventually recommended that the city use a procurement card contract already sourced by the county and available to the city as its vehicle to tailor a solution for the city. Software also was available to reconcile procurement card purchases with the city's financial system. After a pilot implementation, the city moved into the control phase of DMAIC, focusing on the monetary limits of program controls and delegated authority. When this story was written, the city was planning to roll out the procurement card program incrementally citywide.

According to Marian, the prioritization matrix was particularly valuable, as was the fishbone diagram.

"There was a real 'wow' moment using those tools," Marian says. "They visually helped the team find the causes of problems, and they had the side benefit of helping address the fear of change."

The symbols used by the city on the process map (also known as a flowchart) (figure 7-1) are typical. Generally, squares are used to signify steps in the process. Diamonds are used to portray decisions made during the process. Rounded symbols identify the start and end point of the process. The map uses special symbols to identify documents produced in a process, in this case the purchase order and receiving report.

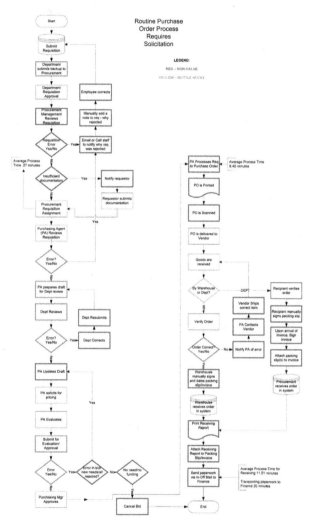

Figure 7-1. Process Map/Flowchart.

Perhaps the best single reference for a description of all of the traditional quality management tools is Nancy Tague's *The Quality Toolbox* (2005). The book categorizes the various tools in terms of the phase they best represent: expanding or focusing. The book includes, for example, a comprehensive explanation of the flowchart, considered one of the basic tools of quality management.[4] The book explains the evolution of the quality models like Six Sigma and contains other useful information like guidelines for effective presentations.

The flowchart in particular enables a visual depiction of the steps in a process (in sequential order), the decision points, inputs, feedback loops in a process, delay or wait time, ties to other processes, and deliverables such as documents. Flowcharts are used to reach a shared understanding about a process among team members and stakeholders.

Some tips and basic steps in developing a flowchart include:

- Self-stick notes are ideal tools for initially constructing a process map.
- Begin by defining the scope of the process to be examined: where it begins and ends.
- Use high-level process flowcharts initially to define the handful of major steps, and then build on them.
- Use brainstorming to identify the activities that take place in the process, writing each on a self-stick note. (Don't worry about sequence initially.)
- Then arrange the activities in a proper sequence.
- Characterize activities as either process steps (square), decision points (diamonds), etc.
- Then draw the arrows to show the process flow.

This tool is used initially to define the "as is" process state. After further exploration and eventual decisions about improvements, a flowchart can be used to define the ideal or "should be" process. They can be used to document a process that later can be used in training or policy manuals describing a process.

Tague (2005) describes useful variations of the flowchart. One is the *top-down flowchart* that begins to build on a high-level flowchart by listing major sub-steps under each major step. This type of flowchart can then be turned into a more detailed flowchart.

A *deployment flowchart* adds organizations or locations to the flowchart, arranging the steps into columns that correspond to the various offices involved in the process steps. Sometime called *swim lane flowcharts*, they can be useful to show the number of handoffs between offices as the process progresses, handoffs that may be adding time or creating inefficiencies.

Tague counsels that the self-stick note process of building a flowchart should be a centerpiece because it requires team members to participate, share ideas, and learn about the process. Do not, Tague warns, use an expert to take control entirely of process mapping.[5]

Ask "Why" At the Right Time to Identify Value and Causes

There are two dimensions to the "why" question in this section: value and causation. The sensitivity about when to ask "why" is related to another tool often used in analysis: the value map. Lean Six Sigma, for example, emphasizes customer value during process analysis. Especially in organizations heavily involved in internal controls—like procurement and finance offices—the concept of "value add" can be controversial and invite a myriad of viewpoints. Make sure there is a clear understanding of the current process before launching into criticisms of it.

There are useful tools for finding causes and assessing value. As Punta Gorda learned, cycle time analysis and value mapping are particularly useful for looking at processes. The objective with these tools is to identify the value and time associated with performance of each step in the process.

Times can be added to process maps to show the duration of each step, where there are delays or bottlenecks, and the time taken for decisions. In the early stages of looking at Colorado contracting, the average contract processing time was derived from data in the financial system that records the dates of various contract approvals. Wait time also can be added to the map. The team then can assess the relative value-added and non-value-added nature of process activities. In the case of the Colorado project, the process efficiency rate could be computed by comparing the wait time (non-value-added) to the remaining review times (value-added) for each office having contract approval responsibilities. Punta Gorda likewise was able to look at process efficiency using the data it collected.

Another important tool is *value added analysis*. Tague (2005) describes this analysis as a useful adjunct to process maps. The colors of symbols used on the Punta Gorda flowchart depicted the nature of the value added by various steps.

For each step on the flowchart, the team asks whether the step contributes to customer satisfaction or is necessary to the output. In Tague's description, steps are color-coded green if they are considered value-added steps because the answer is yes to both questions. If an answer is no to either question, then another question is asked, "Does the activity contribute to the organization's needs?" If so, then that step is color-coded as yellow because its value is derived from organizational requirements. When the answer is no to all questions, the steps are color-coded as red. Typical non-value-added activities include wait time and rework. In Punta Gorda's project, the time associated for returns, for example, was considered a non-value-added step. So was much of the manual paper handling associated with a purchase.

Internal control activities pose a special challenge. While the customer may not see the steps as necessary, in many cases statutes or regulations require certain steps. Punta Gorda, for example, knew that auditable internal controls are legitimate reasons for some steps in a payment process. Still, these organizational value-added activities may be fruitful areas for further examining whether policy changes may be necessary. In the case of Colorado's look at the contracting process, revisions to thresholds for use of bilateral contracts (with the attendant delays for legal review) were driven by reexamination of the reasons for not permitting the use of purchase orders for some services. Said another way, what was the true value of having legal review of smaller dollar contracts?

Punta Gorda used another popular tool—the Ishikawa or fishbone diagram, another of the seven basic quality tools used in quality management. The fishbone diagram is used for identifying, visualizing, and categorizing possible causes to a problem. Along with techniques like the "Five Whys," an Ishikawa diagram can help get to the root cause of problems.

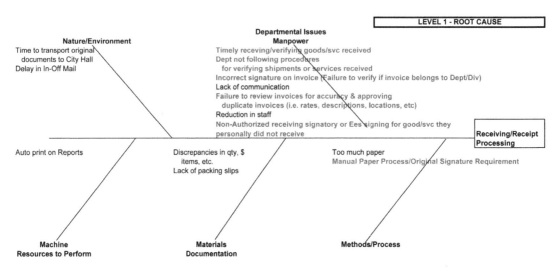

Figure 7-2. Ishikawa (Fishbone) Diagram.

Fishbone (Ishikawa) Diagrams and the Five Whys

Nancy Tague in her book, The Quality Toolbox (2005) describes the use of Ishikawa (fishbone) diagrams and Five Whys. Both are considered basic tools of quality management. The tools are used to explore the causes of problems.

The steps in developing a fishbone diagram are:

- Brainstorm possible causes of the problem and record short descriptions on self-stick notes.
- Draw the fishbone diagram on a surface where self-stick notes can be posted.
- Determine generic headings for the main causes of the problem and use them to name the main branches of the diagram. The standard categories are methods, machines (equipment), people, materials, measurement, and environment. However, these can be grouped with different headings,[6] and the team might want to first decide on the most relevant heading. Punta Gorda used the standard categories.
- Ask, "What are the issues causing/affecting _____?"
- Continue to dig deeper and deeper into the problems by asking "Why does this happen?"
- Arrange short titles for the potential causes and sub-causes as branches under the main causes.

The fishbone diagram helps organize potential causes for further exploration and is useful for setting priorities in a team's analysis. Root-cause analysis goes deeper and is used when trying to uncover the root cause of a problem. Root-cause analysis would be used in conjunction with branches of the fishbone diagram where a team believes further exploration of potential causes is required.

A common tool used for root-cause analysis is the "5 Whys" analysis:

- Ask why a problem occurs. Write all of the answers on notes and arrange them in a column.
- For each cause, ask again, "Why does this problem occur?" or "Why does this situation cause a problem?" Place those answers in a column to the right.

> - Continue until asking five times, or until the fundamental problem, e.g., a policy problem, procedure, etc., is discovered.
>
> Punta Gorda used the Ishikawa diagram at various levels, and they were linked. Figure 7-2 (under Methods/Processes) identified the existence of manual paper processes as a cause. A separate Ishikawa diagram was used to explore the manual process (including signature requirements). That second diagram had "manual process" as the problem on the right side of the diagram and depicted fear of change and absence of automated processes as possible causes.
>
> The root-cause analysis is a critical step in any improvement project. Just as the problem definition is an essential first step, the search for the root cause is just as important and should not be skipped. Problem definitions should steer away from solutions. Just don't forget the root-cause analysis later!

The tools discussed so far in this section are commonly associated with the emergent (exploratory) phase and begin to move the team towards the focusing or convergent phase of the project. Flowcharts or process maps are used to gain an understanding of the process the way it is. (Eventually they can also be used to map the desired end-state, or the way the process should be.) The use of Ishikawa (fishbone) diagrams focuses the team on root causes and potential solutions.

Eventually, the team moves to the ultimate focusing activity. They either make a critical decision, or more often, they recommend a decision. Chapter 6 introduced some considerations in decision making in relation to the use of evaluation spreadsheets and how they can be used to avoid thinking errors. Decision making gets front-and-center treatment now. How does organization of a team's thinking and the decision-making process help promote better decisions?

Organize Thinking and Decision Making

Throughout the project, a team informally sets priorities, determines team norms, and develops performance strategies. At the end of the analytical process, a team encounters the ultimate closing activity: a decision from among various alternatives. The decision can be delegated to the team itself, or the team can frame alternatives and analysis for decision by someone else.

On the way to making decisions or fashioning recommendations for another, thinking needs to be organized. This book does not pretend to cover all errors in logic, but there are some approaches and questions that can be useful to a team's assessing the validity of its thinking. Often the process of making a decision involves movement from the general to the specific, application of assumptions, and examination and integration of beliefs shared by the team.

Fisher and Sharp (2009) call this thinking process the "ladder of inference." From data and information, arguments are fashioned that ultimately lead to a conclusion. Some of the steps in inference use inductive reasoning. Researchers fashion a hypothesis, design an experiment or statistically valid method of observation, analyze the results, and draw conclusions. Teams also use deductive reasoning when they move step-by-logical-step from one conclusion to another. There are useful techniques for assessing the validity of these inferences and the associated reasoning. Consider these questions by a team:[7]

- What are the assumptions in our logic, and are they valid?
- Are we moving logically from symptoms through diagnosis of problems and their causes?
- Has the team stopped looking for relevant, objective data prematurely? What data do we need? What have we left out?
- If data is used, is the team biased towards vivid data? Are we giving undue weight to quantifiable data?
- Is our own preliminary point of view influencing our analysis?
- Are we progressively testing our theories against the objective data?
- Would "role reversal" and seeing the issue from another perspective be helpful?

Also consider these questions derived from the inquiry model of learning:[8]

- Are arguments sufficiency justified? Are they based on opinions or beliefs that are supported by evidence?
- Do assumptions exist that should be challenged?
- Are premises being used in arguments that are debatable?
- Are analogies used in arguments valid?
- Are definitions clear so that ambiguity is not contributing to confusion and relationships among ideas?
- Are there logical fallacies in our arguments, e.g., overgeneralizations or a *false dilemma*, that sets up only two options where there may be more?

Questions such as these test the underlying reasoning processes in a team. This chapter describes some decision-making errors that may provoke other ideas about how to test the team's thinking.

Decision-makers considering recommendations of a team may ask similar questions. But the team also should use these kinds of diagnostic questions to assess the validity of its own thinking. Tools like those already introduced are useful for helping a team organize its thinking. The Five Whys tool, for example, directly tests the ladder of inference relating to causes of problems.

In general, the validity of a team's thinking bounds the effectiveness of decision making. A decision could be the choice of a policy. It might be a response to a specific type of risk. Typically, decisions are considered processes because they evolve. Circumstance may change and require an adjustment in a project or implementation strategy, for example.

Decision making is a theme running throughout this book. The team's purpose guides project decisions. Chapter 4 looks at decision making as a part of team processes. Multi-voting, for example, was described as a useful tool in some circumstances to help teams make decisions in more complex situations where consensus cannot be expected. Punta Gorda used a form of multi-voting when encountering differing opinions about whether the step in a process had value; the team agreed to abide by decisions made in this manner. Agreement on team norms for decision making is especially important to keep a team on track and moving forward. Other decisions involve central choices made at the end of a project that encompass the purpose for the team's existence.

A decision is not an event, it is a process.[9] Much that is written about decision making pays little attention to that point in time when the choice is made. Rather, sound decisions are preceded by clarification of the problem. Decision-makers expand the range of options and consider more than one. They reality-test the assumptions, look at the options from varying perspectives, and find ways to counteract emotional responses. Sound decisions incorporate the use small experiments or pilots to learn about cause-and-effect of various alternatives, and they anticipate and prepare for what can go wrong.[10]

The formality of decisions varies. Some decisions have few alternatives or little consequence. Others have a myriad of considerations that must be carefully managed on the way to making a decision that is very consequential.

Some decisions are constrained by legal and regulatory limits, organizational preferences, or policies that limit alternatives. Even organizational culture can limit available alternatives. In Colorado, for example, there was a strong culture favoring decentralization in procurement. A team's project charter—if there is one—should identify the constraints on decisions and explain them in a way that the team understands. Sometimes, the constraints come from another office who has policy-making authority in an area. Ideally, of course, one would have those stakeholders also at the table during a project.

One can learn from other decisions.[11] If similar decisions have been made before, let those decisions inform the current one. Who had the expertise and participated in the decision? What information or data was used? Was feedback from any stakeholder particularly important? And whose approval was needed?

The tools described so far in this chapter are useful for exploring alternatives and ideas. Once the team begins to close in on specific alternatives, the focusing phase is underway. Eventually, there is a decision to forgo certain ideas or alternatives for others considered most favorable.

Teams and the Brain's Role in Decision Making

Emotion, rationality, creativity. As more is discovered about the brain, studies indicate that how we decide may just be an extension of these basic processes in the brain.

On the one hand, some think that rational thought may only be useful for simple problems, because the brain cannot process more than a half-dozen considerations at any one time. The more we ponder trade-offs in the traditional way, the more likely we are to over think problems and arrive at the wrong conclusion.[12] There appears to be some agreement that over-thinking sometimes does not lead to better decisions than the initial hunch.[13] These are provocative ideas that warrant some examination: the possible risks from over-thinking a problem. Still, procurement professionals work in an environment where rational decision making is expected.

The brain is an argument between rational thought and emotion.[14] For simple decisions with no more than several essential variables, use of analytical portions of the brain may be best. For more complex decisions, however, like buying cars, over-analysis has been shown to lead to decisions later regretted.

(continued on next page)

Teams and the Brain's Role, cont'd.

Lehrer (2009) even says, "Think less about those items that you care a lot about... Don't be afraid to let your emotions choose."[15] But to minimize the unwarranted effect of short-term emotions, consider the expected outcome of a decision in the short term, the mid-term, and long term.[16]

The quantified aspects of a decision can lead to errors in the ultimate decision. Consider a decision about where to live in relation to work. The basic feeling of the importance of being close to work can be overcome by analysis of the distance in miles, and analysis of the actual minutes to commute, eventually leading to a decision that places too little value on the convenience of being close to work.[17]

Still, novel problems require use of reason.[18] Some researchers recommend that the rational sections of the brain be used to collect and categorize the facts.[19] Simulation like that used to train aircrews helps internalize the ability of the emotional parts of the brain to process the information effectively and make for better decisions (especially intuitive ones under stress).

Experts suggest, when there is time, that decision-makers get away for a while from the decision and let the emotional brain, the intuition, govern. Yet, the emotional brain is prone to errors.

Daniel Kahneman's book, *Thinking, Fast and Slow* (2011) identifies more thinking errors found through research. Outcome bias (or hindsight bias) is the tendency to revise what we remember about our own beliefs in light of what actually happened, what Kahneman characterizes as a cognitive illusion. Individuals can be influenced irrationally by recent experiences and intense feelings, a phenomenon known as availability bias. Use of multiple evaluators (commonly used in procurement evaluations) helps mitigate the effect of those errors. Kahneman's prospect theory says that humans are risk averse when there is known gain, and contrary to our expectation, risk seeking when confronted with known loss. Said another way, humans place about twice as much importance on potential loss than gain.[20] Another manifestation of this bias is a preference for the familiar or status quo.[21]

Kahneman identifies other examples of errors or cognitive illusions. The research helps illuminate errors sometimes identified in negotiation texts: susceptibility to vividness (use of facts to establish credibility), framing (advantages to framing as a loss rather than a gain), availability (e.g., having the draft document ready), and anchoring (errors from aggressive opening positions). According to Kahneman, we tend to be overconfident in our ability to estimate prospects for success. Moreover, our last experience is the one that often drives perceptions and decisions.

Other errors include the tendency to generalize from single examples rather than examining other circumstances (the fundamental attribution error). An example might be characterizing all construction companies as "changes contractors" based on one bad experience. Chapter 6 taught that we sometimes confuse data correlation with causation: the fact that data coexist in statistically significant ways does not necessarily mean that one phenomenon causes the other. And business texts in particular sometimes suffer from the halo effect, where existence of attributes is inferred from the existence of one positive outcome without rigorous research.[22]

Teams hold a key to avoiding errors. The individual brain is prone to errors from too much unwarranted certainty." The best decisions emerge when a multiplicity of viewpoints are brought to bear on the situation."[23] Teams can extend the decision-making process to consider the "arguments unfolding in your head," and "always entertain competing hypotheses."[24]

Process can help avoid errors too. Lehrer talks about Cockpit Resource Management (CRM) or more effective use of flight crew team approaches as accounting for decreases in accidents attributable to "pilot error."[25] CRM deters unwarranted certainty and promotes sharing of information. Kahneman (2011) finds value in bureaucracy and organizational processes as well because they slow down thinking, bring varying perspectives to estimates of uncertainty, and help illuminate errors in thinking.

One special value of a team is its ability to evaluate and jettison bad ideas. Teams expand ideas early on then winnow them down. But at some point—not too early—they should include a process for healthy skepticism. Walt Disney was known to use three different rooms to create ideas and assess them. Room 1 was a place where ideas could be generated without any restraints. Room 2 was the room where ideas were clarified, organized, and made into visual storyboards. Room 3 was the place where the entire team would critically assess the project. Criticism was constructive and addressed to the idea. A team's presentation to decision-makers should capture "Room 3" considerations.[26] Use of a devil's advocate, whose role is widely accepted as a constructive one, can accomplish the same thing.[27]

Teams also can help by constantly discussing what is not known.[28] One of Kahneman's recurring messages is that decision-makers sometimes favor conclusions based on their own experience: they may adapt their view of facts so they are consistent with those conclusions.

Much of team achievement is related to overcoming resistance to change. Teams can help. Leaders may make decisions, but teams influence them. Many people need to support a strategy or decision, and teams can serve as their voice.

There is value to teams and the use of structure in decision making. A structured approach, including the use of checklists[29] to capture key considerations, together with collaboration and sensitivity to the types of errors that exist in decisions, improves the prospects of making good ones.

Even simple decisions (with limited alternatives) can be improved by using an organized decision process. Benjamin Franklin's method may be the most well-known: the pro-con list. Described by Ullman (2006) in his book *Making Robust Decisions*, the process for choosing between two alternatives was set out by Franklin in a letter he wrote in 1772 to Joseph Priestley, an 18th century English theologian credited with the discovery of oxygen. Priestley had asked Franklin's advice about whether to take a lucrative offer of employment as a tutor and advisor for a British lord. But the job was in London, and Priestley lived in and loved the countryside.

Ullman describes the Franklin pro/con method as useful when deciding to reject or accept single alternatives.[30] Ullman describes the tool this way:

1. Include a pros and cons column on a sheet of paper.
2. For each alternative, fill in the pros and cons.
3. Eliminate pros and cons by drawing lines through them with respect to their relative importance. Multiple pros or cons may equal a single pro/con in terms of relative importance.
4. One pro or con column may become "dominant" and determine the decision.

To use the pro/con technique effectively, though, there are some suggested enhancements.[31] Include a "do nothing" option. Teams should discuss the basis for their knowledge about each of the alternatives' pros and cons. What is the confidence level in the assumptions, and how was the information or data? Make sure there is a dissenting opinion in the group.

Do not keep the alternatives fixed in stone. Consider other options or alternatives. Use a whiteboard or self-stick notes to promote creativity and flexibility in the evolution of the list. Refine it. Meetings used to explore ideas and make these types of decisions are the ones when open dialogue and discussion need to be encouraged.[32]

The pro-con method of evaluating alternatives is best suited for simple decisions with only two or three alternatives. Heath and Heath (2013) mildly disapprove of the Franklin pro-con list, though. To them, the pro-con list magnifies one of the greatest errors of decision making: narrow framing problems and not developing more options.

They tell the rest of Priestley's story. He eventually rejected Franklin's advice. He created a new option, an eighteenth-century version of alternative work schedules where he would make trips to London when needed. He also sought counsel from others besides Franklin to test his visceral feelings about the offer. Priestley eventually took the offer but on modified terms.[33]

More alternatives—proposal evaluations, for example—make the process of deciding more complex. Prioritization or decision matrices, like those illustrated in chapter 6's discussion of procurement evaluation, may be more useful ways to manage multiple alternatives and various criteria. Matrices involve development of criteria, weighting them, and developing rating scales used for the criteria so relative scores can identify the alternatives considered most favorable.[34] The relative scores can promote meaningful discussion among team members.

Punta Gorda's Prioritization and Decision Making

Punta Gorda's team used a solution prioritization matrix to identify the best solutions from among a range of possibilities. The first step was to identify the criteria for the solution. Marian Pace's team identified five criteria: whether the solution was cost effective (including considerations of the potential revenue such as rebates given by banks), time to implement, process reduction (time and paper), ease of use/implementation, and the level of acceptance by internal and external stakeholders. The team spent considerable time discussing the meaning of criteria in the context of the project. The team documented the criteria definitions, so when they conducted the evaluation, all members understood them.

In the second step, the team used a spreadsheet to perform a "nominal group technique" to determine the weighing of the criteria. Figure 7-3 shows the prioritization matrix used for this step. Each team member individually ranked criteria on a one-through-five scale. Those individual weights were tallied in the column named "Individual Weights." The aggregated criteria weight was computed using the total of the individual weights divided by the total weight available (90). For example, the team members agreed that cost effectiveness was the most important criteria: it ended up being 33% of the weighting.

The third step was to brainstorm ideas for possible solutions. In this case, the team came up with five ideas, including a "no change" option. Among the alternatives was to execute a "linking agreement" to the county's procurement card contract with its own rebate formula. Another possibility was for the city to conduct its own solicitation for a procurement card solution.

Each team member ranked the alternatives in order of preference. An Excel spreadsheet was used to average the ordinal ratings and weight them according to the weights selected by the team. The result? "No change," as might be expected, was the least attractive alternative. The number one alternative was to execute a linking agreement with the county's procurement card contract.

The team then developed an implementation plan. The city council had to approve the approach: the procurement card agreement and purchase of software to permit procurement card purchase reconciliation with the city's financial system. The team planned the steps needed for implementation—a pilot period and the training needed for broader implementation in the city.

There were constraints on the decision. For one, the city wanted implementation by the third quarter of the fiscal year because that period accounted for the highest amount of expenditures in the city. Coordination with the information technology department was required because the payables/procurement card reconciliation system had to be integrated with the city's financial system.

To brief the city council, the team prepared a cost-benefit analysis. The analysis compared the licensing costs of the payables/procurement card reconciliation software system to the financial benefits from the procurement card rebates expected to be received. Financially, the decision was an easy one: procurement card rebates were expected to be more than three times the costs of software installation, licensing, maintenance, and training.

The city council approved the team's recommendation. The city executed a contract and started the pilot program.

When Punta Gorda, Florida, embarked on the project to improve its payables process, setting priorities among various solutions became important. But first, the team had to decide what weight to assign to various considerations. Was the possibility of revenue from a procurement card most important? Was time to implement the predominant consideration? Or was it more important to improve efficiencies by streamlining the process? Other considerations included the ease of use and the acceptance of the new process by both internal and external stakeholders like auditors and vendors.

Criteria 1   Cost Effective
                 Define: Net Revenue (Cost - Rebate)
Criteria 2   Time to Implement
                 Define: Agreement, Policies, Training & Roll-Out
Criteria 3   Process Reduction (Time/Paper)
                 Define: Ability to reduce process, fewer errors, less paper
Criteria 4   Ease of Use
                 Define: Maintain database/policies, training, Understanding policies/processes
Criteria 5   Acceptance (Internal/External)
                 Define: Internal: Dept/Finance/City Manager/Council External: Vendors/Auditors

| | **TEAM MEMBERS** | | | | | | Individual | Criteria |
	#1	**#2**	**#3**	**#4**	**5**	**6**	Weights	Weight
Cost Effect	5	5	5	5	5	5	30	0.33
Time to Implement	1	1	1	1	1	1	6	0.07
Process Red	4	3	4	4	4	3	22	0.24
Ease of Use	3	4	3	3	2	2	17	0.19
Acceptance	2	2	2	2	3	4	15	0.17

TOTAL WEIGHT   **90**

Figure 7-3. Prioritization Matrix.

The prioritization matrix shown in figure 7-3 was used to establish the weighting of the individual criteria. Separate matrices were used to rank specific solutions. The various solutions were individually evaluated by evaluators against each of the criteria using an ordinal ranking of first through fifth. The weights were applied to those combined ordinal rankings. In effect, a separate prioritization matrix was developed for each of the solutions with a consolidated matrix ultimately leading to the preference: linking to the county's procurement card contract.

Another way that teams narrow ideas is through the use of the impact-effort matrix, sometimes referred to as an effective-achievable chart.[35] This tool is a version of a more generic two-dimensional chart used to understand the implications of all combinations of two factors or dimensions relevant to an issue.[36] Ideas or alternatives are entered on self-stick notes. The team can individually or collectively arrange the ideas or alternatives along two axes. One axis is impact or effectiveness. The other axis is the amount of effort required or how achievable the choice is.

The team evaluates how well the alternative accomplishes purposes or solves problems. Effectiveness/impact can look at the strength of the overall contribution to improvement. Achievability or effort looks at how easy it is to accomplish, the resources required and the likelihood of success. Or a team might consider the amount of control over the environment that the team has. The team brainstorms the criteria in the context of the specific project.

This grouping of ideas/alternatives into four quadrants can be used to identify priorities or preferences: easy/high impact, difficult/high impact, easy/low impact, and difficult/low impact. While these kinds of matrices do not make decisions for teams, they are useful for categorizing ideas, generating team discussions, and setting priorities. Teague notes that this tool is not as useful when many criteria are involved, when a prioritization matrix may better model a decision.[37] But they are especially effective for communicating alternatives to stakeholders.

More complex decisions require additional steps and considerations. Ullman (2006) developed a decision checklist that provides a useful approach to complex decisions.

- Recognize that there is a decision to be made.
- Write or state the issue as a single sentence.
- Develop multiple alternatives for resolving the issue.
- List the stakeholders.
- Work to generate a set of discriminating criteria and their targets.
- Understand who thinks which criteria are important.
- Evaluate the alternatives relative to the criteria.
- Identify and manage the evaluation uncertainties.
- Fuse the evaluations using a structured method.
- Base future activity on a what-to-do-next evaluation.
- Document the decision and the reason behind it.

Idaho's Performance and Risk-Based Evaluation System

In chapter 2, we discussed Idaho's project to improve its service procurements. This opportunity was identified because, although the state was spending so much on procurement of services, the procurement team did not feel it was selecting the right contractors needed to obtain acceptable service over the contract life. They realized that evaluators with far less expertise and experience than the vendors were spending more and more time in proposal evaluations, and evaluators were not finding the true differentiators between proposals. So the state tried a best value "Performance Information Procurement System" (PIPS) that proved to be extremely successful in construction projects.

The PIPS system is characterized by the use during evaluation of "dominant information": past performance and abbreviated risk minimization plans. Proposals are less than 30 pages in length, as opposed to the hundreds of pages often filled with information that is less useful in selecting vendors. Initial evaluations are blind with respect to proposer names or other identifying information in the submittals. More evaluator time is spent in interviews, contract risk minimization, pre-planning, and validation of contractor-provided materials. Evaluators spend considerably less time wading through proposal content that does not represent a true differentiator among proposals. Moreover, the selected vendor is able to understand more about the state program's needs before contracts are finally executed.

The state has used the PIPS system successfully for several large procurements outside of the construction area. PIPS was used to purchase information technology systems, health insurance, medical care, and food services.

The Idaho story shows improvement outside of a traditional continuous improvement model. Their project started by questioning assumptions about the way to conduct an RFP. At its core, the project involved a change to the process the state uses to make complex decisions.

Chapter 4 introduced decision making in the context of teams. The Idaho project, however, touches more complex decision making. An award decision involves numerous factors, some of which are critical, and some may not be capable of rational trade-off. The evaluation of alternatives largely is qualitative, cost perhaps being the main exception. Risk and the relevance of vendor experience and past performance are among the considerations that are most complex. There is uncertainty in the application of evaluation criteria. There may be unequal knowledge and experience among evaluators. And there simply may be differences in perspectives among team members. Of course, managing all of these various components of the decision process is very difficult.[38]

Technology-based decision support systems exist that account for evaluator/decision-maker satisfaction (with criteria) and uncertainty through an application of numerical techniques called Bayesian methods. Computerized decision-support systems have been developed that account not only for how well an alternative satisfies criteria, but also for the individual uncertainty of evaluators. As an example of the complexity, with ten factors, five proposals, and five evaluators, along with their attendant uncertainty, complex decisions can morph into an information management challenge involving 2,500 (10 x 5 x 5 x10) pieces of information.

These systems may not apply perfectly to a public procurement environment, however. For example, the models accommodate individual evaluator development of evaluation criteria, while public procurements require a definition of evaluation criteria and their weighting in advance of the solicitation. The systems also permit revisions to the decision criteria throughout the process, while public procurements may not have the option of changing decision criteria midway through evaluation. Finally, these models require individual estimates of decision uncertainty that may not be accurate themselves, leaving yet another numerical rating that is subject to challenge by third parties looking at the evaluation process. The algorithms that consolidate uncertainty estimates into an overall evaluation may be difficult to explain to a judge looking at the rationality of a procurement decisions after a challenge by a bidder. So these computer simulations may not be practical for public procurement offices.

Still, though, they offer insight into effective decision processes. Ullman (2006) himself acknowledges that the underlying computer application may not be used, but he finds utility in studying guidelines for decision making from these systems.

The Idaho PIPS project met headlong one of the key issues with traditional evaluation systems. A proliferation of factors often hides true differentiators. The shortening of proposals and revised focus on cost, experience, and risk helped Idaho target what were considered the real discriminators between proposals for services.

A problem with some numerical evaluation systems is their permitting numerical trade-offs between proposal features that may not really be capable of trade-offs.[39] For example, ease of system use and training factors may permit some trade-off numerically, so exceptional ease of use may offset the need for robust training. Other factors may not be so susceptible to trade-off.

Take the financial health of a company. One occasionally sees offeror financials rated numerically. It is difficult to see how strengths in financials could be estimated as an offset to technical or management aspects of the proposal. By reducing the number of evaluation factors to the meaningful discriminators, one improves the chances of modeling true trade-offs. Proposal risk, cost, and performance history—factors used in the Idaho PIPS model—are three factors reasonably susceptible to trade-off.

Ullman (2006) provides a series of other considerations in the process of complex decisions that are worth highlighting. Agencies commonly use numerical scales to evaluate qualitative criteria, with criteria defined in terms of the goal. Ullman has found people have difficulty performing good differentiation with more than seven choices, and five-point scales are common.[40]

Ullman recommends that one always consider the effect of uncertainty by evaluators. Uncertainty can be the result of two little information, misinterpretation of criteria, or variations in the amount of knowledge of evaluators. Some decision-support models account for evaluation uncertainty. But even without these systems, evaluators at the least can discuss evaluations as a team to clarify criteria and their application.[41] The use of visual evaluation tools, like Excel's conditional formatting discussed in chapter 6, can vividly highlight differences in evaluator satisfaction levels even though that model does not mathematically account for variations in evaluator uncertainty. The sharing of team knowledge is one recognized way to reduce evaluator uncertainty.[42]

When discussing as an evaluation team the apparent differences in evaluations, begin with the criteria most likely to impact the overall decision and having the widest variation.[43] This helps focus the decision on factors with the greatest sensitivity, that is, those most likely to affect the overall decision as they change. Again, the conditional-formatting method described in chapter 6 can assist in identifying those factors.

As a companion consideration, do not load up the evaluation with factors that are important but whose satisfaction is mandatory. Some procurement offices use mandatory requirements as pass-fail criteria, and the literature recommends reducing the evaluated factors to only those that meaningfully differentiate between proposals. Important criteria that can be evaluated pass-fail are called *filters*.[44] This method is used, for example, when solicitations ask that some factors be addressed as yes-no responses.

Ullman identifies fundamental questions that a team must answer before making a decision. Which is the best alternative? What is the risk that the decision will not turn out as expected? Is enough known to make a good decision? Is there buy-in for the decision? What must be done next to feel confident about the decision, given the limitation on resources?[45]

Ultimately, any team—evaluation teams included—must address these decision-making issues. The procurement ideally integrates risk in the evaluation process, assembles adequate information for the decision, has the support of senior executives and stakeholders, and has evaluation processes that organize information and support decision making.

Document the Recommendation or Decision

Documentation of the decision rationale has value. In procurements, many statutes and ordinances require written findings and determinations for various stages of procurement. Award decisions are a common example, as are vendor nonresponsibility determinations that disqualify companies from receiving an award.[46] These determinations are the central focus in bid protests and appeals, for example, that challenge some aspect of the procurement. Perhaps more importantly, they serve as a record of the team's rationale from which vendors can learn, as in post-award debriefings, for example.[47]

When preparing memoranda for award decisions, use succinct explanations that summarize the strengths of the winning offer. Highlight why the winning proposal won using RFP evaluation language as the guide. If an offer wasn't strong in one area, say so. It shows a balanced evaluation. Don't just let the spreadsheet—if numerical ratings are used—speak for itself entirely. People decide. Spreadsheets don't.

Then have the team try on the decision memorandum for size. Does it map to the evaluation factors and criteria in the request for proposal? Will it communicate fairly the differentiators to unsuccessful bidders if they read the memo? If not, revise it.

Documenting the rationale has value apart from satisfying the legal requirements. It is a reference document for answering questions about how the decision was made; it can be reused as a reference by future teams with similar projects.

The ending of a project involves a decision also. Often, a great deal of time and resources are spent in moving a project forward. There are various stakeholders involved, many of them with different perspectives. Quantitative considerations alone are rarely the driving consideration in ending a project. Many times the decision does not rest with the team but resides with another stakeholder (often an executive).

The cooperative Colorado/Utah e-procurement system illustrates decision making in the context of ending a project as well as the value of documenting a decision rationale. The decision memorandum served as a reference when a subsequent e-procurement solicitation was led ten years later.

Deciding to End a Project

"If you build it, they will come." Unfortunately, that isn't always true. Sometimes, it's just not the right solution. In 2000, Colorado and Utah attempted the first ever, two-state cooperative procurement for an e-procurement system. E-procurement systems were in their nascent state at that time. Virginia and Washington had had some success. Not too long after, Georgia, North Carolina, and Florida had procurement systems. Both Colorado and Utah had online solicitation publication systems, but they did not have systems permitting streamlined ordering from vendor catalogs, online quote capability, or broad integration of procurement and financial systems.

At the time, decreasing revenues and budgets challenged states. Self-funded models were being touted by industry as a no-brainer solution. In this funding model, little or no state-appropriated money was required. Instead, industry financed the system development and implementation through fees paid by vendors in the range of 1% of the order amount.

The e-procurement contractor took considerable financial risk, commitment of capital with the expectation that the eventual orders would generate the revenue to offset expenses and make a profit.

The Colorado/Utah contract was structured as a production option contract, with the states having the absolute right to exercise or not exercise the option based on the performance during the pilot phase. Everyone expected that to be a formality. It wasn't.

What actually happened? There were far fewer orders placed through the system than expected. The major expenditure categories in the states were technology, paper, and other office supply products. The world-class suppliers had robust online ordering systems that government buyers liked. They were intuitive, while the new catalog system was viewed as an intermediary system that added no value for the decentralized buyers. They didn't particularly care about the strategic value of a system like this: permitting states to get visibility into expenditures that legacy accounting systems simply don't provide.

In the early days of e-procurement systems, they generally required development of an electronic catalog into which vendor products could be loaded with a description and price. The theory was that vendors would achieve efficiencies in ordering, the aggregation of products on the system would be more convenient for government buyers, and the vendors would welcome the opportunity and be enthusiastic even in the face of a small fee on orders. For some vendors with sophisticated online configuration and ordering systems, however, integration into a third-party catalog looked like a step backwards.

Moreover, there were significant change management challenges that had not been anticipated. Some agency buyers resisted using the system and complained to their senior department directors. Coupled with some unrealized expectations about what the system would do technically, and resistance among sophisticated vendors to integrating with the catalog, senior executives showed little appetite for bearing the pain associated with the project. Overall, the experience proved that the old adage—"if you build it they will come"—could be seriously wrong.

In January 2002, the decision was made not to exercise the production option. Given the significant investment by the contractor, the decision merited special attention and careful consideration. The state had been collecting implementation effort data by the various users during the pilot period, including the time spent by users during implementation. The users also had provided comments during testing. Catalog vendors were polled about their experiences.

The project management team prepared a memorandum to senior officials that explained the contract type, the necessity of an option decision, and the pros and cons of the system. The project team also conferred with the contractor about the recommendation. Despite what had been characterized as a "quick win" by the governor's innovation consultant, ultimately a decision was made not to exercise the option.

While the decision was a difficult one and obviously a source of disappointment for the implementation contractor, there was no challenge to the decision. The decision memorandum subsequently became a useful reference document for the 2010–2011 procurement of an e-marketing system by the state of Colorado on behalf of the Western States Contracting Alliance.

Teams often do not make the final decision. They may be assembled to conduct the investigation, run pilots to test changes, coordinate with stakeholders, and identify alternatives. The team may come up with suggested criteria for a decision. But often recommendations are communicated to an executive or some other person (or group of persons like an executive team) for a final decision.

In my Air Force experience, most formal decisions having broad organizational impact were made above me. Our responsibility as individual officers and teams was to prepare staff packages in a way that permitted effective decisions, often with an accompanying presentation. Over the years, I distilled what I learned into an acronym, ABOARD, for preparing written decision packages that are coordinated with other offices and frame the rationale for the final decision.

ABOARD: Staff Work for Decisions by Others

For over four decades, junior officers in the United States Air Force cowered when they were told they had not "completed staff work." "Completed staff work" means giving the decision-maker all of the information necessary to make the decision. The term is used in *Tongue and Quill*,[48] at first a pamphlet and later an electronic publication that describes approaches to effective oral and written communication, including email.

Many decisions are made by senior executives or others at levels above the team. The communications that aid the decisions must be made in a way that organizes information, states criteria for decisions, analyzes alternatives, and clearly states recommendations for action. The decision packages often have to be coordinated with other offices and stakeholders.

Remembering the audience is the key to effective communication. Who will review the memo or listen to a presentation? What knowledge do they have about the project? What will they be expecting to hear? Clearly identify the objectives. What are the expected outcomes, e.g., providing information or, reaching a decision, or approval? What actions are needed from the audience or the recipient?

Presentations and written communications should answer specific questions. One useful acronym for remembering the essential elements of a written presentation or written memorandum for decision making is ABOARD. Make sure your decision package addresses the following elements:

Authority/Action to be taken. Why is the executive signing or approving this? Describe the authority for the decision. It could be a statutory prescription, executive order or direction, project charter, or other directive. State that the communication is for information only or describe what the decision-maker is being asked to do: decide among alternatives, select a winning proposal, make a staffing decision, etc.

Background. Describe the background for the decision. If a team was convened to conduct the initial analysis, describe the team members and steps taken to get to the recommendation. A brief chronology can be helpful.

Options. What alternatives exist that can or cannot be done? Describe the alternatives or options that have been identified by the team as worthy of consideration. If options or alternatives might intuitively be warranted but have not been considered, explain why. Describe how alternatives are limited by legal and regulatory limits or other constraints—known organizational preferences or policy limitations, for example.

Analysis. What's the best option and why? Explain what role objective data played (if any) and the pros and cons of each option or alternative. If specific decision-making tools have been used, summarize how they were used by the team to identify and prioritize options or alternatives.

Recommendation. State the recommendation and briefly summarize why.

> ***Documents Attached.*** Include the document used to execute the decision. This can be the signature on a policy document, a blank signature page for a procurement selection decision, etc. Also, depending on the style of the decision-maker, include copies of key source documents such as statutes, background reports, etc.
>
> ABOARD is a useful organizing acronym for assembling a decision package. Where there are other coordinating offices, make sure to route the package for their review and comments.

When developing recommendations, it may be useful to understand what senior executives are told about evaluating them. Kahneman, Lovallo & Sibony's 2011 *Harvard Business Review* article, "Before You Make That Big Decision,"[49] is particularly helpful to guide teams into further questions about their analysis and recommendation process. The authors suggest that executives ask various questions in order to test the reasoning of teams bringing them recommendations. Among their questions:

- Is there any reason to suspect that self-interest on the team has colored by the recommendations?
- Have the people making the recommendation fallen in love with it?
- Were there dissenting opinions within the team?
- Have credible alternatives been considered?
- If you had to make this decision again in a year, what information would you want, and can you get more of the information now?
- Do you know where the numbers came from?
- Can you see a *halo effect*, that is, the story is more emotionally coherent that it really is?
- Is the team overly attached to past decisions?
- Is the team overly cautious (or optimistic)?

This chapter covers a lot of territory on thinking and decisions. How does one improve the quality of decision making? The answer it turns out is practice. More will be said about practice in chapter 9, but one particular tool is worthy of mention now: decision retrospects. Opportunities to practice real decisions sometimes are rare. So teams need to learn as much as they can from decisions they make or recommend.

Use Decision Retrospects

To improve decision making, debrief. One author recommends keeping a decision journal as a way of improving later decisions.[50] In complex projects, well-documented decisions or recommendations serve as an artifact that a team can then reevaluate.

Decision retrospects are a way to look back and learn from decisions. Did the decision resolve the issue? What information, presentation, thinking, or data could have been used to filter out options faster? Were the project's purpose, requirements, and organizational policies of value? Were they used effectively? Did the decision help the project's progress? Were the right people involved in the decision process? Were there unintended consequences from the decision, and could those have been forecasted? Were the risks, the things we worried about, the right things? Did the team have sufficient authority to make the decision in a timely and effective way? Overall, what was learned in the decision process that could help future projects?[51]

Chip Heath and Dan Heath's book, *Decisive* (2013), points the way to a retrospect about the decision to end the Colorado/Utah e-procurement project. That project was designed with a useful "trip wire," an approach the Heath brothers advise. The end of the pilot phase required a decision about whether to exercise the option for full production (and statewide implementation).

The memorandum clearly identified the project purpose that guided the decision. The goals were specified in the RFP, never changed, and included: automation of the overall procurement process; system ability to support more dynamic supplier pricing capabilities using the system catalog features; and expected reduction in the costs of procured goods and services through, among other things, enhanced competition achieved through broad supplier acceptance and integration into the system.

Broad supplier acceptance and a streamlined ordering system were key goals. Neither was on the near horizon in the judgment of the project team.

The decision memo framed options other than just abandonment and exercise of the project option. Heath and Heath caution against narrow framing, that is, not fully exploring available options, because decisions are improved by having more than one or two alternatives. Extension of the pilot phase, development of success metrics, and a more targeted selection of suppliers for catalog integration were considered but not recommended. One of the fundamental problems with the implementation was the absence of mature technology that would permit vendors already having sophisticated configuration and ordering catalogs to integrate without having to go backwards in terms of technology and customer satisfaction.

Heath and Heath caution decision makers to reality-test assumptions. The consultant assessment of the self-funded model was that it was a "quick win," a common belief at the time. "Zooming in" for a more in-depth understanding of industry's readiness for catalog integration would have been useful, as would a "zoom-out" reality-check about the expected acceptance of the system by users across the state. As it turned out, the level of system use was much lower than expected. Moreover, despite what Daniel Kahneman and others recommend, the state never considered the base rates of information technology implementation success as an historical window into the likelihood that the project would succeed. Information technology projects were known to have grim statistics in terms of the number of large projects that met original expectations of scope, time, and budget. Some additional analysis should have been done to evaluate the basis for the unwarranted optimism that this project was a "quick win."

A bigger picture view might have triggered another of Heath and Heath's suggestions: that teams should prepare to be wrong. The Colorado/Utah project did not use a pre-mortem (more about that in chapter 8) in order to identify potential risks that eventually materialized. Users considered the system complexity unnecessary; they preferred to use their favorite vendor catalogs.

Further, the technology simply had not matured enough to integrate sophisticated computer and office supply vendors already possessing robust online catalogs.

A retrospect would have illuminated considerations that could improve the prospects for success in future attempts at acquisition of an e-procurement system. As it turned out, the decision memorandum later was useful and did identify some key challenges: change management, user resistance, the need for executive commitment, and encouragement to overcome the "pain" in adopting the new technology.

Retrospects have the advantage of drawing on tacit knowledge and lessons learned while the project is in the minds of the team members. The Colorado/Utah memorandum achieved many of the objectives of a retrospective: it identified key reasons for the eventual project outcome in a way that could be used for learning in future projects.

It's a Process

Decision making is a process, not an event. It involves examining, analyzing, and selecting ideas and alternatives, and a variety of tools of varying complexity are available to support the process. Teams can use specific tools to engage the convergent (closing) thinking necessary to focus and decide on ideas. They can study past decisions to gain a better understanding on how to approach them. Perhaps the most important factor, however, is stakeholder buy-in. Indeed those who study decisions identify stakeholder buy-in as a key objective of complex decisions[52] because it often drives successful implementation.

PART III

—◆—

SUSTAIN THE TEAM'S EFFORTS

8   Manage Risk and Change

Risk means the possibility that an event will adversely affect achievement of objectives. Thus, risk management encompasses planning, organizing, and controlling resources and activities to minimize the effects of loss. In many respects, risk events can be identified, impact and likelihood estimated, and treatments planned and implemented. However, resistance to change is one of the most significant risks that teams encounter, and, as such, it is usually addressed separately as change management.

Project Risk and Procurement Risk

Risk management is defined as the process of planning, organizing, directing, and controlling the resources and activities of an organization in order to minimize the adverse effects of accidental losses at the least possible cost.[1] There are heuristic guidelines for managing risk: don't risk a lot for a little, don't take risk purely for reasons of principle or losing face, never risk more that you can afford to lose, consider the controllable and uncontrollable parts of the risk, and consider the odds and what your intuition and experience tell you.[2] Try to achieve a "balance between affordability and practicality."[3] This section of the chapter will describe the more formal risk-management framework, explain its relationship to project management, and highlight some particularly relevant procurement considerations.

Risk has been managed in procurement and contracting for years. Risk is considered during subcontract management by commercial vendors and an explicit consideration in planning in complex projects. Earlier models used in procurement focused on contract types, size and complexity of the work, and costs/financial considerations to be assessed in every procurement.[4] Risk management, more recently, has been elevated to a discipline akin to project management, financial management, and procurement management. With the expansion of advanced contracting and project delivery systems, and performance-based contracting, a greater understanding of risk management is required. NIGP has a separate course on procurement risk management built around Elizabeth Wright's *Risk Management in Public Contracting* (2007) Resistance to technological change is identified as an example of risk in NIGP's principles and practices.[5]

Risk management extends from procurement planning to contact administration, even contract closure. Risk management embraces boilerplate contract language, e.g., insurance, indemnification and limitation of liability clauses that allocate potential liabilities and other risk.[6] But it goes far beyond to market research, statement of work requirements, evaluation strategies, and contract administration approaches. Risk management begins before a project even starts towards objectives, at the time when decision-makers are deciding how to proceed.[7]

This section develops concepts of risk and its applicability to all projects. The application of risk-management practices is on a continuum. Even small projects involve some risk, but planning can be informal and at a high level. Other large, financed infrastructure projects may involve sufficient complexity, stakeholders, and risk to warrant formal risk-management planning. Moreover, financial institutions may require it. Procurement professionals should develop the habit of thinking "risk" in any project, no matter how small. Push the project through the identification, assessment, treatment, and monitoring phases of risk management.

Take a public event for example. As told in chapter 5, the law firm of McKenna Long & Aldridge LLP hosted an annual event in Denver to bring industry and procurement leaders together to learn about current developments in public procurement. Outside speakers were used, the agenda was published well in advance, and people traveled from out of town to attend.

In an event of this type, there is a sizeable investment of peoples' time. Organizers hope to minimize the risk of things going wrong. How does one mitigate the risks in conferences? The legal secretary who oversaw this event, Lisa King, used planning effectively. She started early, expected success, but in Lisa's words, "Planned for the worst." Lisa King explains, "Getting down to the final days, you're just trying to follow-up and anticipate what can go wrong. This starts with visiting the venue the afternoon before the event to make sure the resources are in place."

The day before the presentation, the firm and hotel tested internet connectivity and audio-visual systems. In one instance, where an out-of-town speaker's schedule changed, the hotel and firm set up a remote call-in/audio capability for the presenter in case the speaker had an irresolvable conflict. The firm's IT professional pre-installed presentations on the primary computer and had a back-up computer available (with presentations available also on a flash drive). Lisa emailed the program director and panel moderators' cell phone numbers to panelists for emergency notification in case there were last minute cancellations or delays. The panel moderators—McKenna Long and Aldridge attorneys familiar with public procurement law—were ready to fill in for speakers who might unexpectedly have to cancel.

The firm had written handouts with enough content for attendees so they could be used to conduct seminars in case of equipment failures. The PowerPoint three-slide-per-page printing format is a useful note-taking tool and serves as a good backup presentation handout.

On the day of the event, the firm tested the computer, projector, and files. They turned off computer hibernation so speaker presentations were not interrupted. Lisa and the program director met with panelists and moderators to discuss how allotted time would be managed and time remaining signaled and how the remote controller/laser pointers operated.

Cell phones were used to monitor speaker status. Some risk—severe weather, for example—is residual or inherent and can never cost effectively be mitigated. That risk is considered "accepted" using risk-management jargon.

Complex risk-management models need not be used on all projects. But like Lisa King and her firm demonstrated, risk-management considerations at least informally should be incorporated into project planning.

The COSO Risk Management Framework

Risk management enjoyed resurgence with the 2004 publication by the Committee of Sponsoring Organizations (COSO) of *Enterprise Risk Management—Integrated Framework*. COSO is the organization that also developed and published the 1992 guidance on internal controls, *Internal Controls—An Integrated Framework*. COSO describes internal controls as encompassed within enterprise risk management.

The essential aspects of internal controls relate to processes, compliance, and financial reporting. Procurement offices are familiar with the compliance and reporting obligations surrounding sound financial management, as in procedures involved in management of procurement card programs. Compliance with procurement rules likewise is a key ingredient of satisfying legal requirements for fair and reasonable pricing.

Risk management expands its scope beyond reporting and compliance to operations. Moreover, enterprise risk management adds another consideration not in the internal controls framework: strategic objectives of an organization. According to COSO, "enterprise risk management is applied in a strategy setting, as well as in working toward achievement of objectives in the other three categories [operations, reporting, and compliance]."[8]

COSO's model encompasses the larger enterprise, although the framework is a familiar one even for projects. COSO envisions establishment of a "risk officer" but concludes that "virtually all personnel play some role in effecting risk management."[9]

Government risk management in some circles is associated with insurance. The COSO model—and the way that risk management is taught by NIGP—goes well beyond insurance, however.

Risk is defined by COSO as the possibility that an event will occur and adversely affect the achievement of objectives. The COSO model for strategic risk planning engages a broad range of stakeholders: the community, customers, employees and suppliers.

Risk management begins with an analysis of the internal environment. Entities need to determine their level of risk appetite, or the amount of risk that an entity is willing to accept in pursuit of its mission. The entity's culture may influence an agency's appetite for risk also. Through dialogue internally, an entity develops an overall management philosophy with respect to risk.

In the Port St. Lucie neighborhood-stabilization grant story, the city's Office of Management and Budget (OMB) worked with the Risk Management Department to adjust insurance limits and clarify the city's tolerance for risk.

"We didn't have long to get this done," Cheryl Shanaberger, OMB's deputy director explained. "Our partners knew we had to adjust processes. Risk management was an example. Our insurance requirements made participation difficult for some vendors. Given the small size of most of the renovation projects—$25,000 maximum in many cases—both Risk Management and legal counsel were on-board about modifying insurance requirements."

The project also addressed cash flow concerns by using the procurement card to pay for the modest project costs in advance. There would have been some risk associated with that strategy as well, but Cheryl Shanaberger persisted.

"I advocated advance use of procurement cards, given the low dollar value of the projects. Yes, there was some push-back, but eventually, we all realized the value to the project, that the opportunities for the vendors outweighed the city's risk."

COSO says that objective setting is a pre-condition to the later steps of event identification, risk assessment, and risk response that is central to risk management. The objectives frame the operational context for identifying possible risk events, for example. These are derived from the high-level goals that spring from an agency's mission. COSO categorizes the objectives consistent with the risk categories: operations objectives, reporting objectives, and compliance objectives. Compliance in this context includes compliance with legal requirements.

Sophisticated risk management planning can use more advanced statistical functions not normally encountered in a procurement office. NASA engineering, for example, uses sophisticated quantitative methods to assess risk in design alternatives. It is more common in public procurement contexts to use narrative descriptors of risk tolerance in documents like strategic plans or policy documents.

The COSO framework is closely aligned with Wright's (2007) description of risk management in government contracting. Moreover, the COSO framework is essentially identical to that used by project manager professionals as outlined in the Project Management Body of Knowledge (PMBOK®). For the purposes of this book, the normal procurement-planning process serves as a good point from which to further understand the relevance of steps in risk management planning.

Procurement and Risk Management Planning

The first step in risk management is to fully understand the context. Authors who write about effective risk management in complex construction or infrastructure projects describe a process for identifying the context for the risk-management process that is closely akin to procurement planning.[10] They advocate use of cross-functional teams to leverage experience and tacit knowledge in identifying an approach to risk. These teams meet to understand the objectives of the organization and project. The teams identify the essential elements of the project that define its success.[11]

Risk is assessed using the likelihood and impact of potential events that can threaten success in meeting procurement objectives. In identifying the objectives, there typically are multiple stakeholders. In other than simple projects, one of the initial planning tasks is to brainstorm and identify the range of stakeholders and interests that must be met to achieve project success.

These include not only the users, but other government departments, the potential contractors, regulators, procurement staff, and even the vendor community.

The team defines the criteria for success. On e-procurement implementations for example, one criterion for success could be to reduce the disruption to existing business processes during the implementation. The procurement office, accounting office, and users all would share this objective.

Risk provides a different perspective for looking at project requirements, and later, a different way of evaluating merit in competing proposals. While statements of work often are written with desired objectives or goals, the key elements of the project also can be written in terms of risk. In general, except for simple projects, a better assessment of risk can be attained by breaking down the work into component elements. The statement of work, or work breakdown structure, is a good starting point for identifying the elements. These elements can include the various business activities, functions of the service, locations, project phases, and schedule. Gaining an understanding of these key elements of performance forms the basis for subsequent reviews and assessment of risk.

This context development for risk management should already be part of sound procurement planning. In many instances, using organizations are performing this breakdown analysis as they develop the statement of work. They may also be conducting threshold analysis of risk when they write the SOW. For example, a desired feature of an IT implementation that off-the-shelf software be used in the solution represents a decision that software or technology maturity is a significant risk element. These considerations can be integrated into the evaluation and award.

Identify the Risks

After the context for the project has been fully developed, an agency identifies potential risks. This is the process—often using brainstorming—of identifying potential events that could affect achievement of objectives. These events can be internal and relate to infrastructure, personnel, process and technology. External events can pose risk. They include economic, natural, political, social, and technological conditions. The Japanese tsunami's interruption of auto-parts supply chains was such an event, as well as the follow-on failure of the transportation system to adapt to the disruption.

Representative event categories in the COSO framework that might be relevant to procurement include:

- Suppler effectiveness
- Process efficiency
- Process effectiveness
- Asset management
- Intellectual property
- Leadership and governance (e.g., project management)
- Systems (upgrades and enhancements)

- Economy
- Employee safety
- Changing regulations and statutes
- Employee capability and loss
- Data confidentiality

In complex procurements, the list can be longer. Wright (2007) adds other key risk indicators in a procurement context. Among them:[12]

- Unclear or vague specifications or statements of work
- Unrealistic delivery or performance schedules
- Product immaturity in the marketplace, or unproven processes
- Pricing methodology/contract types not suited to the requirements
- Lack of experienced, available resources
- High attrition rates for necessary personnel
- Negative industry or economic trends
- Unrealistically low prices
- Supplier requirement for financing during performance

Tapping the expertise of experienced personnel is vital to identifying the risks. Moreover, the expertise of experienced personnel can later help categorize, prioritize, and develop strategies for handling the risks.

Checklists may serve as useful tools to identify risks on routine projects or projects where the team has deep experience. But brainstorming approaches are superior on novel projects. Checklists can have a tendency to inhibit creativity when dealing with new or unfamiliar types of projects.[13]

In strategic sourcing, for example, a risk matrix may emphasize the risk from supply disruption, on the one hand, or the critical importance of a commodity because of the amount spent on it. A checklist can identify general considerations. But strategic sourcing is an example of a project where brainstorming among experienced stakeholders may lead to better risk identification than checking off a list of considerations. Success in strategic sourcing requires application of tacit knowledge derived from experience, like the possible indirect effects of subordinating established vendor relationships to measurable, sometimes minimal, cost savings.

One innovative way to integrate risk in planning is to conduct what has been called a pre-mortem. Its sibling is the pre-parade that accounts for unexpected success.

Pre-mortems and Pre-parades

"If we'd known then, what we know now . . ." —Unknown

Gary Klein (2003) introduced the world to the pre-mortem exercise, a twist on after-action reviews designed to detect potential problems early. According to Klein, barriers to detecting potential problems include the nature of the problem (e.g., subtle or gradual problems or those that are ambiguous), expertise (mindsets that create errors or interfere with the ability to detect patterns and clues that promote richer mind models), fatigue or competing priorities that interfere with alertness to problems, and organizational barriers like reliance on historical procedures, production pressures, or inadequate data.

The pre-mortem exercise is conducted during project planning, after the contours of the project plan are understood but before performance fatigue sets in. It begins with a question that makes it easier for dissenters to express their reservations. The team is asked to imagine a fiasco in which the project has failed. It is a total catastrophic failure. Each member is asked, "What could have caused the fiasco?" Each team member writes down what happened to cause the fiasco, applying his or her own intuitions and judgments. The facilitator then asks each team member in turn to read one reason from the list and describe it, until the reasons are exhausted. The facilitator consolidates the causes, and the team discusses the list. They can use it as a basis for formulating a plan, revisiting it as necessary during project performance. Essentially, the team applies its collective experience and intuition in voicing concerns and identifying risks.

What is learned can be incorporated into future solicitation planning. A team could decide to use more industry meetings during market research, revise boilerplate contract clauses that allocate risk, change contract types, or request specific proposal information that can be evaluated and discussed. This tool helps identify and address the risks that are considered the most significant. The team should review the list periodically.[14]

Heath and Heath (2013) revealed a similar tool in their latest book on decision making. Sometimes unexpected success can overwhelm a team's capacity. A pre-parade exercise starts with imagining a wild success. Then the team asks, "Are we ready for it?"[15] New products sometimes suffer from unanticipated demand as consumers line up to snatch products off shelves. In a procurement environment, a solicitation may unexpectedly generate dozens of proposals, requiring a lawful strategy to eliminate proposals not reasonably susceptible of being awarded a contract.

These tools permit users to reflect on what choices might lead to disaster or unmanageable success by tapping into the intuition of experienced stakeholders.[16] Those who promote the tools believe they solve the problem of learning always occurring at the wrong end of the project.

In complex procurements, integrating risk considerations during procurement planning provides opportunities for better proposal evaluation. Not all projects require comprehensive risk management plans. But in projects on the scale of an enterprise e-procurement implementation, with varying levels of technology maturity among proposers, system integration challenges, and broad enterprise change management issues, risk becomes a key ingredient.

Assess the Risks

After identification of risks to a project, risks are assessed. Assessment consists of two parts: risk analysis and risk evaluation.

Whatever method is used to identify risk, consider supplementing the risk descriptors with scenarios. Having experienced people describe the potential scenario and potential impact helps in later assessment phases. For example, indemnification and limitation of liability clauses address potential events that pose risk to contracting parties. Having attorneys describe such things as litigation and liability scenarios, likely defenses, potential costs, and the effect of the various clauses on recovery of damages can help procurement professionals and teams better understand the risks when they assess them. Asking proposers to describe risk-management scenarios can also help illuminate the practical nature of the risks, the implications for the procurement, and the proposers' understanding of the requirements.

Risk analysis requires two estimates. The likelihood of the event is estimated. Scales are used to identify a range of estimated probabilities from rare to almost certain. Then the consequence of the event is estimated, also using a scale that ranges from negligible impact to extreme. After each event is assessed, often across various elements of performance, an aggregate risk factor is developed.

This aggregate risk factor then permits the evaluation. Assessment methods can combine the likelihood and consequence ratings into a numerical risk factor. These can be displayed in tabular or graphical ways to show the relative seriousness or priority of the risk.

Matrices often are used to visually portray risk. The matrix uses likelihood and consequence as the axes. Quadrants are commonly used to categorize risk as high, medium, and low. Then the matrix is used to focus more closely on risks and set priorities for their treatment.

Looking back at the event planning for the McKenna Long & Aldridge LLP procurement update, certain risks were present. Had a formal four-quadrant risk-management matrix been used, it might have looked like figure 8-1.

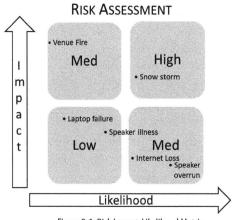

Figure 8-1. Risk Impact-Likelihood Matrix.

A team can use this kind of quadrant to discuss potential risk in projects. In a winter program in Denver, snow storms can and have had significant impacts on programs. A venue fire may have very low likelihood of occurring, but the impact is significant enough to perhaps be categorized as a medium risk. Both of these risks could be "treated" by planning a means of notifying attendees after the event is cancelled.

The more likely risks are in the lower right (medium risk) quadrant. Internet losses and panelist time overruns require some planning about how they are handled. Use of handouts and a method for informing speakers of time constraints are easy ways to minimize less catastrophic risk.

Likelihood of risks may be difficult to estimate in procurements. Risk-likelihood ranges are determined after discussing the work and possible conditions that will increase or decrease the probability of events. Complexity of hardware or software, the maturity of the technology, integration with other systems, and the number of contractors/subcontractors on a team all may influence the likelihood of certain adverse risk events occurring in an information technology project, for example.

Risk categories can include inherent risk—part of the activity itself—and residual risk that remains even after risk treatment.[17] The risk of event cancellations from unusually severe weather is an inherent risk. Inherent risk in an internal controls environment is that which exists even in controlled activities where there can be credible breakdown of controls. Post-transaction reviews of procurement card activity address both residual and inherent risks that policies and procedures sometimes are not followed.

According to COSO, studies have shown that decision-makers are overconfident in their ability to estimate the amount of uncertainty.[18] Teams offer a variety of perspectives that can help minimize the overconfidence error.

Assessment methods can be both qualitative and quantitative. This chapter has described semi-quantitative methods used most often in procurement offices. Some are *semi*-quantified because they permit ordinal comparison, as in priorities, and in a modest way relatively measure severity and priority. But they do not absolutely measure risk in a way that permits financial decisions to be based on the measures. Formal, quantified cost-benefit analysis is not usually required in the types of projects encountered by procurement offices.[19]

There are professionals who specialize in use of more sophisticated risk assessment tools. The California Office of Systems Integration highlighted in chapter 3 uses a more robust risk-management assessment framework for major projects.[20] Other tools may be more appropriate in making financing decisions or evaluating alternative project delivery approaches. Projects with long performance periods, complex cash flow models, significant environmental or regulatory considerations, and large capital expenditures may require quantitative risk-management modeling to assist in decision making.

In a procurement, the risks from the various proposals often are considered. The relative merits of offerors' past performance and experience, technical and management approaches, and their plans to manage risk can be evaluated. Some proposals might involve high risk of excessive agency involvement in contract administration or late performance, for example.

After risks have been identified and assessed, an appropriate response is selected. All projects involve some risk, and risk response should be considered, no matter how informally.

Risk Response

The primary risk response in a procurement is sharing risk with the best vendor and having the vendor take steps to mitigate significant risks. Of course, there may be other elements of risk in a procurement—inadequate contract management and government employee training, for example. After the selection decision and contract execution, most risk-response activities are a responsibility of the contractor, but the agency shares risk management through contract management. Other procurement projects also require risk response after risks are identified and assessed.

The COSO model uses four categories of risk response: avoidance, reduction, sharing, and acceptance. Contracting essentially involves some amount of sharing or even transferring of risk. Risk response is dependent on judgments exercised in the context of trade-offs about benefits, likelihood and impact from risks, and the costs of treatment. In some cases—e.g., purchasing of insurance and bonds—these can be quantified. In others, they cannot.

In general, the risk should be the responsibility of those best able to control it.[21] The contract is the main vehicle for risk sharing.[22] But offerors may in the best position to integrate considerations of risk in their proposal approaches.

Risk and Solicitation Planning

In a procurement, the application of risk management depends on the context. In strategic sourcing, for example, a risk matrix may emphasize the risk from supply disruption, on the one hand, or the amount of the dollars spent on the commodity.[23] Financial and procurement system IT implementations often have resistance to change as a key risk.

The last section of this chapter covers approaches to managing the resistance associated with change, some of which can be integrated into procurements and contracts.

Many methods for addressing risk are fixed contractually. For example, most governments use boilerplate provisions for the contractual allocation of risk relating to liability to third parties.

The initial decision about contract type and project delivery method allocates risk between the government and contractor. Fixed-price versus cost type, traditional project management delivery versus iterative approaches, and design-build or construction manager/general contractor (CM/GC) contracts in construction all involve allocation of risk.

Cost-type contracts tend to shift risk to the government. Some construction-management delivery methods shift risk more to the owner. Construction management/general contractor delivery strategies share risk between the owner and contractor, with the owner assuming cost risk up to the contract price ceiling. Above that amount, the contractor bears the risk. From a financing perspective, firm, fixed-price contracts place risk on the contractor.

The choice of contract type is made up-front in a procurement and is difficult to change later. Risk sometimes is controlled by including price indexing or other economic adjustment allowances, building in contingencies where appropriate, including re-pricing or price redetermination provisions, using incentives to share savings or control schedule, and opening estimating and cost-accounting records.[24]

Some project management considerations relevant to risk were covered in chapter 5. Business strategy meetings and procurement-planning checklists should address risk. The checklist can be useful when creating agendas for procurement-planning meetings. Cross-functional teams are valuable in part because they can spot risk issues that are not covered by standard planning checklists.

In the solicitation, instead of requesting general descriptions of risk-management approaches, proposers can be asked to identify the risks in the context of the environment the project faces. Offerors can be asked to identify, assess, and discuss the top three to five risks. They should describe their plan to manage the risks. They can be asked to include a discussion about the agency's role in risk management, topics like the engagement of senior executives in a steering committee, use of phased implementations in information technology projects, or early identification of the skills and knowledge needed by agency personnel to support the contract.

This response could be evaluated to gauge whether the offeror understands the project context and has a sound approach to performance. The responses could be used also to assess the risk that an offeror's proposed approach may require excessive contract administration (beyond expected project communication and other involvement required by the proposed approach) in order to maintain schedule and achieve a successful outcome within the proposed cost.[25]

Some proposals might demonstrate such a firm understanding of the requirement, and have such a sound approach, that the risk of excessive agency involvement or schedule slippage is judged to be minimal. Similarly, the range of proposers' past performance may suggest varying risks of excessive agency involvement beyond that normally needed to make the solution viable and delivered on time.

In procurement and contracting, much of the risk "treatment" is performed using contract clauses. Force majeure clauses provide contractual protection from adverse weather, for example. Unknown subsurface conditions encountered during construction are a risk for both owners and contractors. Differing site conditions clauses are typically used to manage those contingencies.

Some of the greatest contract negotiation challenges arise from the risk of liability arising out of third party claims related to contract performance. Governments use a combination of liability shifting clauses to deal with those situations. Indemnification and hold-harmless clauses shift the claims and litigation risks for injuries or property damage caused by a contractor during contract performance. From a contractor perspective, there is risk of unforeseen indirect liability caused by performance issues, and contractors may try to align the potential risks to the contract value using limitation of liability clauses and/or pricing contingencies.

The next story illustrates a particularly solid approach to providing guidance on how to manage contractual risks. One of the frustrations for practitioners is translating theoretical risk knowledge into actionable procurement strategies and contract clauses. The solution often involves fixing responsibility for advising agencies and making decisions regarding liability allocation. North Dakota in particular has a good approach.

North Dakota's Integration of Risk Management and Procurement

North Dakota's Procurement website prominently displays links to the Risk Management Division's Risk Management Manual and guidelines on contract risk management, as well as the Attorney General's Contract Drafting and Review manual.

Risk management offices often provide guidance regarding how to handle claims against the government. Those offices typically, with their counsel, manage the funds that are used to pay for personal injury and property claims made against the government. They may purchase casualty insurance to protect government assets or other insurance needed to protect their entity from liability arising out of its operations.

What is unusual about North Dakota's approach is the amount of collaboration between the Risk Management Division, Procurement, and the Attorney General. The state's risk management manual describes the state's approach to risk management: systematic risk assessment, risk control, risk financing, and administration. The risk-management process includes the traditional steps of risk treatment: risk acceptance, avoidance, transfer, and reduction. In addition to describing the activities around loss reporting and claims administration, the manual includes detailed descriptions of insurance and an entire chapter on contract risk. The Attorney General's contract-drafting manual talks in terms of risk and refers to the Risk Management Division's manual for sample indemnification and limitation of liability language.

North Dakota has statutory provisions that prescribe policies and responsibilities regarding use of indemnification provisions and limitation of liability. The Director of the Office of Management and Budget (OMB) has certain responsibilities, including the approval of use of some contract-liability allocation provisions. The Risk Management Division exercises those responsibilities for OMB.

On its website, the State Procurement Office links to Risk Management's comprehensive "Guidelines to Managing Contractual Risk."[26] Although the guide contains detailed explanations of insurance types and certificates of insurance, more importantly, the guidelines describe the importance of screening contractors and the role of contract risk transfer using approved clauses.

The guidelines also contain a risk-management analysis matrix (and sample agreement analysis) that defines risk categories (low, moderate, and high). The guidelines provide recommended indemnification and insurance coverage. The sample agreement analysis includes text of clauses for the various categories of risk.

North Dakota has centralized the approval authority for use of certain provisions. Requests are made to the Risk Management Division for approval to use certain indemnification and limitation of liability provisions. For example, contracts for construction or maintenance of state buildings or highways may require different indemnification provisions that must be approved by OMB. The state policy clearly makes the State Management Division and Attorney General the advising offices for state agencies having questions about these contractual risk provisions.

The North Dakota approach is uniquely comprehensive. It establishes the Risk Management Division as central to the management of all risk—including contractual risk—and goes beyond limited roles of some risk-management offices who limit their activities to insurance administration and management of claims against the entity.

Monitoring and Controlling

Monitoring and control activities follow the implementation of risk responses. Like internal controls, these can include various approvals, authorizations, reviews, segregation of duties, reconciliations, exception reporting, and other operational control activities. Physical asset or security procedures are examples, as are administrative controls on IT systems. Monitoring and control for risk-management purposes typically is linked with other project management activities, such as weekly or monthly reviews. Lessons learned while monitoring activities may include revisiting risk identification, risk assessment, and risk response.

Even though formal risk management plans may not be used in most procurements, keeping a risk register may be advisable. A risk register lists risks, risk assessments (based on likelihood and impact), and the treatment. The state of North Dakota, for example, provides examples of a register used to periodically monitor risk, making adjustments for risk categories and treatment as necessary. [27] In procurements, these adjustments could require revisiting contract management approaches.

Review and auditing are essential to risk-management monitoring. Like internal controls, oversight and review are integral to risk management. Review of procurement card approval and review processes in agencies helps identify situations where abuse might be possible. In a procurement, analysis of industry questions and answers regarding a request for proposal is a form of monitoring. The questions might require reassessment of risk mitigation approaches on bonding and insurance, for example. Even more significantly, the absence of acceptable bids at the time of bid opening may signal the need to reexamine the contract type or procurement strategy.

Effective contract administration, however, may be the most important element of risk monitoring and control.[28] Beginning with post-award kickoff meetings, careful monitoring of project schedule, status, and aggressive resolution of contract issues as they arise become central to monitoring the risks of a procurement project and assessing the need for adjustments. Recurring project status reporting like that in figure 5-3, Project Status Report, helps monitor and control risks.

Effective contract administration uses sound communication strategies to minimize risk. Beginning with post-award meetings, recurring dialogue between government and contractor personnel keeps expectations aligned. Not only are issues like waivers and unexpected contract changes avoided, communications promote broader objectives of establishing relationships that are more like partnering and less adversarial.

Litigation may be an unfortunate outcome where other kinds of contract management tools are not effective. Issue-elevation provisions, or collaborative partnering relationships, are proven ways to minimize the risk that a project will descend into litigation before other more effective means of resolving project issues have been exhausted.

The last part of this chapter discusses models used in planning with a specific type of risk. One of the most significant risks in large projects is the natural resistance to change that everyone exhibits.

Integrate a Change Management Model into Planning

Change management is treated here as the flip side of risk management. Change management is an issue when project complexity increases, the solution scales across an enterprise, and the number of stakeholders increases.[29] This book has touched on elements of change management throughout. Resistance to change is a risk to project success and must be accounted for in every phase of a project or continuous improvement effort. These projects often involve change to future behavior, and people naturally resist change.

In fact, in the consulting world, the difficulty in effecting lasting change is called "resistance." Fundamentally, a team must develop strategies to overcome resistance and foster change that sticks. There are planning models for improving the odds of success on projects where resistance is a central consideration.

Change is not an event, it's a process.[30] This book adopts a model that accounts for successful strategies used by the projects described in this book. John Kotter's book *Leading Change* (1996) described an eight-point model for change. His later book with Dan Cohen, *The Heart of Change* (2002), and a book by Dan and Chip Heath, *Switch* (2010), built on the model. They address the challenges from change and identify strategies for overcoming resistance. From the perspective of the individual who is undergoing significant change perceived as a threat, the resistance to change generally is reduced by providing people "as much prediction, understanding, control, and compassion as possible."[31]

People undergoing change ask very fundamental questions. "Am I able? Will it be worth it? Do I trust you?" [32] Said another way, "What's in it for me? What problems does it solve? What values does it serve? What are the benefits?"[33]

Like other problem solving, planning for change first involves expansive thinking to identify the kinds of forces at play that affect resistance. One of the better known tools used for this purpose is the force-field analysis. The Punta Gorda team used a "force-field" analysis in the presentation to senior executives about the recommendation to use the county's procurement card contract as a way to improve its payables process.

Force-Field Analysis

A force-field analysis identifies possible leverage points to address change issues in a project. Nancy Tague describes use of force-field analysis in *The Quality Toolbox* (2005). The tool is used to identify both supporting and opposing aspects of a desired change when a solution is being considered.

The steps in the development of a force-field analysis[34] include:

1. Identify the problem or desired change on a flip chart or whiteboard.
2. Split the chart or board into two halves with a vertical line, naming one side "for" and the other "against."
3. Brainstorm all the forces that inhibit the change or solution, or that support its effectiveness. Put short descriptors for the forces on either the "for" or "against" side of the chart as appropriate.

---

4. After brainstorming, lines can be used between each force and the center line to characterize the strength of the force, e.g., a longer line indicates a stronger force.

5. Discuss as a group ways to limit the forces that tend to oppose the change or solution.

6. Discuss as a group ways to harness forces that support the change or solution.

7. Think of forces as pushing the centerline back and forth. Ideally, strategies are found to enhance the supporting forces and reduce the opposing forces against the change/solution so the line moves in support of the project's success.

8. The force-field analysis can also be used in conjunction with the fishbone/Ishikawa diagram. It can be used to evaluate the strength of potential forces that affect solutions to root causes of problems. It has particular value in that teams visually can see the dynamics of situations where opposing forces work to support or oppose the implementation of change or solutions.

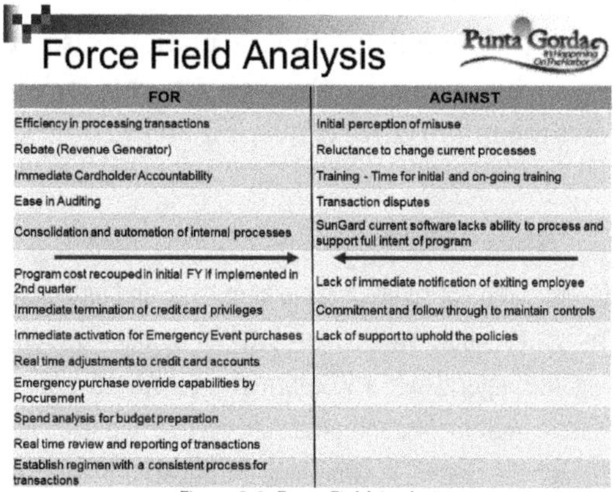

Figure 8-2. Force-Field Analysis.

The "force-field" slide shown in figure 8-2 was used by Punta Gorda's process-improvement team during executive presentations to capture the qualitative considerations in the decision. Forces in support of moving forward on the project included the rebate and increased efficiency in processing, improvements overall to the city's internal controls, and better payment support for the city's emergency management program. Forces working against the decision to adopt the program included initial perceptions of risk (from misuse) in procurement card programs, resistance to change, and resource and other barriers to effective implementation of the program. Brainstorming is a useful way to identify possible resistance to a project.

There are few better examples of change-management challenges than the award-winning Georgia Procurement Transformation project, a story told in *Contract Management* magazine.[35] Their four-year initiative required early integration of effective change strategies to overcome resistance among some employees who had spent years in the Georgia procurement system. In the 1990s, a project like this would have been described using the term "reengineering." Georgia called it "transformation," but the effect was the same. Whether in industry or government, change initiatives of this scale pose special challenges. And overcoming resistance is among the greatest.

The Georgia project illustrated essential elements of a change strategy that was managed using early planning. Governor Sonny Perdue's consultant reports and the state's economic conditions created a feeling of urgency and defined a clear purpose. Special steps were taken to build a good team—the "right people on the bus"—to undertake the reform. Consultants also helped script the critical moves—Chip Heath and Dan Heath's phrase—that included a sound project management and communications plan. The plan was adapted as necessary when the environment changed, and organization changes were made so the environment did not impede project success. The team molded the environment by changing policies and regulations, and they leveraged technology effectively. Projects of this magnitude require especially early planning to incorporate change management strategies at the right time in a project.

Arizona's ProcureAZ, an e-procurement implementation, also required significant effort to manage change. Anyone who has been through an enterprise-wide deployment of an e-procurement system knows the importance of keeping an eye on resistance. ProcureAZ's story provides great lessons.

Arizona's ProcureAZ E-Procurement Solution

Arizona's ProcureAZ e-procurement solution came in on time and on budget. In just the first 100 days, the system gave the state a single, web-based portal for vendor registration, sourcing, and state contract/catalog ordering. The project led to a 50% increase in cooperative procurements, streamlined ordering for state and local governments, and processed over $550 million in requisitions, purchase orders, and contracts through the system. In two years, the project achieved the first-ever integration in Arizona of procurement and financial information systems. In 2011, ProcureAZ received the NIGP Innovation Award. Well deserved!

The urgency for change was created by dire economic conditions in the state, an estimated $1.4 billion budget shortfall. The state had no integrated system for tracking expenditures statewide that could be leveraged for achieving procurement savings.

Jean Clark, State Purchasing Administrator, saw e-procurement as a transformational solution. The state could achieve the advantages of centralization in data collection despite decentralization in procurement operations. Data could be used to leverage volume in achieving better pricing, not just across state agencies, but for local governments as well. The single system would help vendors manage their state contract portfolios, provide additional opportunities for Arizona vendors, improve efficiencies for state and local agencies, and free procurement professionals to pursue other value-added activities. The system also would make training easier. The system promised to be one that local governments could leverage also as they looked to further automate their procurement functions.

But ProcureAZ involved a big change in procurement processes. The project would span dozens if not hundreds of state and local government agencies. Users were key stakeholders. So were the vendors. Jean knew what it takes to succeed with a project of this magnitude. "It starts with having the right people on the team."

Jean wanted Tanja Schmitt. Tanja had over 27 years of experience with the state's information technology (IT) department. She also had previous experience with the procurement office's implementation of a system to streamline the request for proposal process. Jean considered Tanja's participation critical. As it turned out, one of the unusual aspects of this project was the shared leadership by IT and procurement.

The team also had a great contractor, Periscope Holdings.

"Having the right people involved includes the contractor," Tanja emphasized. "The contractor is key."

Experienced contractors provide implementation strategies to help overcome resistance. Tanja explains, "The RFP statement of work included a very detailed scope of work, and the solicitation required the contractor to describe its change and project management strategies." Jean agreed with Tanja's assessment of the vital importance of getting the right contractor. The solicitation placed special emphasis on experience with projects of this magnitude. According to Jean, "Periscope was particularly strong."

There were various other stakeholder groups. As a result, representative teams were used to manage the effort. The CORE team consisted of representatives from a select group of agencies that participated in user acceptance testing and training. A user group was assembled to provide feedback on the system and to help communicate information and share ideas. A financial integration team was assembled to brainstorm and identify the best possible option for designing, developing and implementing the financial system interface.

The CORE team selected members for the initial user group based on their enthusiasm, readiness, and capabilities. According to Tanja, Jean was particularly good in selecting the agency representatives to participate on the CORE team so they would have a broader cross-section of agency purchasing scenarios. One of the original CORE team members eventually become the leader of the user group, which helped build momentum among the user community and move the project along.

A steering committee of executives from key agencies met monthly to provide executive oversight for the project and assist in decision making. Jean was the primary connection between the steering committee and other teams.

Tanja, working in conjunction with the Periscope project team, provided the project management expertise that initiatives like this require. Together they developed a detailed planning and control system identifying the project milestones, deliverables, tasks, schedules, and team resources. She also knew how to use Periscope's project management software, which was used to communicate project status and serve as a document repository and collaboration tool for sharing important project documentation.

Jean communicated the vision constantly. In Jean's "mantra" (as she called it), she described the e-procurement implementation as the most important, transformational event since the state modernized its procurement system by adopting the American Bar Association model procurement code in 1983. There was early resistance by some local governments, some were very vocal. But Jean kept telling the story and promoting the benefits of the system. She used emails, one-on-one meetings, letters, and personal presentations to municipalities and the League of Arizona Cities and Towns to explain the potential benefits of the system.

Communication with vendors was vitally important as well. The funding model depended on the collection of an administrative fee on some orders placed through the system. As it turned out, 90% of

(continued on next page)

Arizona's ProcureAZ E-Procurement Solution, cont'd.

the vendors said there would be no change in contract pricing. Vendors saw a real value to being able to receive orders through a system of this nature without having to engage in manual transactions or procurements with local governments. This was a story that needed to be told, and Jean did.

Jean and her project team also helped overcome obstacles with senior management. When the project moved into financial system integration, the nature of the interface ("real time") was far superior but took more resources. The state's accounting department had received another statutory mandate that required the same IT resources. With assistance of senior management, Jean and Tanja were able to negotiate assistance from another department that had enough experience with the financial system to provide the needed technical resources.

Tanja coordinated and exchanged information between Periscope and the state's General Accounting office, IT administrators and development teams, and the CORE team. Jean communicated with the executive steering committee and Department of Administration leadership, letting them know project status, rollout schedules, and when resources were needed. She was also involved with CORE team oversight. According to Tanja, "The CORE team really appreciated Jean's personal involvement."

One communication theme was especially noteworthy. Senior executives were on-board. They insisted on state agencies making milestones during the rollout.

Periscope and the team used a phased implementation schedule to first get vendors registered and a catalog established for state and local government ordering. Phased implementation helped demonstrate the system's value and ease of use, creating early advocates that were members of the state's user group. As part of the phased implementation, Periscope met with agencies, mapped out a procurement process flow for them (the "as is" state), and identified the "to be" state for the agency. The direct user-contractor contact was invaluable. It permitted the users to be part of the implementation, understand the change, exercise some control over it, and plan for it.

With a train-the-trainer strategy, agencies could be more in control of an implementation tailored for their agency. The trainers also served as eyes and ears for the CORE team; they were able to provide prompt feedback on aspects of the implementation that needed reexamination.

ProcureAZ had the ingredients to sustain its success. Senior leadership was committed to the system. Later phases of the project added data mining and analysis capabilities that won additional recognition in 2012 by the National Association of State Procurement Officials. ProcureAZ promises to aggregate spend across the state to enable more strategic procurement, improve efficiencies in ordering, and streamline procurement processes.

Many of the stories in this book involve change. ProcureAZ is particularly valuable because it vividly illustrates the elements of effective change management.

Create the Change Imperative: Increase Urgency

Facts are important but they are not enough. To motivate people to adapt to change, connect peoples' emotion to the subject.

One of the stories told by Kotter and coauthor Dan Cohen in their book, *Heart of Change* and retold by Chip Heath and Dan Heath in *Switch*,[36] is a purchasing story. A company was looking for ways to reduce procurement costs, but the purchasing office faced resistance from senior executives and managers content to continue their own parochial buying habits. So the purchasing office created a vivid experience.

One example of waste was the purchase of work gloves. The purchasing office rounded up the various work gloves ordered by various units of the organization. They not only found varying types of gloves. They found identical work gloves with prices ranging from three dollars to eleven dollars.

The team tagged them with prices and displayed them in a conference room at a meeting with senior managers. Managers were astonished at the variance in prices and, needless to say, became believers in the need to address procurement practices. Did they really need all those different types of gloves?

Emotion may be difficult to trigger in procurement projects, but try. Arizona's urgency was related to a well-accepted financial fact: the state was in dire economic straits. Jean Clark connected the potential of the e-procurement system to the pride felt about the state's modernization of the procurement system years ago. Arizona was able to integrate these facts into an emotional component used for its communication strategy.

Enlist the Guiding Team

Team leaders must demonstrate enthusiasm and commit to drafting the right people into the group needed to affect the change. This element—enlisting the right team—is a linchpin of Kotter's change management formulation. In the Georgia procurement transformation, getting the "right people on the bus" was considered essential to the project.

Find team members who can model the trust and teamwork required.[37] Jean Clark knew she needed an experienced information technology professional to help with the project management. As it turned out, that PM was invaluable when the financial system integration began to compete with other priorities levied on the information technology department. The opportunity summary discussed in chapter 2 may be one way to recruit and start a dialogue with potential teammates about possibilities in a project.

Get the Vision and Strategy Right

Develop and communicate a clear vision. But be careful about jumping to vision and strategy too early. One needs to create the sense of urgency first, ideally through a connection to emotions.

In an era when vision and strategy get so much attention, there is a tendency to jump to fixing the problem before the necessary precursors are in place. If the urgency already is high, getting to vision may be appropriate, but often that is not the case.[38]

In procurement projects, the strategy in large measure is set at the time a solicitation is published. ProcureAZ's solicitation had the offerors address project and change management strategies in their proposals.

Jean Clark saw the importance of enlisting senior executives into achieving buy-in for the project. This strategic focus was a key to the team's getting enterprise-wide acceptance of the project and commitment to the resources needed to make it succeed.

Communicate the Change Vision

John Kotter teaches that communication is more than sending an avalanche of information. There has to be a deeper, broader connection with those affected by the change.

Encourage questions from stakeholders. Practice fielding questions so answers are given with confidence. Kotter and Cohen (2002) tell a story about what were essentially organizational town hall meetings to discuss a company's change to a new team-based organization. Some employees felt threatened by the change. Managers talked to union employees, but they first engaged in question and answer preparation sessions where members of the team practiced answering questions that might come from the audience.[39]

Jean Clark communicated the vision well. Her mantra, as she called it, compared the ProcureAZ program to the transformation that occurred in state procurement over a quarter century before with the adoption of its progressive procurement code. This approach was positive, challenging people to be part of a new identity in the state that turned out to be unique and recognized nationally.

This positive approach draws on intrinsic motivation. People want to be part of a unique, winning team. Communications that accentuate the positive point to an encouraging future at the beginning of change. This optimism helps shape a new identity and harness the power socially of being part of a worthwhile group.

Communication strategies such as these not only help others forecast the future. They also build understanding of the change and give people some element of control. In ProcureAZ, the train-the-trainer strategy and robust communications permitted agencies to adapt the implementation to their needs.

Deploy the Tools of Influence

Sometimes people have to be persuaded to change. Individuals want to know "what's in it for me?" (WIIFM).[40] Chip Heath and Dan Heath (2010) take a slightly different angle on the emotional and psychological dimensions of change. They advocate techniques to change the identity of the group and grow it.

Social proof and social capital[41] traditionally have been considered a means of influence when change is hard. People want to align with others in the group. Building an identity also promotes consistency, as people behave in ways that are consistent with their behavior, values, and goals.

In ProcureAZ, the establishment of user groups during the implementation created social leverage by assembling people with common goals and who supported the project. Add the credibility of a first-class contractor, the authority of a governor and her executive team committed to the project, and even the scarcity of knowing that a state project is one of very few that succeeds, and the tools of influence are deployed.[42] The behaviors, habits, and shared identity catch. In many respects, this creation of identity supplants the narrower motivation of WIIFM, or "what's in it for me?"

Project teams are often reminded of the importance of communication. But they also can use the levers of influence to help evolve an identity where behaviors, habits, and change become part of a new culture that embraces change.[43]

Empower Action

We borrow from Kotter and other recent authors on this element of change. There are various things that can be done to empower action and promote success.

One is scripting the critical moves.[44] ProcureAZ's use of a well-regarded contractor having e-procurement experience helped identify the best practices and a path forward to making the implementation successful. Sometimes it is difficult to know where to start on complex projects involving change. Having experienced consultants and contractors can certainly help.

Heath and Heath also counsel to find the bright spots in an organization, and copy what they do.[45] Finding a project manager who has succeeded on a large scale can bring energy to a team and improve the prospects of success. Jean Clark did that when she convinced Tanja Schmitt to join the e-procurement team; Tanja had been a big part of an earlier success by the state, while not as large in scope, also involved multiple stakeholders. She knew the procurement office and its operations.

Sometimes the best practices of colleagues can point the way.[46] NIGP's discussion forum is a useful place to find questions and comments that point the way to other offices who have tackled similar problems. The nominations and descriptions of NIGP and NASPO awards include enough information to assess whether the context and challenges were similar in those projects. If those successes appear to be relevant, contact their project leads and learn from them.

John Kotter emphasized the importance of removing system and other barriers during implementation. This is largely a leadership role, one that Jean Clark fulfilled. When the implementation faced competing priorities levied on the information technology office, Jean creatively went to another department to line up the needed expertise to assist the contractor with e-procurement/financial system integration.

Create Short-Term Wins, Consolidate Gains, and Produce More Wins

Another of Kotter's principles is the importance of creating short-term wins early. Some change is daunting and must be broken down into smaller portions.

Emotionally, large projects can be demoralizing. It is difficult to know where to start.[47] In a continuous-improvement project looking at organizational policies and procedures, this means setting priorities and tackling one or two at a time. That way, people can plan around the tasks, focus their efforts, and integrate existing work. In an e-procurement system implementation across an entire government, shrinking change often means tackling an implementation in phases. That is what the state of Arizona did in its ProcureAZ implementation when it first rolled out vendor registration and catalog functionality and later the total e-procurement implementation progressively across state agencies.

ProcureAZ effectively used phased implementation to get buy-in. The state of Indiana did also.

Their award-winning K12Indiana project was aimed at aggregating requirements and coordinating sourcing in order to achieve savings on maintenance, repair, and operations expenditures in schools and the state. The state conducted a "case study" with a broad cross-section of eight schools to pilot the program and demonstrate savings in office supplies as well as maintenance, repair, and operations (MRO) expenses. Some schools considered their situations unique, and demonstrated success was useful in achieving buy-in. The project demonstrated savings opportunities of 20%, leading eventually to establishment of over 50 contracts and coordinated sourcing among schools for a variety of requirements. The initial pilot evolved into expansion of the e-procurement capabilities to integrate with some school financial systems. The program also launched a similar strategic procurement project aimed at leveraging volume in library purchases and adding new capabilities such as electronic books.

Chapter 2 told Thomas Linley's story about how he used a pilot phase to demonstrate the value of office machine consolidation to reduce costs. Perhaps on a smaller scale, this approach helped deal with the well-known area of resistance. People resist changes to their office machine locations and configurations, but like most of these stories, short-term wins can be consolidated and produce more success.

Keep at It: Build on the Change and Anchor It in the Culture

Momentum can be a fleeting ally sometimes. Arizona's ProcureAZ project enjoyed great success in completing Phase I in the first 100 days. But Jean Clark was leery about the team's losing momentum for Phase II, the full procurement functionality phase. To avoid the loss of momentum (that can happen after achievement of significant milestones), Jean elevated her communication with teams as Phase I drew to a close. Jean kept at it!

Effective implementation of an e-procurement system involves a change in culture. But a change in culture is not planned, it evolves over time. Until behaviors become anchored in habits, organizational change doesn't stick. But Arizona had some things going for it.

Executive leadership in the state had clearly communicated an important expectation: agencies were expected to use the system. The system provided data from which the state could assess requisition numbers, processing and approval times, and numbers of solicitations, contracts, and purchase orders. State leadership could easily see how the system was (or was not) being used.

Perhaps the most significant practice that made the change stick was the Procurement Office's continuous engagement with agencies so they could see the value of the system firsthand. Some agencies were not sold until they really saw and used the system. Even after they initially used the system, they came back to the Procurement Office with lots of questions. As Jean Clark describes it, though, the concerns usually were training issues.

ProcureAZ developed excellent habits in terms of gathering feedback, revisiting their processes, and learning from them. The system gives the state excellent capabilities to reap the benefits of a transformation project in the future, sustaining the value of the system as people turnover. ProcureAZ has become a habit in Arizona state government!

Use Checklists to Build Risk and Change Management into Projects Early

At the beginning of this book, readers were cautioned to not see chapters as linear steps in continuous improvement. We've all encountered situations when we had to go back to a project purpose when making later decisions, for example.

Risk and change management are no different. The types of risks a project will encounter may drive early decisions like team membership. The state of Arizona, for example, recruited an IT project manager who was able to bridge the connections to the information technology community. She helped avoid schedule slippage when competing priorities threatened the project's financial system integration phase.

Even less transformational projects like the McKenna Long & Aldridge LLP procurement update event took concrete steps to reduce risks associated with the program. Up-front planning is required to effectively respond to with speaker cancellations and bad weather.

How are risk and change considerations built into a project early? How does a team keep track of all the considerations and potential risks to a project? And do this early so a project's schedule is not compromised? Checklists, it turns out, can be a useful tool—along with collaborative techniques like brainstorming—to guide project planning teams in the identification, assessment, and treatment of risks.

The Colorado contracting reengineering project, a story told in chapter 6, not merely improved the efficiency of state contracting. An equally important part of the initiative was reaching a comfort level regarding the quality of contracts as well. Relaxing contract review and approval policies can increase risk.

In Colorado's case, there was incomplete data about the quality of state contracts overall. The financial systems had codes showing the reasons for contracts that were "rejected" by the central approvers. What data existed indicated that the rejections in some agencies were in excess of 20% of the number of contracts reviewed. But it was not clear whether all rejections were substantive or were mere matters of form. The Attorney General's legal sufficiency reviews are designed to catch significant contracting errors, so there was some reluctance to eliminate a part of the process that was widely regarded as reducing risk to the state.

The Two Faces of Contract-Review Checklists

The Colorado contracting reengineering project used checklists to assist in identifying high-risk contracts.[48] High-risk contracts require centralized review by the State Controller and, sometimes, legal review by the Attorney General's office. Examples of high-risk contracts included information technology contracts, contracts with proposed revisions to indemnification clauses, or contracts using limitation of liability clauses. The policy identifies a series of considerations for determining risk.

Amendments that simply extend the contract expiration date by a year or less are considered low risk, as are amendments that merely adjust prices or rates consistent with the terms of the contract. Other technical amendments not changing scope of work, or amendments to contracts to conform to changes in state laws, are also considered low risk. Interagency contracts and contracts using pre-approved formats also are considered low risk and do not require central review.

High-risk contracts include those involving inherently dangerous activities, hazardous materials, and debt collection. Intergovernmental contracts with the federal government are in the high-risk category because of the extensive compliance requirements levied on contracts with federal funding. Contracts involving third-party financing, such as certificates of participation or lease-purchase agreements, are regarded as high risk. Contracts having provisions limiting liability also are considered high-risk contracts that require central review and approval. Information technology contracts and contracts for the operation of prisons also are in the high-risk category.

Comprehensive policies, like Colorado's contract review policy, sometimes involve so many considerations they are easy to overlook. Harry McCabe, contracts director for the Department of Human Services, was well-known for his development and use of a contract "wizard" in his department to make it easier for the program offices to write a contract with the required state and federal terms and conditions. Harry had also successfully developed a checklist to simplify the requirements of contract routing and approval. His checklist system accommodated the new risk review process nicely. He was able to incorporate the risk assessment criteria in the program checklist, collect the relevant information, and complete the risk assessment checklist consistent with State Controller instructions. The department's program offices answer questions on Harry's checklist regarding work complexity, nature of the contract statement of work, the program experience with the project type, and reliability of and prior experience with the vendor.

Harry found other value in checklists, too. They helped with knowledge-transfer challenges. New employees assigned contract-management duties in Harry's department get his checklist, and it is a roadmap for training. The risk considerations in the checklist provide an easy entry into learning and understanding the contract review process. At monthly contract user trainings that Harry conducts for his contract users, he focuses on the process basics and explains the reasons behind the rules. Ultimately, the checklist became what Harry describes as the most significant tool that he ever developed in the department. He relies on the checklist to help mitigate the effects of staff turnover in the department. Harry's contracts are known as some of the best in the state.

The state's reengineered process not only has satisfied State Controller internal control concerns. In the case of Harry McCabe's department, it also facilitated the improvement of skills and knowledge by agency personnel involved in the contracting process.

Checklists are widely accepted as valid ways to minimize risk. People get busy, and they often overlook essential facts that, had they been less pressed for time, they might have caught. Atul Gawande's *The Checklist Manifesto* describes how surgical operations were improved in the World Health Organization using checklists; the lessons are relevant to procurement as well.

Gawande (a surgeon) first studied the use of checklists by aircrews in cockpits. He then developed simple checklists that could be used in hospital operating rooms to prevent infections, eliminate mistakes prior to incisions, and reduce the risk of post-operative mistakes like loss of instruments and confusion about the post-operative treatment.

The checklists curiously had some unanticipated effects. They permitted a redistribution of power[49] in operating rooms by giving nurses explicit authority to monitor and verbalize completion of steps. They were expected to intervene when they saw a mistake. Indirect benefits of the use of checklist included providing executives the ability to see supply shortages—the checklist highlighted issues with availability. The author called this *activation phenomenon*: giving people a chance to say something at the start of a team activity activates participation and a willingness to speak up. In some hospital implementations, one checklist item was simply to have an informal early discussion before incision about basic context facts: a brief recitation of the surgeon's plans, amount of blood loss expected, and incision location. In construction projects, the author noted that the use of visual issues logs and schedules promoted communication among members of the project team, subcontractors, and trades.[50]

Under conditions of complexity, people need room to act and adapt. Checklists can help facilitate that action and prevent critical mistakes under trying conditions.[51] Checklists are not a substitute for expertise but are intended to prompt memory on key steps.

Checklists are best used at significant "pause points," times when a pause for reflection and completion of a checklist is most important. In aviation, those points tend to be pre-takeoff, pre-descent, and pre-landing. In surgery, the pause points may be before administration of the anesthetic, incision, and leaving the operating room. In procurement, we would surmise, checklists could be useful at the solicitation planning stage, award, and post-award at the contract administration kick-off.

Contracts can include requirements that act like checklists in triggering risk-management actions. David Lee Roth, leader of the rock band Van Halen, notoriously was known for his apparent dislike for brown M&Ms. The Van Halen tour was an early leader in large multimedia stage productions. A clause was included in the band's contract that permitted cancellation of a performance and full payment if a brown M&M was found backstage. In one Colorado contract, Roth and the band exercised the cancellation right.

As Roth later explained it, however, an issue with M&Ms was a sign that there may have been problems with the promoter's implementation. The band didn't require perfection, but they saw an M&M defect as symptomatic. They would then go and walk the setup, looking for errors. In the Colorado concert, they reportedly learned that the stage was insufficient to support the weight of the production equipment and was in danger of failing. The M&M contract clause provided a risk-monitoring trigger that gave Van Halen a legal basis to cancel.

Checklists can be useful for early identification of potential risks. In Harry McCabe's case, they also helped frame training, a topic we'll turn to in the next chapter. In any event, considerations of risk should accompany early project planning.

Besides risk issues, early planning is needed to identify change management challenges as well. A project of the magnitude of Arizona's ProcureAZ requires getting the right people on the management team, reaching agreement about the project objectives, and developing a communication and implementation strategy that fosters user buy-in and can be communicated to the offerors on the procurement. Pertinent provisions need to be included in the contract. Training, for example, becomes central to the success of implementations from a change perspective, and training costs and approaches are early considerations in procurement planning.

Plan, Communicate, and Listen

Risk management is a discipline in itself, but procurement professionals must know the essentials. Very complex procurements or other team activities may, however, require the use of specialized risk-management professionals, change management experts, and subject matter experts. Stakeholders play a critical role in change management; therefore it is essential to identify all affected groups, listen to them, and cultivate their support.

9 Keep Learning and Make It Stick!

"Purchasing gone wild!" —Barbara R. Johnson, CPPO, CPPB

◆

Barbara Johnson developed and presented purchasing training under this title. It's hard to resist; it has "stickiness." Stickiness generates traction for projects and learning. It is created through simplicity, emotion, unexpectedness, repetition, and stories.

Organizational learning is another dimension of continuous improvement. At the team level, learning occurs through project reviews and project adjustments and through pilots and phased implementation. The knowledge and competencies of most experienced employees are tacit. Therefore, experiential learning is needed in order to re-create this knowledge.

Learning and its sibling, *knowledge management,*[1] have broad dimensions relevant to large organizations. This chapter introduces fundamentals of knowledge management that procurement teams may encounter and find useful.

If one searches government human resources websites nationally, *knowledge transfer* appears as a topic in many HR departments. Transferring knowledge sometimes is equated with traditional training activities, even though more learning takes place informally. At a team level, learning from project experience and adjusting actions and strategy going forward is a dimension of learning.

Sometimes just trying to get ideas to have traction is a challenge. Total Quality Management (TQM), a quality management system widely used in the early 1990s, may be an example. It started off as an idea with a bang and then quietly slipped away as other models became more in vogue—reengineering, Six Sigma, Lean, Lean Six Sigma are some. Teams often encounter the challenge of making policies, procedures, and other ideas "stick" and last beyond the limited timeframe of a team or project's life.

As team members move in and out of teams, they must find ways to transfer needed knowledge to new members. With so many procurement offices and their teams relying on training, this chapter begins to satisfy a need for exposure to learning and training concepts of particular relevance to small group activities.

Teams face training challenges in various contexts. Chapter 8 told the story of Arizona's ProcureAZ project. That information technology system was acquired by the state to automate procurement and collect data useful to its strategic management of procurement expenditures. The team managing its implementation had to integrate training into the implementation strategy. State employees needed to learn the new system. At the other end of the spectrum, the team designing the Multnomah County, Oregon, online learning system described in this chapter had learning as the primary objective of the team's activities. Teams commonly have to design, deliver, or at least integrate training into project goals.

Project reviews are a form of learning also. The various flavors of project reviews come from the knowledge management world and are important tools for team learning.

Build Review into Projects Early

In one sense, learning refers to the lessons that a team encounters during a project that help the team evaluate the wisdom of an approach. Fisher and Sharp (2009) deal with team learning from the perspective of the prepare-act-review cycle. Their basic premise is that what we learn from planned action is superior to simply relying on thinking and models.

Beginning to act adds experience to the learning equation, permitting teams to validate thinking or perhaps adjust their plans and approaches based on what is learned from actual practice. Action promotes learning: the ability to learn from experience and make needed adjustments in performance strategy. The Port St. Lucie story told in chapter 1 exemplifies the value of review during the project.

What Port St. Lucie Learned

As we have seen, Port St. Lucie's Office of Management and Budget (OMB) used federal grant funds to improve neighborhoods severely impacted by the economic downturn. Vendors were central to the project; they renovated the distressed housing. However, some vendors were not proposing in the second phase of the project. When the team asked why, they learned that some vendors were bidding based on what they thought was needed instead of the precise language in the solicitation. They weren't getting contracts as a result. The review caused the city to revisit the solicitation requirements and redefine what they were trying to achieve. They modified the objective, clarified the requirements, and more local businesses got involved.

What did OMB take away as the larger lesson? "One thing was our relationship to vendors. We learned the absolute value of engaging the private sector in problem solving. We had group meetings, and the vendors were constructive about proposing solutions. We had to overcome the 'we don't dare talk to vendors' mentality," Cheryl Shanaberger says. OMB was surprised by the willingness of vendors to give unbiased advice.

How does one create this environment? "The City Manager sets the tone of cooperation," Cheryl explains. "Everyone pitched in as true partners—Community Services, Risk Management, the Building Department, and legal counsel. Even simple things required us to work together, things like getting access to the homes for appliance delivery so that schedules were not impacted."

Jim Pritchard, who managed the project, came to the project management position from a different agency. He noticed a difference in Port St. Lucie. "I really noticed a difference in the openness of OMB, in tolerating and even encouraging constructive conflict. It truly is a collaborative environment."

The Port St. Lucie story illustrates team learning that can be derived from mid-project and after-action reviews. The gravamen of a project review is the willingness to encourage criticism and sometimes constructive conflict. When a team has built the trust that Port St. Lucie obviously had, they are able to freely ask the essential questions:

- What did we expect to see happen?
- What actually happened?
- What are the reasons for the difference?
- What do we learn that can be used in the future?[2]

Then a team takes the lessons and rolls them into the project delivery strategy. At the end of a project, a team may take the lessons about how it worked together as a team and adjust the team norms or working strategy going forward. If the team does not integrate the lessons from reviews into its activities, though, the exercise is not worthwhile.

These occasional project reviews should be held at key points during the project. Why are we encountering unexpected resistance or pushback on the procurement card implementation? Have we enlisted the right executive support? Is the training too complicated for occasional users? Is the review and approval process way too burdensome? Or in Port St. Lucie's case, why have some vendors stopped participating unexpectedly?

At the end of the project, teams may want to review the other dimensions of their collaboration. Did we have the right people on the team? Who else should have been on the team, and how could the planning process have been changed to get the right participation? Did we have an effective communications plan, and who else should have been in the loop on updates? Was the way we conducted meetings valuable? Could other approaches to meetings have been better?

After-Action Reviews, Retrospects, and Learning Histories

One way to create a learning opportunity is the after-action review. A "retrospect" (sometimes called retrospective) is a term commonly used to describe a similar review process after the project is closed. The purpose of an after-action review is to find ways to learn from a project during its project life.

Some teams have looked at after-action reviews as activities only done after completion of a project. However, they should be used during project performance while memories are fresh.[3] For example, a procurement has a series of steps before beginning contract performance: planning, solicitation development, evaluation and award, and contract execution. While a retrospect could be conducted on the entire procurement after the award, there is value to conducting incremental after-action reviews. After the solicitation is published, a team after-action review might reveal weaknesses in the request for proposal that could be corrected by solicitation amendment. An after-action review after a request

(continued on next page)

After-Action Reviews, cont'd.

for best and final offers could uncover some information exchange issues, or even ambiguities about requirements, that conceivably could be corrected with a second request for best and final offers. A team loses the opportunity for these midpoint-project completions if periodic reviews are not conducted.

Team leaders must be sensitive to the need to create "safety." Often, the process of looking back and critically evaluating performance can spark emotional response. These kinds of reviews should not be done until the team has had a chance to meld and develop working norms that include open, candid communication. Also, in order to create the right climate of openness, it's best not to invite spectators or management who were not part of the team.[4]

Scott Belsky (2010) describes an approach to group feedback called *appreciations* that he learned from a workshop run by storyteller Jay O'Callahan. When a story was told by a participant and the group started the feedback, each person providing feedback was asked to comment on the elements of the story that they most appreciated.[5] This is a means of creating safety in a group that has not had the time to bond and develop more intimate trust necessary for candid exchange of ideas. Starting with those elements of the story that members appreciate might pave the way to constructive criticism later.

The term *retrospect* is associated with after-action reviews after project completion. A task force, for example, could use a retrospect to learn from a large project that has gone badly. A retrospect done long after the end of the project may require a team's revisiting the objectives and deliverables of a project. A retrospect requires a step-by-step return to the project history. Because one of the objectives is to capture tacit knowledge about a project, stories of project participants are sometimes recorded.[6]

A retrospect team explores whether there were external conditions that explained the failure or success. There may have been internal team factors that contributed as well, and the team discusses what could have been done differently and what should be used in future projects. The review also looks at unintended consequences arising out of a project.[7]

Shore and Warden (2008) describe a software development project retrospective.[8] First, the team issues what they call the "prime directive," that everyone makes mistakes and the retrospective is not the place to place blame or attack individuals. The assumption is that everyone on the project did the best they could with what they knew at the time, their skills and abilities, the resources, and the given situation. The team asks for affirmative acknowledgement of the prime directive by each participant.

Then they brainstorm ideas or thoughts about the project in categories. What was enjoyable and needs to be done more? What was frustrating and should be done less? What was confusing?

After a chance to reflect, the ideas are written on separate index cards. Even ideas outside of the team's control are fine. Anonymous cards facilitate participation. The cards are read and put up on the whiteboard. They are discussed, with new ones added as the conversation naturally unfolds about each idea.

Then the team uses a process called "mute mapping," a version of affinity diagrams. Everyone is invited to go to the whiteboard, group related cards together, and move unrelated cards far apart. There is no talking. If two people disagree on where to put a card, they work out a compromise without talking. This exercise usually lasts about ten minutes. The facilitator then draws a circle around each group—still no talking. Then the facilitator asks the team to name the category.

Once categories are named, the participants multi-vote on which categories should be improved for the next iteration or project. They use five self-stick dots to vote. They can place them all on one category or spread them among several.

The team then comes up with options for summarizing the idea embraced in the category. They invent summarizations, and the group decides which is best. If there isn't a clear consensus, they vote. The final vote becomes a retrospective objective.

The authors emphasize that—especially in software development retrospectives—it is easy for the objective to languish without action. Someone should be responsible for following through to push the team and remind it when actions are due.

After-action reviews can be applied to decision making as well. In Klein's (2003) decision-making critique, he has the team write down the key decisions that were made. Telling a story chronologically may be helpful to uncover the decisions. Identify the tough decisions. Then ask the expert or decision-maker, why was this difficult? How were you interpreting the situation? What clues or patterns should have been picked up? Why was the action chosen? In hindsight, should a different action have been chosen?[9]

Some state workforce development websites list another version of the retrospective: a critical events review. They work the same way, but the impetus for the review is an unexpected event. The same four questions are asked, however. An example might be a disaster response that involved mobilization of the procurement-response team. The lessons that are learned are rolled into the procurement disaster preparedness plan.

A learning history is an extension of after-action reports or retrospects. They are more resource intensive and involve interviews by a cadre of people who were not necessarily involved in the project. They are reserved for critically important events where recapture of the tacit and explicit knowledge from a group of people is necessary.

A learning history involves more resources and is performed well after the project is closed. A team of 3–5 people is usually convened, and interviews are scheduled with the key stakeholders in the project, including project managers and decision-makers. Interviews are recorded or detailed notes taken. After collection of the information, the team meets to determine what should be part of the recorded history, the episodes of the project's history. Some quotations are used in the subsequent narrative that includes comments and insights by the team regarding what lessons can be derived from the history: themes that arise, questions that the narrative poses, and other issues that can be considered by future teams. The idea is to have a product that future teams can review and discuss before launching on new projects where the lessons are relevant to critical choices that the new team may face.[10] Estimates in the time to complete these histories range from one half day to two days per interview.

The McKenna Long & Aldridge LLP procurement update event was used previously to illustrate essential elements of project management. The Denver event portrays essential risk-management concepts described in chapter 8. Teams like these learn from the project and incorporate what they learn into future projects. Lisa King, the legal assistant who coordinated the event, explains.

"I keep a folder for this event, and right after the event I talk to the attorney directing the program and panel moderators and get their feedback. I add the tips and lessons-learned to my folder. Unfortunately, we haven't found a way to stop snow storms!"

Build after-action reviews into project strategy. A team derives useful information by asking, what do we learn from this experience in terms of future projects?" This is team learning.

The use of pilots is a type of planned experiment that can be incorporated into a project to build-in learning during project execution. When a policy change is piloted for a segment of an organization and observations made about the effects, for example, the feedback is useful for helping the team and entire organization learn. This is a way of creating project learning on a smaller scale before a decision that could have wide-ranging impacts on an organization. Thomas Linley's office-machine project in Ohio used pilot consolidations of multifunction machines in select offices, permitting midcourse adjustments in the strategy had they been necessary.

Likewise, phased implementations in information technology projects are examples of the use of feedback and learning. Arizona's ProcureAZ project used phased implementation and user team feedback to learn and identify needed adjustments to implementation strategy.

Strive for "Stickiness"

Apart from the process of learning from recurring project reviews, learning also implicates the concept of stickiness. How do teams add traction to an idea?

Humans propagate physical properties genetically. Other customs, attitudes, habits, and ideas—sometimes called *memes*—spread through other means. Chip Heath and Dan Heath in their book *Made to Stick* (2008) identified various strategies for making ideas sticky.

Strive for simplicity. Find the core of the idea and try to simplify its message. Ideas that are credible and concrete are more prone to stick. Vivid, clear images can help.[11] Package ideas so they are surprising and unexpected. Harness emotion to the extent possible.

Tapping emotion in procurement may be a challenge. Chapter 8 told the story of a company trying to get senior executives to understand the value of strategic sourcing. One can talk over and over about potential cost savings from standardizing on high use items so demand can be aggregated and prices reduced. Or one can haul in a pile of work gloves to a conference room table, tag them with prices varying 300%, and have the executives visually see the problem. That is use of emotion—and unexpectedness and concreteness—to get an idea to stick.

Stories also help promote stickiness. Stories are used in this book to bring concepts to life.

Barb Johnson, the former procurement manager for Columbus Regional Airport, developed a unique approach to helping her students learn and share from a rich variety of experiences.

"Purchasing Gone Wild"—Stories that Transfer Knowledge & Expertise

Failure isn't final. In fact, Barbara Johnson, the former procurement manager for the Columbus Regional Airport Authority, focuses on failure and resiliency in her "Purchasing Gone Wild" workshop. Barb finds that it encourages folks to share their experiences if a foundation of "It's okay to fail" is laid.

And it teaches us all that failure is indeed not final.

Johnson borrowed the concept from an article in the *Harvard Business Review* about how we don't sit around the fire and tell stories anymore in our culture. She evolved the related concepts of failure and resiliency as a learning tool when she was the purchasing manager of the city of Columbus, Ohio. Her office was leading the implementation of the city's first automated procurement system. Barb wanted staff members to model failure and resiliency as a learning tool so that the staff and the client business unit purchasers would not be afraid to use the new system, to fail, and then to try again to succeed.

They adopted two slogans that incorporated failure and resiliency into learning. The first was "refuse to be a victim," encouraging system users to see success as pushing through mistakes, doubt, and challenges. System users were also told to, "Ask me again," encouraging them to ask questions a second time if they did not understand the first explanation. The central Purchasing Office staff members understood that not every user would "get it" the first time; they hadn't either!

User group meetings allowed the system users to share ideas, failures, and fixes with their stories presented on a large projection screen. In the end, the system implementation was an overwhelming success.

In the Purchasing Gone Wild seminar, Barb tells stories of procurement professionals who have learned from mistakes.

"Screwing up is not fatal," Barb reminds attendees. She even draws parallels with engineers and scientists, who use prototypes and testing to learn, even though the prototypes often fail. She sets the stage by introducing students to a concept that many of them may find unusual, that we learn through failure. And resiliency is the ability to spring back from adversity.

The handful of slides Barb uses emphasize the power of stories. "We are more interdependent than ever. Information and regulations are growing and growing. More can go wrong in a procurement than can go right. We share stories to make sense of changes in our environment, to create new knowledge, and to make decisions. We celebrate failures to learn from them. It helps us develop resiliency."

Barb shares some of her stories: bad specifications, problems in specifying contract types, failure to reach agreement in contracts. Then she lets the attendees share their stories.

They break into small groups, and each person tells the group their "failure and resiliency" story. Names can be changed to protect the innocent! The group then picks one story to tell to the full class. There is lots of sharing. The entire class decides which story is the "best," and the winner receives a bead necklace. Barb presented the first workshop during spring break and Mardi Gras, so the prize and theme aligned especially well: purchasing gone wild!

Barb Johnson's presentation title illustrates the elements of the Chip Heath and Dan Heath model for sticky ideas. The title is unexpected. Just reading the title evokes a feeling that this presentation is going to be a bit unusual. It helps cement one of Barb's central themes: we learn from our experiences, even failures. Later, we tell the story of this book's lead, "Do you have art in your procurement manual?" The curiosity and surprise that these titles evoke help remind us that there is room for creativity in procurement.

For your projects, develop a succinct story or elevator speech that conveys a vivid, compelling story about the reasons for the project. Even better, use vivid images and pictures to capture the imagination. Use metaphors in team meetings to come up with creative ways to frame the project.[12]

Malcolm Gladwell (2000) added other elements to the idea of stickiness or conditions that cause certain ideas to achieve a "tipping point." He found that various individuals in networks fulfill roles associated with propagation of ideas. Some people are the repositories of information about the idea. Other people are influencers or persuaders. Identify relevant networks and find those networks and key people in them who fulfill these kinds of roles. They often can easily be identified—others often look up to them—making them useful members of a team where traction of ideas can be a challenge. In many ways, Jean Clark was successful in finding people who were networked and able to communicate vivid messages about the value of ProcureAZ. Jean obviously was one of those people herself.

And repetition—the repetition of the right behaviors—is another key to stickiness. Observing, doing, and explaining is an on-the-job training approach that mirrors repetition using various ways to promote practice and reflection. Creating job aids, checklists, and taking notes also helps repeat concepts.[13] With respect to internal controls like procurement procedures, teams may need to construct formal reviews, training, newsletters, briefings, meeting agenda items, or other creative means to build repetition and follow-up into projects to make ideas stick.

Help Create Tacit Knowledge

This chapter turns now to another dimension of learning: the way that knowledge is created (and transferred). Teams often either train or manage projects where training is a component. As chapter 4 described, team members may turnover and—even if on a small scale—relevant knowledge has to be transferred or created. But organizational learning starts with the individual.[14]

This section uses the word "create" in its title because in many respects knowledge is not transferred. While information can be provided, and insight and experiences shared, knowledge *creation* has to occur at the individual level. What is called knowledge transfer may be more accurately described as recreation of the ability to deal with new situations, events, information, and contexts.[15]

Tacit and Explicit Knowledge

Older, more experienced employees often have deep knowledge and ability. I once had an employee in my central collections office who was the only one who knew how to maintain and generate reports out of our *legacy* (meaning really old) debt-collection IT system. There was documentation about the system, but she had developed workarounds for some of the peculiarities of the system's behavior. No amount of documentation alone was enough for another employee to create the knowledge necessary to effectively use that system. Employees stepping into the shoes of departing or retiring staff have to learn what was once known. This really is knowledge creation.

In 2008, NASPO published a research brief on challenges with the aging workforce.[16] The paper concluded by acknowledging the difficulties in tacit knowledge transfer—what this chapter calls knowledge creation—but stopped short of comprehensively identifying solutions.

As the NASPO paper explained, knowledge is categorized into two categories: explicit and tacit knowledge. The distinction and interplay between tacit and explicit knowledge, the role of socialization, and the spiral of knowledge were introduced in 1991 by Ikujiro Nonaka in *Harvard Business Review*.[17] Explicit knowledge can be readily identified and transferred; it often consists of manuals, documents, and procedures. Tacit knowledge is more difficult to articulate and share; often people are not aware they even have it. Tacit knowledge is difficult to recreate. Recreating tacit knowledge requires more personal contact or hands-on experience. Current writing about knowledge management has focused less on resources to make learning available (often through computer systems) and more on the structures in organizations that promote informal learning. Some commentators maintain that the knowledge management of the 1990s focused too heavily on explicit knowledge, incorporated too much structure and logic, overemphasized technology, and sacrificed creativity and insight.[18] Jay Cross (2007) believes that "know who" and "know where" are more important than the "how and what" of learning. Informal structures promote networking that is essential for people to access learning communities.

Yes, it is important to know the information and where to find it.[19] Too often, though, the focus is on traditional, formal training delivery without paying enough attention to the opportunities to use a variety of strategies such as structured follow-up, creation of action plans, or other opportunities to practice.[20]

Barriers to Knowledge Creation

Culture is an important ingredient in fruitful learning environments. Fear remains a barrier to open communication, fear of being considered deficient. Informal learning tools aimed at encouraging candid feedback may be one way to promote psychological safety necessary to learning where there are demanding goals and accountability.[21]

Individuals accumulate over a lifetime their beliefs about what is true through their upbringing, education, training, experiences on the job, and individual trial and error. Newly created knowledge can be inconsistent with those beliefs. Or individuals create scripts for responding to situations, and new information may require development of new actions, a process called accommodation. When that process is too difficult, some peoples' self-image may be threatened.

Complexity is another barrier; simplicity is a recurring element of successful learning. Hackman (2002) identifies access to critical information as necessary to supporting teams. On the other hand, establishing supportive context must also take into account the fact that "a flood is as bad as a drought."[22] Managing the flow of information requires attention as a team to tasks where information volume is challenging. Effective use of information, feedback, and incorporation of the lessons in the organization learning cycle—and achieving simplicity—may be a challenge.

Knowledge creation can confront other barriers.[23] Absence of a common language is one barrier; a common understanding of terminology is necessary for sharing knowledge. Trautman (2007), a practitioner who developed a peer-mentoring model, includes *jargon* as an element of his five-minute meeting plans used for individual mentoring sessions.[24] The NIGP *Online Dictionary* creates a common professional glossary. But in a cooperative procurement between states, for example, even fundamental vocabulary about procurement types—negotiations versus request for proposals, for example—may require clarification.

Likewise, while organizational procedures can be valuable and promote consistency, they also can impede innovation and get in the way of crossing functional boundaries in organizations. An organization's culture and paradigms are embodied in mission statements and other documents. They help define the organization's vision and align thinking, but they also can be an enemy of learning, constructive change or innovation. Some practices endure simply because they have always been done that way. In Port St. Lucie, Florida's, case, the city had to overcome a historical reluctance to talk with vendors in advance of solicitations. In short, some knowledge needs to be discarded.[25]

Models for Learning

Researchers have defined broad models for learning. Davis and Davis (2000) took trainer-centric descriptions of teaching models and converted them into trainee-centered suggestions for people managing their own learning. They identified seven strategies: behavioral, cognitive, inquiry, mental models, group dynamics, virtual reality (simulation), and holistic (experiential). Behavioral learning, for example, is best suited to procedural skills like those involved in teaching someone how to create an evaluation spreadsheet. Other strategies, like cognitive, mental models, and experiential approaches are used for much of the knowledge-based learning that procurement professionals encounter.

Learners internally integrate concepts (cognitively) with other learning when they sit in presentations. They might use inquiry to deconstruct and learn from a bid protest experience. We learn and apply mental models whenever we use a problem-solving approach in a project, as when we build a staff package to support a major decision. Procurement practitioners use group-dynamics learning when they debrief after a procurement-planning meeting and discuss how the meeting might have been improved for the next procurement. And disaster-response simulations are an example of how simulations are used in procurement.

Some approaches to learning may not work well for all learners. Some students may not learn verbally as well as others. They may be less able to construct cognitive frameworks by reading, for example. They may prefer to jump into doing a task as opposed to reading about it. Younger adults may not have the background to learn through problem solving. Some adults do better with group process learning than others who prefer to focus on substantive tasks.[26] The adult learner can guide trainers into the methods that work best for them—at least initially.

This chapter implicitly applies a simple model that teams can use for learning and teaching others using a variety of learning approaches. Figure 9-1 depicts the essential elements.

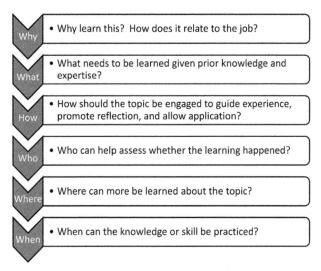

Figure 9-1. Five Ws and a How of Learning.

The model depicted in figure 9-1 can be used by individuals to manage their own learning. It can be used by teams or peer mentors for informal training.

The model works this way. Answer the "why?" or "what's in it for me?" (WIIFM) question. Sharpen the reasons for and relevance of the learning. Identify what experience and knowledge the learner already has. Clearly map out an outline for the learning and its objectives. Sequence and chunk the content appropriately. For learners with deep expertise but new to a team, at least cover the new jargon.

Determine how to engage the topic. Vary the approaches to learning:[27] often a mixture of reading, showing, doing, and talking about the topics. Talk to the learners about their preferred style. Identify who and what approaches can be used to assess whether the material has been learned.

Provide information about where additional resources for learning can be found. And creatively find ways to practice what was learned.[28]

This chapter begins to illustrate how some offices have used various approaches to learning. And effective learning starts with conversations.

Foster Conversation and Dialogue

This chapter spans a range of activities that focus on learning in contexts that teams often encounter. Von Krogh, Ichijo, and Nonaka (2000) identified conversation as one of pillars of knowledge creation.[29] Jay Cross (2007) likewise emphasizes conversation as more important to informal learning than other more formal training approaches that organizations rely on. Effective conversation encourages active participation in which everyone contributes.

People good at conversation use a certain conversational etiquette. They "check authority at the door," permit some level of chaos, and avoid moving towards closure too early. They are orderly, brief, acknowledge other points of view, and avoid ambiguity. Effective conversations have healthy amounts of editorial judgment, effectively narrowing the number of concepts at the appropriate time, using objective data and justification to decide on the merit of a concept, and moving toward closure at the right time. Good conversations also are characterized by experimentation with new concepts and meanings.[30]

Technology is supporting conversations among people who have never met. The next story illustrates one important use of technology to promote learning, however informally. Communities of practice are accepted ways of networking professionals to encourage informal learning.

Using NASPO and NIGP "Communities of Practice"

Chapter 3 described NIGP's discussion forum and how it is used to identify best practices. In the example there, the inquiry was about performance measures purchasing offices are using to provide information and statistics to senior agency executives. NASPO also has a network community that state members use to exchange ideas.

NASPO and NIGP's online resources create a true "community of practice." A community of practice is a group of professionals or employees who communicate with each other because they share common work practices, interests, or aims.[31]

The NASPO Network Community and NIGP's Nsite are online communities where NASPO and NIGP members can discuss procurement topics, get information on procurement processes, and share documents and best practices. They are available to members only.

Nsite has discussion communities that address specific topics. In addition to the general members section, there are separate discussion-communities topics such as technology in procurement, K-12, and higher education, among others. The NASPO Network Community has separate discussions for its committees, e.g., committees working on the state law survey, the NASPO Cronin awards, emerging issues, and professional development. There are topical discussions relating to cloud computing, law enforcement procurement, and disaster preparedness.

Nsite has over 2,000 discussion posts in the general purchasing community. Nsite has included discussions about such things as model solicitations, organizational issues like centralization-decentralization, preferences, ethics and conflicts of interest policies, governance issues such as the role of city and county elected officials, and questions about use of various kinds of contract clauses.

Both sites permit document sharing and have resource libraries. NIGP's Resource Library has model-solicitation language and contracts, reports and articles, NIGP publications and research, and other documents.

One caution is advised about context. Governance and legal requirements often vary between jurisdictions. In Florida, for example, the rules regarding solicitations and award, as well as open record/freedom of information requirements, are quite different from other jurisdictions. One often saw discussion posts asking for input only from Florida procurement professionals. They now have their own community.

One best practice that can improve the quality of online discussions is the consolidated reply.[32] These include the original query, but they also succinctly summarize responses. Sometimes these summaries are useful because responses may be done off-line by email and not captured in the discussion community. The consolidated reply also can list related resources that are known to be relevant to the topic, or perhaps discovered as a result of the discussion. A consolidated reply can help inform other members of the community whether more research is being done, whether the inquiry is over, and what if any conclusions were reached regarding the topic.

These sites not only are solid communities of practice. Nsite also is the platform to support online courses hosted by NIGP. Students who actively learn to use Nsite for community discussions are in a good position to effectively collaborate in NIGP's online courses. NASPO's community and online collaboration tools are used for committee work coordination and to hold Cronin Award webinars where members can learn from award-winners about their innovative projects.

The next story is one that introduces the importance of being attuned to principles of adult learning, perhaps in a surprising context. Multnomah County's story about computer-based learning breaks the paradigm of traditional training by illustrating how technology can be used to make information available when adults need it.

The second edition of Stolovitch and Keeps's *Telling Ain't Training* (2011), the book used in NIGP's instructor training program, added two new chapters about technology and training. The authors emphasized two key points about technology and learning in particular. According to them, technology has not been found to improve effectiveness of training, although it has been shown to improve efficiency and availability. Their other key point is that that the instructional and learning principles apply equally to e-learning and face-to-face learning.

Multnomah County's project shows how computer-based training can supplement and enhance more traditional face-to-face training. Most of all, this story illustrates the relevance of training principles and how important training skills are to procurement offices.

Multnomah County's Computer-Based Learning System

Multnomah County, Oregon, turned a major system upgrade into an award winning training vehicle. In 2012, the county received NIGP's Innovations in Public Procurement Award for its in-house-developed, computer-based learning system. The history and technical features of the project were described by *Government Procurement* magazine.[33]

The genesis for the program was adoption of the procurement modules in the county's enterprise resource planning (ERP) system, SAP. Like other government entities, the county started implementation with the financial modules, and when the procurement system aspects were added, the county faced a training challenge. Along with system implementation, the county was reengineering its contracting process.

(continued on next page)

Multnomah County's Computer-Based Learning System, cont'd.

The county's procurement organization had elements of both centralization and decentralization. Many of the agency personnel performing procurement and contracting functions were not procurement professionals, but they performed procurement work in conjunction with other duties that were their primary responsibilities.

Brian Smith, the Purchasing Manager for Multnomah County, led a team that researched training alternatives. Because of cost considerations, though, his team opted for in-house development using open-source software and commercial products familiar to the human resources department. The system was able to leverage existing PowerPoint presentations already used for training and add other features like audio to presentations for online learning.

The NIGP Innovation Award was a testament to the creativity of Brian and his team. They zeroed in on project objectives that included training of high volume users as well as development of a reference resource. They assembled a qualified team and adapted project implementation strategies as they learned more about available technology and its capabilities. Their training system combined technology (including interactive aspects that provide learners with feedback) with a management system to help track training of the county's employees. They used metrics regarding completion rates, satisfaction ratings, and completion scores to measure the success of the project.

In *Government Procurement* magazine's article, Brian emphasized that the human resources department brought adult-learning principles to the team. The system is especially useful for adult learners because the training modules are always available as a resource. The course content is appropriately "chunked," and learners can self-manage training and learn at their own pace. The slides include associated audio with context explanations, and learners can return to individual modules if they need refreshers about specific topics.

Agency employees often shadow more experienced persons when they are learning their jobs. However, this system provides more training consistency and less variation in procurement practices. The documented training supported by the system fosters continuity.

An unexpected value of the system is its ability to support face-to-face training. Some learners prefer face-to-face interaction over purely online environments. Brian considers training competency a core for personnel in his organization; in a decentralized environment, he has seen his organization's mission evolve towards training and oversight. Brian is quick to emphasize, "As a profession, we are trainers. Maybe one of the most surprising lessons from development of this system was how well it expands the teaching resources of our staff."

As a result of the project, the procurement office has been recognized for its leadership in computer-based courses. The system has been expanded to include content in over 20 other county courses.

E-learning has improved the ability to make knowledge available when adults need access to it. Like Multnomah County's, these systems can chunk information into digestible forms in order to improve the odds of beating the knowledge loss that occurs after lectures: only 15% is retained three weeks after a lecture. Practice improves the retention, but so does breaking the information into smaller chunks (that also promotes on-demand access).[34]

In some respects, assessment is facilitated better in these programs because they integrate self-testing as the course progresses, as opposed to face-to-face courses that often rely on general instructor notions of whether the class "gets it" or end-of-course assessment tests. With properly designed assessments, these systems can tap into learning by making questions meaningful and requiring some amount of reflection before the response.[35]

Not every government or agency will have as sophisticated a training platform as Multnomah County's. This story is important, however, because it vividly illustrates one agency's surprising realization about how central learning is to its mission. What started as a traditional search for training about ERP and contracting systems evolved into awareness that training is a core capability that is essential to procurement team missions.[36] The project represented collaboration between the procurement and human resources.

Workforce-development offices may have resources that are useful to knowledge creation in small groups or organizations. Sometimes they focus more on strategic issues like those related to succession planning: knowledge capture before it leaves the organization. Still, these tools can be adapted to the various objectives that teams are likely to encounter. For example, guidance on capturing and transferring key knowledge before critical personnel leave an organization can be turned into approaches to making checklists and informal approaches to integrating new employees into teams. What does a new team member need to know about the team history, its norms, and method of working? Who will mentor their transition into the team? How will it be done; is inviting them to the next meeting enough?

The Multnomah County computer-assisted learning project cements the value of knowing learning principles, especially when technology is used. Informal learning has become a centerpiece recently of knowledge management. Systems like Multnomah's, the NASPO network community and NIGP's Nsite provide virtual opportunities for conversations, a key ingredient of learning in teams.

Use Guided Experience to Learn and Teach

We learn by doing, not by reading books alone. Public procurement practice, for example, is not unlike the practice of law and medicine. We have a series of recurring challenges, projects, or problems. We apply skills, knowledge, and cognitive models to solving or completing the problems or projects. We learn from those experiences, adapt approaches in some cases, improve competencies, and repeat the process for new assignments and challenges. It is called *practice*.

Much of what we need to know in procurement cannot be experienced firsthand. Disaster preparedness planning and response are examples. We have to find alternative strategies for learning that we hope sticks so that it prepares us adequately when the disaster arises. Formal training programs, along with more informal interactions with our peers, help us learn what we need to be successful.

When we attend training, or otherwise engage peers in learning new things, we are exercising what are often called *adult learning principles*. For teams, some of these principles are relevant as they tackle learning challenges associated with team performance. At one end of the spectrum, a team may have to integrate a new member on a team. At the other end of the spectrum, a team's charter can involve development of a formal training program. In between those two ends of the spectrum, training might not be the primary project objective but an essential ingredient nonetheless. Marscy Stone's Oregon disaster-preparedness workgroup had a training element as the procurement tools were developed and agencies shown how to use them.

Done right, training may be one of the richest environments for learning opportunities. Or done poorly, training can be a directive, unilateral experience for participants—the "sage from the stage" model—where little learning occurs. The key is to try to involve as many senses and varying experiences as possible.

Adult Learning and the NIGP Instructor-Training Program

There is life without PowerPoint! NIGP's instructor training program is an excellent example of how adult learning principles are used. It also illustrates some approaches to learning that groups can use in transferring knowledge during training.

I entered NIGP's instructor training program in 2008. The instructor program began with a three day course in Reston, Virginia. The core textbook was the first edition of Stolovitch and Keeps' *Telling Ain't Training* (2011), an excellent book that covers a good deal of learning and training theory while offering practical solutions and approaches.

For potential instructors like me, molded by the PowerPoint culture, the course was essential. We learned that adults need to be learning-prepared (what Stolovitch and Keeps call readiness), often by answering the "what's in it for me?" (WIIFM) question. Adults need a clear understanding of why a particular topic is important.

Adults bring a breadth of experience to a course, so early assessment of expectations about a course is vitally important. Said another way, some adult learners have deep experience with parts of a course, and that experience should be tapped so they do not lose interest.

Adults tend to be practical and focused on goals. They also want to be involved in managing their learning. Seminars for adults sometimes include surveys of activities and enlist the class in helping to map out the activities to be used. In short, they participate in design of the learning experience.

Our train-the-trainer class threw away PowerPoint for a while, as we experimented with use of flip charts, movement, and other learning approaches. Some students learn better by listening. Others can learn by speaking or articulating a concept. Some like visual clues, as when we designated a flip chart as a "parking lot" to capture concepts or ideas that we hadn't fully explored. Movement in a room has been found helpful to learning, making it more interesting. We moved around in different groups for various exercises to be exposed to the perspectives of other students and the energizing effects of movement.

At the end of the course, we practiced teaching. We chose a topic to plan and present for a short fifteen-minute training session. Our presentations were videotaped. We used the mock training to self-assess our performance and get feedback from other students.

We were exposed to a sound instructional development method, one used in NIGP courses. I personally was reacquainted with Bloom's taxonomy, a classification of educational objectives at varying levels of sophistication using action words like identify, know, define, describe, compare, differentiate, use, apply, evaluate, etc. The creation of objectives in any training module is the prerequisite to further instructional development, such as planning of in-class activities.

Our training and the model lesson plans incorporated other adult learning principles:

- Adjust the class to the level and needs of the participants.
- Use icebreakers to get students comfortable with one another. Suggested icebreakers are made available to NIGP instructors on the NIGP instructor website.
- During student introductions, include expectations/goals from each student and what they want to learn.
- Write goals on chart paper and post them on the wall. Reconcile student goals with the course class objectives/agenda blocks of instruction. Explain any goals that the course cannot meet.
- Tell a personal story that relates the importance of the topic in the practice of public procurement. Use the stories to illustrate principles.
- Ask participants if they have a story to tell about why knowing the topic is important.
- Give an initial pretest to assess the level of attendees' knowledge of the material.
- Use activities that involve the participants in the course content and allow assessment of their current level of knowledge and interest. Adjust course delivery accordingly and get the participants involved in relating their own experiences to the course content.
- Pause frequently to allow reflection. Questions allow learners to process information. Don't fill in the silence too quickly after a question is asked.
- Check off goals as they are achieved during the class.
- Remember that frequent use of examples helps students understand and remember.
- Encourage students to provide their own examples.
- Plan activities that provide a change of pace during the class. Adults learn about 10% of what they read, 20% of what they hear, and 50% of what they hear and see. Learning jumps to 70% of what students say and 90% from what they both say and do.[37]
- At lunch breaks and after each day assess progress and make any necessary adjustments in the schedule and activities.
- At the end of the course, review student expectations gathered on the first day to determine if all expectations were met.

After the class, the instructor certification process included two mentored trainings, where course delivery was shared by a master instructor and student instructor. This approach gives student instructors the chance to observe and practice in an environment where feedback is provided. Barb Johnson was my first instructor mentor, and she helped me learn that there is life after PowerPoint!

What made the NIGP instructor course *experiential* was the use of real training techniques in a guided environment. We not only were learning <u>about</u> training. We were practicing approaches <u>to</u> learning, experiencing in real time the lessons we were learning. We taught mock training modules and got feedback from the instructor and class. The use of guided experience continued into the student teaching mentored by master instructors.

The principles that NIGP teaches instructors are relevant in other learning contexts. Readiness is a condition precedent to any effective learning, and the WIIFM focus helps open learners' minds and attention to training content. Instructors build on adult learners' expertise; pre-course assessments help identify the levels of the various participants. In courses I teach now, I am able to use other students' experiences to supplement my own to illustrate how course material is applied.[38]

Another principle is to get participants to take charge of their own learning. Change of pace and use of small group discussions help attendees participate in various ways and find their own meaningful ways to contribute. As Stolovitch and Keeps (2011) explain, "The key in this case is to build numerous exercises that require participation and contribution. Develop scenarios, role-plays, cases, brainstorming, and practice activities that require learner involvement."[39]

At its core, learning is achieved through action and experience. Leonard and Swap (2005) in their book *Deep Smarts* use the term "guided experience" to describe tools and techniques used to leverage experience in learning. Practice is key, so long as the learner is repeating the right behaviors. That is where experienced practitioners can design learning experiences to guide practice, observation, problem solving and experimentation.

Some guided experience is low cost. See, do, and lead approaches to knowledge coaching;[40] decision-making exercises; and after-action reviews do not require sizeable investments of anything other than time.

Some experience is direct, as when a novice purchasing agent shadows a more experienced procurement professional during a request for proposal project. Other experience is vicarious, as when one professional asks another about considerations in using various evaluation scoring methods. By using real examples or experiences to share relevant stories, or creating realistic experiences, a mentoring peer can help make ideas vivid and sticky and vicariously impart experience from which others can learn.

The process of using experienced people to train new or less experienced people can be called many things. In my military career, a formal on-the-job training program was used. More recently, *job shadowing*, *mentoring*, and *onboarding* are terms that are used to describe the process of using guided experience to train. This next story introduces some elements of peer-to-peer training, and the discussion that follows illustrates how that training might have been made even better.

The Colorado State Purchasing Office Training Plan

In late 1990s, the Colorado State Purchasing Office (SPO) faced a structural personnel challenge. It was difficult to recruit talented, experienced people into the central State Purchasing Office. The solution: a comprehensive training plan to facilitate upward mobility for purchasing agents.

Some of the SPO's difficulty was a result of a change to state personnel classifications. In the past, *purchasing agents* had been a separate classification. But the state reduced the number of classification categories, putting purchasing agents into a general professional class. The classification criteria were so broad that often there was no specific relationship to the responsibilities of purchasing agents. Despite the fact that agents in the State Purchasing Office had wide-ranging responsibilities with a variety of agencies and institutions, including some oversight, it was difficult to get human resources professionals to understand the difference between working in the state's central purchasing office and in individual departments.

Sometimes fairly novice purchasing agents in other departments were classified at the same (sometimes higher) level than State Purchasing Office procurement professionals. This classification anomaly existed despite the SPO professionals having responsibility to source statewide contracts, manage complex solicitations for non-delegated agencies, and participate in oversight and reviews of other agencies. It was difficult to recruit from other agencies when there was little incentive from a pay perspective.

The SPO director had two objectives. First, he wanted to convey a clearer picture for human resource professionals of the nature of work at the State Purchasing Office. Second, he wanted to revitalize the dialogue between senior, experienced managers in SPO and purchasing agents who had been newly hired.

As is typical, the position descriptions for the office's purchasing agents were fairly uniform. Fulfill requisitions. Conduct market research and surveys. Administer and award invitations for bids or requests for proposals. However, the historical language used in position descriptions did not distinguish between the standard sourcing responsibilities in all agencies and the different central SPO responsibilities associated with statewide price agreements used by state agencies, institutions of higher education, and local governments.

The director researched the Department of Personnel policies and learned about the classification distinctions between staff level responsibility and line responsibility. The guidance provided some examples that, although not procurement specific, were useful. The SPO purchasing agents provided advice to other offices in other departments and were recognized authorities. They also had line authority for their own large procurements.

As a result, SPO developed a "State Purchasing Office Purchasing Agents Training Plan." The plan's introduction stated that the job skills and knowledge points in the plan were intended to highlight the knowledge and/or experience necessary to fully function as a lead purchasing agent in the State Purchasing Office. The plan stated that "a unique application of procurement expertise is required for procurements and contracts having statewide impact," concepts derived from classification guidance at the time. The introduction generally noted the role of fully functioning purchasing agents as resources for and advisors to other agencies, their role in development of policy direction for the state, and the agents' autonomy in taking actions.

The four-page training plan was essentially an outline of job skills and knowledge (in one wide column), with a second column for recording the date and initials of the person who had either observed work or discussed the various skills and knowledge sufficiently to determine whether the necessary level of competency existed. Some of the topics were completed by the director after either observing work or having conversations with the purchasing agent. In one case, he worked directly on a complex request for proposal with a purchasing agent, and they explored a new method of evaluation. In other cases, the SPO procurement manager or procurement programs manager recorded completion of certain skills and knowledge.

(continued on next page)

> *The Colorado State Purchasing Office Training Plan, cont'd.*
>
> The plan did not cover every aspect of procurement commonly covered by procurement certification programs (e.g., the NIGP foundation courses) or other widely available training. Instead, it focused on the unique aspects of the position. These included such things as: the special market research and surveys conducted for statewide contracts; special terms and conditions required in statewide contracts used by local governments; surveys regarding improvements to state contracts; management of ordering volume reports; liaison activities with state agencies and local governments; interpretation of state procurement laws and regulations; leading peer review teams to conduct procurement reviews of other agency procurement programs; technical assistance using the state's e-procurement system; and working effectively with all other statewide approving authorities like the State Controller, Office of Information Technology, and Attorney General. The plan also included some specific statutory and regulatory references of particular relevance.
>
> For the most part, these were the knowledge areas and competencies that procurement professionals in other departments did not require. This plan not only outlined activities for learning. The completed plan was attached to requests for personnel actions to upgrade the general professional level for purchasing agents.

The Colorado training plan had elements of more comprehensive onboarding or on-the-job training programs. It was limited in its purpose, however, and used primarily for recording competencies in central procurement office activities that were different from other public procurement professionals. One special value of the approach was its describing the work in a conceptual framework familiar to human resources personnel performing classification. Moreover, the plan promoted important dialogue in the State Purchasing Office essential to training. It also served as a record of the dates when competency was demonstrated or determined. It became useful in achieving earned upgrades.

There were aspects of the training program that could have been improved.[41] Figure 9-1 is a useful guide for identifying possible improvements.

A threshold question is answering why training is important. An early meeting with the trainee could better have set the stage for training. The SPO managers, one of whom supervised the trainees, could have participated in the training plan development and attended the first meeting. The first meeting could have been used to discuss the objectives of training, outline the training plan, and discuss on-going communication. At that meeting, the trainee's role could have been discussed: their responsibility for coordinating training times, updating the training plan as training evolved, etc.

The director could have involved the employee more in the tailoring of the training plan. So, for example, only office-specific training might have been required with more experienced employees. In some cases, only the unique use of vocabulary might be covered. Some professionals coming into SPO may have had extensive experience working with local governments and even leading statewide price agreement procurements. Training roles may change as well.

For more experienced trainees, or targeted training by subject matter experts, the trainer's role might be more passive, that is, the trainee will ask for assistance and training when they need it.

The "how" of training is a function of effective learning styles. Involving trainees in plan development can help identify their learning styles. Trautman (2007) identifies essentially four approaches to learning one-on-one: reading, watching, doing, and talking while doing.[42] While some combination of all of these generally is preferable, the trainee could have helped determine the order of training activities. Some people, for example, prefer discussions to get the big picture before reading. Others may like to see an example before reading further and discussing a topic. The idea is to use approaches that engage the trainee in a variety of ways that permit application and meaningful, internal reflection using discussions and other methods of training.[43] Whatever mixture of training approaches is selected, Trautman recommends that training be conducted at least weekly.

The SPO training plan had a useful format for recording dates of training, the training topics, and identifying some written resources. However, the plan was not "chunked" in terms of training intensity and the time allocated to topics. Overall, the planning could have been improved by addressing the frequency and duration of training sessions.[44] Moreover, the plan could have been improved by sequencing. While position descriptions may provide good guidance for topics and even the nature of the learning, e.g., know, be able to explain, be able to locate, they often are not sequenced in terms of what topics need to come before others.

Learning needs to be periodically assessed. The plan could have been improved by specifying an assessment technique. Assessments tend to be the most challenging aspects of any training and the most often overlooked. While behavioral-training practitioners often use the "repeat it back" method of assessment while demonstrating skills, in a knowledge-based environment that may not be very effective. In retrospect, answering the "who" question in figure 9-1 might have led to useful assessment conversations with other managers in SPO. During those discussions, the trainee could summarize what was learned during discussions with the director or other trainers, or from written materials the trainee had read. The trainee may have ideas about how their understanding of the topic could be assessed, e.g., who they would like to talk to about a specific topic in order to self-assess their learning.

Knowing "where" learning resources can be found is an important part of adult learning. Besides Colorado statutes and rules as references, the plan could have included key references to NIGP textbooks or other written resources for major knowledge/skill areas that trainees should read before the face-to-face training sessions. Building receptors for additional learning, e.g., using cognitive models like those in this book or the knowledge framework in NIGP textbooks, are useful adjuncts for experiential learning.[45]

Sound Transit, the Seattle metropolitan area rapid transit system, uses an exceptional tool for training its procurement professionals. Called a Procurement Activities List (PAL), the checklist is organized in an intuitive way to match the common steps in procurement. There are links in the online checklists to other resources available online. A copy of the first page of the PAL (for requests for proposals over $100K) is shown in figure 9-2.

SOUNDTRANSIT
Procurement and Contracts Division
Materials, Technologies and Services Group

PROCUREMENT ACTIVITY LIST
For Request For Proposals ≥ $100,000

This is intended as a simplified guide when using the Request for Proposals method. Deviations from this guide are at the discretion of the Contract Specialist (CS), except where indicated by a red/blue folder as a mandatory approval task. Unique circumstances or situations should be discussed with the Supervisor or Contracts Manager. Templates, forms and samples are hyperlinked.

ACTIVITY/TASK

PRE-SOLICITATION

Review and log in the Requisition
- ✓ Assign e-Bid Procurement No.
- ✓ Enter into Log 1 (keep log updated throughout the process)
If Kick-Off Requisition, submit a copy to Contracts Help

Conduct intake with Project Manager (PM)
- ✓ Discuss procurement schedule and evaluation team
- ✓ Determine if Derivatives/Liquidated Damages are relevant (if yes, notify Supervisor/CM)
- ✓ Submit completed Diversity Analysis Worksheet to DPO Administrative Specialist

Set-up procurement file
- ✓ Create N Drive Folder
- ✓ Start hard copy file folder
- ✓ Start Procurement Summary Memo

Draft solicitation document(s)
- ✓ Review Scope of Work/Technical Specifications with PM
- ✓ Send Insurance Requirements Review to RM for review
- ✓ Determine evaluation criteria & discuss evaluation procedures with PM

IF FEDERALLY FUNDED:
Review Required Third-Party Contract Clauses and advertise with federal requirements

Seek Approval to Advertise

SOLICITATION

Publish notification of the solicitation
- ✓ Send DJC advertisement by Email, no later than 3pm the day before intended publication date
- ✓ Upload solicitation documents to eBid & send notifications to identified business classifications
- ✓ Notify Reception of solicitation deadline and any pre-proposal meeting

Conduct pre-proposal meeting
PRE-MEETING:
- ✓ Discuss Agenda & define participant roles with PM
- ✓ Invite Diversity Representative
- ✓ Coordinate with Board Administration and Security (if using the Board Room)
AT MEETING:
- ✓ Direct to e-Bid for question submittal and official answers
- ✓ Collect business cards and sign-in sheet for the file

Respond to Request for Information/questions/other
- ✓ Seek Approval of Supervisor/CM (initials on Addendum/Clarification document)

Prepare evaluation packets for evaluators (before RFP closes)
- ✓ Modify evaluation instructions as necessary

EVALUATIONS

Conduct responsiveness review and price scoring
- ✓ Check Bonds/Letters of Credit (LOC) – If LOC/Money Order/Check send original to FIT & CC file
- ✓ Calculate price scores

IF FEDERALLY FUNDED:
Check for Buy America Compliance, Rolling Stock Pre- and Post-Award Audit Checklist; Lobbying Certificate Procurement Desktop Procedure for Rolling Stock Buy America compliance

Assemble and deliver evaluation package to evaluators
- ✓ Obtain Evaluators' signatures on Non-Disclosure and NCOI Form

Conduct evaluation meeting to determine rankings
- ✓ Notify shortlisted firms (if moving forward to site-visit/interview/demo)

Conduct site-visit(s)/interview(s)/demo(s) – (with all firms within at least 10% of top firm)
- ✓ Document evaluations on site-visit(s)/interview(s)/demo(s)

Figure 9-2. Sound Transit Procurement Activity List.

Hyperlinks in the PAL make access to additional learning resources easy: they point to online resources where additional resources can be found.

Another important question is "when" learning can be practiced. The SPO plan, for example, could have integrated often-overlooked learning opportunities, like attendance at pre-solicitation meetings, listening on conference calls with client agencies, attendance at department or other meetings with SPO managers, or mock award debriefings with vendors. These experiences might have vividly made other learning sticky and provided additional opportunities for discussion.

With some of these improvements, SPO would have been on its way to developing a master training plan checklist. Such a checklist could have been adapted for employees with varying levels of experience. Novice purchasing-agent training might use the entire plan over an extended training period, beginning with the portions most essential to immediate success on the job. Experienced procurement professionals might need to use only a portion of the plan.

Trautman (2007) recommends use of a tailored one-page meeting plan (outline) in advance of every training session. A mini-version of the larger training plan, it includes the main purpose of the meeting, the relationship to the job, an outline of the main points, the new vocabulary specific to the job, ways to practice or gain further knowledge, and identification of additional resources. Figure 9-1 is a useful guide for developing abbreviated plans in advance of every training session.

Although various Colorado SPO employees were involved in mentoring employees, the office did not have an open discussion about "coaching." For example, when showing someone how to do something, it helps to think aloud. Discuss what could go wrong. Examine consequences once a mistake is made. Ask open-ended questions to test thinking. Acknowledge improvement and progress. Go beyond just explaining procedures. Use questions to create hypotheticals to get deeper into the decision making.[46]

For the most part, the learning in this chapter involves learners and trainees engaged with one another, however informally. What happens when the guided experience may involve tacit knowledge of someone leaving? Ideally, there is overlap between departing employees and those who will perform their functions. Or strategies have been used repeatedly to tap into the tacit knowledge and create the knowledge in others across the team. But that is not always possible.

"Capturing" the Tacit Knowledge of Transitioning Employees

You cannot write down everything. Tacit knowledge by its definition is difficult to capture and requires human interaction and time. Use checklist approaches that facilitate conversations.

When planning transitions, add to the checklists developed for new employees or upgrade training. While the original checklists retain value, adding insights to those checklists might make them better. Add important "know who" contacts, critical steps associated with the job, workflow descriptions or maps, priorities, key due dates, critical reports or plans associated with the job, and lists of other peers who have similar work. The state of Wisconsin has a knowledge journaling template in its knowledge-transfer website that may be useful.[47]

(continued on next page)

"Capturing" the Tacit Knowledge of Transitioning Employee, cont'd.

To set priorities on knowledge capture for transitioning employees, sometimes a goal of succession planning, identify the key positions and the knowledge "at risk." Much of tacit knowledge is "know who" knowledge. Identify the other thought leaders or experts that could be a resource.

On plans and checklists, include topics where more experienced mentors or peers can guide learners though experiences that touch a variety of activities requiring rich tacit knowledge. Consider using experienced employees in guided problem solving to examine approaches to solutions or guided experimentation (such as their use of pilots) to identify considerations in how and why the problems were approached and pilots used.[48]

Some knowledge capture techniques involve interviews of transitioning employees to identify critical knowledge, knowledge they wish they had when they started the job and were forced to relearn, etc. The Tennessee Valley Authority, for example, has a process for capturing the undocumented knowledge of employees nearing retirement. The process is aimed at getting to task, information, and pattern recognition knowledge of those employees and developing knowledge retention plans for critical knowledge.[49]

Debriefings are less effective than job overlap. But whatever strategy is used, identify the most important decisions that have to be made or recommended. What are the constraints on decision making that may not be written, political or otherwise? If there is time, perform a retrospect on critical decisions made by the departing employee. What risk was not accounted for? What information was needed but not obtained? What assumptions should have been challenged? If there is no job overlap, record enough information so an intermediary can help a learner decipher the clues or approaches used by the departing expert.

Include systems considerations. What might have been unintended consequences of changes or decisions?

The learning history approach introduced earlier in this chapter might be useful for these kinds of knowledge capture challenges. Retired, experienced employees might be willing to come back temporarily to help train successors. If not, though, use of media and recording might be an alternative way to capture their tacit knowledge before they leave.

Ideally, the creation of this kind of knowledge begins well before an employee leaves. Using co-presentations, meetings, and informal discussions is more effective for repetitive sharing of experiences and insight necessary to this kind of tacit knowledge creation.

Find Creative Ways to Share Knowledge, Expertise, Experience

So far, this chapter has looked at the use of after-action reviews, retrospects, one-on-one peer mentoring, and more traditional learning models. In this section, we look at other approaches to creating knowledge.

In procurement offices, there sometimes are few opportunities to practice actual skills. A team may have a chance to lead a request for proposal project or evaluation only occasionally. Thankfully, mobilization of procurement disaster teams happen rarely. Teams may have limited opportunities to experience unusually complex procurements. Then vicarious experience may have to be created to learn and practice. These learning opportunities can take a variety of forms.

Developing a strategy to more broadly leverage expertise takes creativity. Perhaps the best part of the NASPO George Cronin Award for Procurement Excellence is the way that NASPO facilitates tacit knowledge creation. After the awards are announced at the NASPO annual conference in the fall, NASPO hosts webinars with the award finalists. Procurement professionals from offices throughout the United States are able to hear award-winners discuss their projects. In the case of Idaho's performance information procurement system (PIPS) project, the story told in chapter 7, the project lead conducted the webinar. The webinar attendees discussed issues of scope definition, how the process evaluated cost, potential risk issues, and the interplay between open records laws and the PIPS process.

The state of Washington won a 2008 NASPO Cronin Award for use of video in its training program. When I followed up with the state three years later, Matt Ackerman explained how the state was creatively using new technology to build on what had already been an innovative approach to training. Matt's use of technology was not on the scale of Multnomah County's, but it was simple, agile, and made just-in-time training available.

Washington's YouTube Training Platform

When Washington wanted to increase their state contract usage, they went high-tech. The state had taken several steps to increase use of the state contracts, including an improved state portal and training tools for central procurement purchasing agents. The most innovative tool, however, was the use of video. As a result, Washington received the 2008 NASPO George Cronin Award for Procurement Excellence for its Contract Adoption Rate project. In the words of the award narrative: "An online streaming video was developed to educate the enterprise as to the benefits of leveraging collective buying power and utilizing master contracts."

In 2011, I talked with Matt Ackerman, the Procurement Integration Manager in Washington's Department of General Services. As Matt described it, the state had moved beyond the use of streaming video. The original video production approach was fairly expensive. Low-cost software called Snagit enabled easy recording of screenshots and integration of voice as a training tool. Using the tool, Matt could create the video of the Web pages from his desktop computer along with his recorded voice, and upload the video to YouTube. This was much easier and cheaper than the previous production of streaming video. YouTube provided an adequate (and free) platform for distributing the video to users.

When vendors visit the Washington procurement website, the page includes instructions for registering on the state's e-procurement portal. For vendors, the website has videos that cover the registration steps, including vendor profile information, searching for commodity codes, and geographical location designation.

The department maintains The Washington Channel on YouTube, and Matt's voice explains the registration steps as he moves through webpage images that he has captured using Snagit. The Washington Channel also includes the original six-minute video that was recognized in 2008 when the state received its Cronin Award for Procurement Excellence.

Washington's approach to training used adult learning principles in an important way. It assumed that many employees could navigate widely popular video websites. Matt Ackerman's solution may be a modest application of "just in time" learning, but it permits users to access the information when they need it. NASPO also records and uses YouTube for publishing its Cronin Award webinars, enabling states to learn about innovative projects from the award winners.

Perhaps as important, Washington's approach permits the state to keep the information current easily. While the earlier use of video was innovative, this newer method is more cost effective. Limited resources are a common challenge. So public entities have to be innovative to create learning opportunities.

Informal learning is the buzzword now. The technology-centric knowledge management systems from a decade ago have in large measure given way to less formal methods of creating conversations and leveraging the power of informal learning. Employees are going to talk and learn. The challenge for an organization is to create supporting structures that influence what is being discussed: nurturing constructive dialogue. As an example, the state of Oklahoma used brown bag lunch training sessions to help promote procurement learning across the state.

Oklahoma's Brown-Bag Learning Sessions

Let's have lunch. Lee Johnson, contract manager for the Oklahoma Central Purchasing Division, led a series of training initiatives and developed an online training program. His most popular efforts, however, were his brown-bag sessions, which featured informal discussion about issues common to the state's contracting officers.

Lee sent out a list of proposed sessions, requested additional recommendations, and eventually conducted 12 Brown Bags. Attendance ranged from twenty-five to fifty people, and sessions were free. The topics included:

- Contract management
- Sole source procurements
- Evaluations
- Integrity
- Information technology procurements
- Negotiations
- Performance-based contracting
- Protests
- The procurement card program and changes from the selection of a new vendor

Lee used various "host" agencies. Going to their sites encouraged agency procurement leaders to participate in the discussions about how their agencies differed and how those differences affected procurement. Sometimes, Lee co-facilitated the sessions or used panels of contracting officers to vary the presentation methods and gain different perspectives.

The Brown Bags were helpful in spreading awareness of upcoming division initiatives and getting informal stakeholder input. Lee found that the attendees in these sessions were not shy about voicing their thoughts and opinions about particular issues; in other environments, they might not have spoken so freely. Stakeholder feedback on future training was also an important goal of the initiative.

According the Lee, "The Brown Bags were a success. When we looked at the evaluation comments that followed, the sessions had been well received. Almost everyone preferred the informal dialogs as opposed to the typical one-way monologues that often characterized traditional training."

Lee Johnson's Brown Bag series built on the power of informal conversations to promote learning. They afforded opportunities for people to discuss issues, engage their own cognitive abilities, and move away from the declarative type training in which presenters often learn the most. With an environment that encourages discussion, attendees exercise their own cognitive processes, creating knowledge that has a chance of sticking.

Lee sometimes co-presented. Pairing up experienced and novice procurement professionals on presentations can help transfer tacit knowledge. The process of developing a presentation involves setting priorities. Allocating slides among topics requires presenters to make judgments about the importance of content. Sequencing slides and developing conclusions likewise can promote a discussion that goes deeper into the underlying assumptions, related considerations, rules of thumb, experiences, and similar considerations that promotes learning. Consider using paired presentations as a tool in helping transfer and create knowledge.

Creative simulations also can be useful in learning.[50] Marscy Stone, whose story was told in chapters 1 and 5 to illustrate the value of purpose and project charters, used table top exercises in the Oregon disaster preparedness workgroup to test the intuitiveness of procurement tools that the team was developing. This permitted the team to work through steps of a process and associated considerations in decision making before an actual disaster. Simulated practice of course is critical in disaster planning. Carefully planned, these kinds of exercises create realistic experience as a learning tool.

Most procurement offices have some kind of oversight or pseudo-auditing function. Can those ever be leveraged to add learning as a central objective? Colorado's "peer-review" program promoted learning but also helped satisfy the requirement that procurement offices monitor or oversee their delegates.

Colorado's Delegation Oversight "Peer Reviews"

The legislature wanted us to oversee delegated agencies more aggressively," said Kay Kishline, former Colorado State Purchasing Director. "However, the agencies wanted more of a partnership. To address both sides' concerns, we developed a 'peer-review' program." The peer-review program was an on-site review of a delegated agency procurement program with help from volunteers from other state agencies and institutions of higher education. The program satisfied, in part, the requirement that the central office oversee and monitor its procurement delegates. Perhaps more valuable, though, the program permitted procurement professionals across the state to share knowledge and experience.

(continued on next page)

Colorado's Delegation Oversight "Peer Reviews, cont'd.

Peer reviews started with the SPO's selection of agencies due for review. In some cases, agencies requested the review themselves—a tribute to the success of the concept. SPO designated a lead procurement professional from its office who coordinated the visit. Other peer-review team participants were recruited from suitable agencies or institutions. For example, another university procurement professional usually participated in the review of a higher education institution. As the program matured, other central reviewer offices, e.g., the State Controller's Office, were also invited to be members of the team.

The team reviewed solicitation files, sole source justifications, purchase orders, procurement card program records, and the agency's use of the state's online Bid Information and Distribution System. Later reviews also addressed findings and recommendations of past peer reviews.

Typically, the review team would meet at the agency purchasing office in the morning, review documents and procurement files, and arrange an out-briefing in the afternoon. The dialogue between the review team and purchasing agency went beyond document review, though. The opportunity was used to learn about short- and long-term challenges faced by the agency, how training is conducted, and ways that the central state purchasing office could provide additional support.

At the end of the review, the team leader prepared a summary memorandum for the State Purchasing Director. Good practices were noted, and a risk assessment was completed that reflected the nature of the risk posed by any noncompliance with regulations. The gravamen of the risk assessment was whether adequate procedures, processes and controls were in place with reasonable assurances that state monies were protected. Assessments of medium or high risk carried specific follow-up requirements. The director then sent a transmittal letter with the memorandum to the agency, thanking them for their support, congratulating agencies having "clean" reviews, or noting any follow-up action required.

Importantly, the agencies were asked for their feedback about the peer-review process. They were asked to rate and provide recommendations about the customer-orientation of the peer-review team, what the agency learned, whether issues were adequately discussed, if the time set aside for the review was adequate and overall impressions of the process.

The State Purchasing Office was clear about the scope of this review. It was not an "audit." All peer participants were equal members of the review team. One primary objective was to keep the doors of communication open and peers part of an interconnected professional network.

Thirza Kennedy, former Procurement Programs Manager in SPO, described the process metaphorically using a chain as an example. "You cannot push a chain. You need to work collaboratively and avoid one person bearing all the weight." When Thirza briefed the division on the peer-review program, she included these words in her slides. "New leaders can appear . . . this is where the other peers bring expertise, knowledge, friendly guidance versus governance and intimidation. . . . Peers can provide valuable information and recommendations. . . . Peers are critical to future relationships."

According to Thirza, the overarching objective of the peer review was to "help—not harm," while at the same time protecting public funds and the image of the profession. Well said, Thirza!

Unfortunately, the peer-review program became a victim of limited resources. There was significant time required of the agencies being visited, other peers, and the State Procurement Office to manage the program, coordinate the visits, and conduct the reviews. Time between reviews stretched out and exceeded three years. That is why some agencies to their credit asked for reviews, especially when they had leadership changes, staff changes, or program growth affecting the procurement functions.

The program adequately fulfilled the delegation oversight responsibility, while at the same time permitting peers to share perspectives, knowledge, and experience. Professionals learned from one another.

One of my most intriguing, creative learning experiences was conducted by Carol Hodes who manages the NIGP Instructor program. I didn't realize the power of what we were doing until after I had a chance to reflect on it. I had read about, but never participated in, an approach to learning that was known as a *café*.

Speed Learning: The NIGP Instructor Development "Café"

How do you break the ice and establish a collaborative environment? A year after I completed my NIGP instructor course, I attended the NIGP Forum in San Antonio. One of the breakout sessions was created for NIGP instructors by Carol Hodes, the Director of NIGP Education and Professional Development. She named the session "speed learning," apropos because we did it all in 75 minutes!

We were divided into groups of six to eight instructors. The room was arranged with chairs at four stations with a flip chart at each. Each station had a topic for discussion, such as, "What methods have you used to break the ice and begin establishing a collaborative environment?" or "What creative assessment tools have you seen used?"

Each topical discussion location had a facilitator who stayed there. The small groups met and discussed the topics for about 15–20 minutes. Ideas were put on the flip chart. Then the groups circulated to another topical discussion location in the room. Each facilitator was able to provide some sharing of concepts.

After the last round, we all met as a group and shared some ideas we considered most powerful during the rotated sessions. In some cases, patterns emerged even between sessions that evoked some common insights. For example, for me some tools that instructors described during the discussion about icebreakers also seemed relevant to later assessments of student learning.

Carol Hode's "speed learning" shows the value of informality and conversation. A similar technique is described in the literature as a "world café."[51] The café can be used to discuss single questions, or a series of related topics like we did. Other versions of the café leave a person or two behind while the rest of the group rotates, or even counter-rotate a group member or two, mixing up group membership to add some different perspectives.

The holy grail of training involves a comprehensive suite of training experiences designed specifically for adults. It would promote progressive improvements in professional knowledge and skills and build a community of practice among procurement professionals. We found one in Virginia: the Virginia Institute of Procurement.

Virginia's Solution to a Graying Procurement Workforce

Virginia faced a dilemma common among states, the graying of its procurement workforce. Seasoned procurement professionals were retiring in record numbers, and state agencies were finding it difficult to attract and hire qualified replacements. Although Virginia has had an excellent procurement training and certification program since 1990—the Virginia Contracting Officer (VCO) program—the VCO program focuses on complex procurements processed by professional buyers and contracting officers. Missing was a comprehensive training program specifically designed for buyers just starting their careers in public procurement.

In 2004, Linda Morris, Training Manager, and her supervisor, David Nims, started with the Department of General Services/Division of Purchases and Supply. They examined the VCO program with an eye toward improving outcomes and potentially adding classes to address unmet training needs. They noticed that the pass rate on the VCO exam was below 60%, and classes were crowded because the VCO certification was really the only training aimed at the commonwealth's procurement laws. Frequently, state employees who were not in complex procurement jobs were taking the training because it was the only procurement training available. The training—aimed at more experienced procurement professionals—was not tailored for novices, which made learning more challenging and contributed to a low exam pass rate.

Dave and Linda addressed the problem by creating a multi-faceted training certification program focused on small purchases—up to $50,000—as the first step in training for a career in public procurement. The Virginia Contracting Associate (VCA) program is the result. In concert with the VCA program, the Virginia Institute of Procurement (VIP) was created as the overarching brand identity for all DGS/DPS training programs.

The VCA curriculum is based on adult learning theory and is designed around a typical small purchase life-cycle using case studies. Instructors are drawn from the professional procurement staff of DGS/DPS and all hold Virginia and national procurement certification. To prepare the instructional staff for a student-centered approach to training, they attend a two-day class on facilitation techniques. The class was designed to enhance their knowledge of adult learning principles and guide them through the assertive facilitation style selected for all VIP certification programs. The instructors learn that some learners are better at auditory learning, others visual. Still others are kinesthetic learners who prefer hands-on practice, role-plays, and simulations. Some students prefer social learning. Some learners are detailed-oriented, while others tend to be more focused on the big picture. The fact that VIP emphasizes facilitation skills further exemplifies the nature of the VIP training: it is learner centered. Most of all, it uses a variety of learning styles in training.

The VCA procurement training uses the case-study method. Participant guides are used during the class that turn into job aids when students return to work. As the class unfolds, students refer to material already in the guide, but they also help build the guide's contents through exercises, quizzes, and other classroom activities they receive as instructor handouts. This approach both reinforces learning and gives students a sense of ownership of the guide content—they see first-hand the value of the guide as a job aid.

The three-day curriculum includes a review after each step in the procurement life-cycle and a comprehensive course review with a practice exam to prepare participants for the certification exam. Like the VCO program, successful completion of the VCA program results in a five-year certification. Continuing education is required for VCA recertification.

DGS/DPS launched the VCA program in 2006 and continues to offer the class six or seven times annually to meet the demand. By spring 2013, approximately 800 state and local government employees holding more than 70 different position titles had earned certification with a 92% pass rate, a tribute to both the budding procurement professionals and the dedicated procurement team that trains them.

There are other indicators that the VCA program is successful and has become institutionalized in Virginia. They include a dramatic increase in attendance at the annual Public Procurement Forum by VCA designees. Beginning in 2011, the fifth anniversary of the VCA program's launch and the first re-certification period for the inaugural VCA class of 2006, approximately one-third of the 600 conference participants were VCA designees. Their on-going attendance in significant numbers is a clear indication of their efforts and desire to maintain their professional certification and continue their procurement education. The annual Public Procurement Forum—co-directed by Linda and Dave—is evolving to match the different levels of training needed to help all VIP students maintain professional certification at whatever level they have earned it.

The number of VCA designees applying for the Virginia Contracting Officer certification continues to increase. In recent years, the number of VCO applicants who already hold VCA certification has reached nearly 50%. This is evidence that the VCA program is fulfilling a key step in procurement education by facilitating career advancement from small to complex purchasing.

Agency hiring managers are recognizing the value of the VCA certification program. Increasingly, postings for procurement positions are published with VCA designation as a preferred educational background.

After seven years, the VCA certification program is thriving and continues to offer valuable training to purchasing staff in agencies and institutions across the commonwealth. As Virginia's procurement workforce continues to shift toward a lower age and experience profile in response to a graying workforce, the commonwealth can take comfort that it has in place a professional training and certification program that will have its younger procurement workforce prepared and ready to step into more senior level roles.

Outside trainers retained by VIP to supplement its training curriculum comment on the energy and excellence surrounding the VIP programs. Linda concluded our interview this way, "There are a lot of fingerprints on the VIP training program that make it work. The continued success of the program is the collective effort of senior management support, the training team, dedicated members of the procurement staff and, of course, our students."

Keep At It

These creative approaches to learning are effective because they tap into adult learning principles. They jettison the concept of directive presentations and encourage collaborative learning. They use the power of movement and give participants opportunities to use different modes of learning: seeing, hearing, speaking and articulating positions, and looking for patterns among related concepts.[52]

"Keeping at it" requires a culture of learning and an understanding that learning is never over. An abiding purpose requires more than a mission and vision statement; it means continually linking progress and evolving circumstances to performance and the underlying purpose. Procurement offices can always find ways to improve, but excellence requires an on-going focus on opportunities for continuous improvement and learning.

The practices of effective teams are cyclical, as well. Good teams are always scanning the environment, looking at adjustments to be made in team norms and performance strategies. As team members move in and out, the team finds ways to ease the transitions and sustain team learning. Project management, analysis, and measurement all involve a cycle. The team plans, acts, and adjusts project strategy based on feedback. Effective leaders also foster continuous learning and creation of a learning environment. After all, exemplary leaders model the way by remaining active learners.[53]

Excellent teams and managers find creative ways to share knowledge, expertise, and experience. They learn and make it stick.

10 Lead Laterally: Choose to Help

"Choose to help." —Roger Fisher and Alan Sharp (2009)

———◆———

Today, most teams are structured horizontally, with little or no vertical or supervisory relationships. Effective team members influence action and lead laterally "from the side" to nudge their teams toward better performance.

Richard Hackman (2002) counts himself among those who believe that total shared leadership is difficult for teams, that most teams need one person who is considered the team leader. Still, even studies of moral leadership, which measure leadership effectiveness by the collective "happiness," recognize that community members move in and out of leader and follower roles.[1] John Kotter (1999) forecasted the kinds of behaviors discussed in this book that are valuable in creating indirect influence.[2]

This book and its stories raise questions about other dimensions of leadership, from the transformational theories of moral and political leadership—often associated with heroic or charismatic leaders—to leadership that is critical to team success. The topic of leadership is broad and complex.

This chapter is not a comprehensive study of leadership, though. There are books widely considered classics that describe the characteristics of charismatic leaders or leadership at the intersection of power, broad social change, and varying managerial and operational levels of large organizations. Theories based on leadership traits and styles counsel that behaviors need to be adjusted based on the situation.[3] This book like others derives certain insights and offers practical approaches for leaders.[4]

But this chapter directs its attention away from charismatic leaders engaged in deep moral and social transformation. After a short section on other dimensions of leadership, this chapter focuses on the leadership skills that teams need. I borrow the term "lateral leadership" to refer to this style.

I first encountered the term "lateral leadership" in a small book by Roger Fisher (of *Getting to Yes* Harvard Negotiation Project fame) and Alan Sharp (2009). The central premise of their book was that there are opportunities for team members to contribute to the leadership of teams even though they have no formal management or supervisory relationship with team members. They can lead by helping the team perform. They ask questions, propose solutions or offer ideas, and then model the way by taking constructive action.

Fisher and Sharp concluded their book by counseling, "choose to help," as the book's synthesis. This chapter will weave their concepts into lessons already learned in this book to illustrate how lateral leaders are shaping public procurement by helping teams perform.

While this book's examination of leadership is somewhat narrower in scope than others, it is relevant to all leadership. It may be helpful to see where lateral leadership fits into the broader dimensions of the subject of leadership.

The Dimensions of Leadership

We'll depart for a moment from the team leadership focus to see where it fits into to the broader topic of leadership. One encounters various words to describe the traits of effective leaders: change agent, innovator, charismatic, optimistic, collaborative, integrity, self-actualization, resilience, persistence, trust, competence, and visionary among others. Some leaders serve in a political environment. Others are community leaders. And bookstores are full of profiles of leaders in business and industry. But traditional concepts of leadership tend to be so dominated by images of charismatic and political leaders that one "forgets that the vast preponderance of personal influence is exerted quietly and subtly in everyday relationships."[5]

Figure 10-1 visually depicts the range of dimensions of leadership. James MacGregor Burns was a Pulitzer Prize winning historian who in 1978 introduced the theory of transformational leadership in his book, *Leadership*. In many ways, Burns framed the endpoints of the discussion: transformational leadership and transactional leadership.

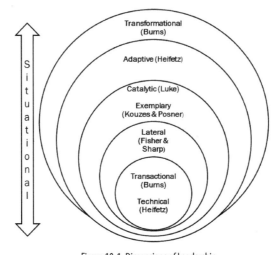

Figure 10-1. Dimensions of Leadership.

Transformational leadership[6] is a theory with leaders at its center who are charismatic and visionary and can inspire followers to transcend their own self-interest for the good of the organization. Transactional leadership, on the other hand, was a term used by Burns to describe a different kind of leadership. Burns used the term to describe the give-and-take between leaders and followers necessary to obtain resources to achieve objectives.[7] To Burns, the dialogue between leaders and followers about issues of integrity, ethics, standards of conduct and the like was transactional, albeit critical, to effective leadership. Burns saw small groups defined more by transactional leadership characterized by behavioral quid pro quo between leaders and followers.

Ronald Heifetz, a Harvard professor in the John F. Kennedy School of Government, developed his theory of adaptive leadership over a period of 30 years. His theory also frames the dimensions of leadership. At one end of the spectrum, the leadership that Heifetz describes as *technical* means problem solving largely drawing on technical skills. When a procurement team sits down to learn how to use an evaluation spreadsheet, for example, the technical context involves a different kind of leadership. The other end of the spectrum for Heifetz is *adaptive leadership*. Adaptive challenges involved competing purposes and often a need to revisit loyalties. Organizational culture and habits become a centerpiece. If you have heard that "leadership is lonely at the top," Heifetz explains why.

Jeffrey Luke (1998), a professor at the University of Oregon, created a model he called *catalytic leadership* that eventually spawned a leadership academy in the state of Oregon. Written for the public leader, in many respects the book more completely bridges the gap between technical and transformational aspects of leadership. Luke's theory was that leadership in the public sector has unique challenges. The nature of interconnected groups having diverse purposes, often fragmented authority, and shared power requires special skills. His book spans topics from Burns' transformational leadership to the technical skills of negotiation and brainstorming.

Kouzes and Posner's *The Leadership Challenge* (2012), one of the most comprehensive recent studies in leadership spanning 30 years, brought us practices of exemplary leadership: model the way, inspire a shared vision, challenge the process, enable others to act, and encourage the heart. *The Leadership Challenge* does not center solely on traits and personalities of leaders, though. The authors cover tangible behaviors that can be learned.

As figure 10-1 depicts, leadership is situational. That is, the traits and behaviors of effective leaders are related to the specific situation. The leadership required of a small military unit might be described as *technical* or *transactional* during operations. Dr. Martin Luther King Jr.'s moral leadership was adaptive and transformational. When a procurement officer is promoted to executive positions in an organization, leadership takes on dimensions that may not permit as many personal connections with individual members. There may be changes that cannot achieve consensus, people may face loss as a result of some decisions, and loyalties may shift. This is an adaptive challenge: leadership considerations evolve as contexts change.

No one begins a career leading hundreds or thousands of people, though, and most never do. For procurement professionals, much of their early work involves helping a group achieve a goal or complete a project. Roger Fisher and Alan Sharp coined the term "lateral leadership" in 1998 to describe the characteristics of effective team members who can influence action. Lateral leadership is an approach to leading "from the side" to nudge teams and groups towards better performance.[8] In teams, though, influence can be shared along with leadership by all team members.

There is broad agreement that leadership in the current age has changed. Leaders and followers are more connected horizontally now. All of the leadership theories and models now acknowledge the move away from hierarchical relationships. Many procurement teams have no supervisory relationship among most team members. As a result, leadership has had to become more facilitative.[9]

Fisher and Sharp identified five dimensions of personal and group effectiveness: purpose, thinking, learning, engagement, and feedback. At its core, lateral leadership is a belief in the importance of demonstrating patience, acknowledging the value of everyone's contribution, and building trust. For some teams, this takes time, involves stops and starts, and requires a great deal of patience. This chapter takes a modestly deeper dive into behaviors that can be learned at the team level to fulfill leadership roles needed by all teams.

Help the Team Keep Purpose in Mind

One finds purpose consistently identified as a key ingredient in effective leadership of teams.[10] Members join groups in part to satisfy specific individual needs that cannot be found only in the technical objective of a team. Understanding these purposes is important to understanding what motivates team members.[11]

There is a flip side to the importance of purpose. Chapter 4 taught that sometimes aligned purpose can be misapplied and can lead to consensus in small groups that can be counterproductive. *Groupthink* has various contributing causes, not the least of which is confusing purpose with intolerance for dissent. Various authors emphasize the importance of protecting dissenters so that a group does not turn a blind eye to purpose.

Still, a central principle in this book is the role of purpose. And leaders must align their own actions with the shared values.[12] Walk the talk.[13]

Purpose frames the objectives of a team. It defines the nature of the opportunities that a team will explore, influences the makeup of the team, and sets the contours of the project management and decision-making approach. Like Marscy Stone illustrated in the state of Oregon's disaster-preparedness workgroup project, the purpose remains the touchstone for the team when it gets off track. And purpose may be the most important yardstick for setting priorities.

A consequential and inspiring purpose can be a motivating tool for attracting other team members. People join groups and engage with them often because they see others pursuing common goals and values. My experience with the use of the opportunity summary (described in chapter 2) was that it began the process of connecting the team's purpose with the higher aspirational goals of those who were invited to be a part of the team.

The Colorado Procurement Technical Assistance Center (PTAC) story below illustrates the importance of purpose. And it shows how leadership in today's modern environment can cut across boundaries when there is a shared purpose.

Leading Across Boundaries: The Colorado PTAC

High praise indeed. In May 2011, the Air Force publicly recognized, on its Small Business website, a Colorado team and best practice, the Monthly Small Business and Industry Day. As described by the Air Force, "The monthly Industry Days offers a practical approach to educating small businesses about how to market their products and services to government clients. The events have proved to be very valuable for companies that have had little previous interaction with the government. Attendees are able to gain insight from experienced government-contracting professionals as well as other participating companies."

Dennis Casey is a counselor in the Colorado Procurement Technical Assistance Center (PTAC). PTAC is funded by the Department of Defense, the state of Colorado, local governments, and donations from Colorado businesses. Its mission is to help Colorado businesses do business with federal, state, and local governments. In the first three years after the Colorado PTAC was created in 2009, the number of clients grew to over 3,000. PTAC's program director was dean of the Air Force Logistics School at the Air Force Institute of Technology. PTAC counselors and members of its board of directors have deep experience in federal, state and local government procurement and contracting, as well as first-rate industry experience.

Dennis Casey retired from the Air Force after a career in medical logistics. After a position in industry, Dennis moved to Colorado Springs. PTAC was just forming there. Peterson AFB at the time was hosting business outreach events in partnership with other Department of Defense agencies. Dennis met with the various DOD small business liaisons, and they thought that further development of a training network for small businesses might be useful. PTAC was particularly suited to host these kinds of training events. Dennis explains, "PTAC didn't have the security concerns of DOD installations. Access to the installations was difficult for many companies, and PTAC was developing a relationship with the Colorado Springs Technology Incubator that gave us a more accessible venue and space for these events."

The end result was that small business specialists from Peterson AFB, Schriever AFB, and the U.S. Air Force Academy teamed up with the Army's Space Command and Fort Carson to hold Industry Days—the event the Air Force recognized. The team coordinated with PTAC, the Colorado Springs Small Business Development Center (SBDC), and local offices of the U.S. General Services Administration (GSA) and the U.S. Small Business Administration (SBA). The purpose of the event was to provide small businesses with the information they need to be more successful in working with local military installations and other agencies.

As an outgrowth of this collaboration, Dennis started a monthly outreach event for PTAC in conjunction with those other government partners. According to Dennis, "Companies learn that there are no secret handshakes. The key is forming relationships." Dennis and the other PTAC counselors help companies understand the process.

The initiative has been a great success for all participants. Presentations have included a "Small Business 101" training course and briefings on business opportunities from each of the front-range

(continued on the next page)

Leading Across Boundaries: The Colorado PTAC, cont'd.

agencies. Additionally the SBDC, GSA, and SBA give presentations about how their organizations can assist small businesses.

The business outreach expanded to the Denver metropolitan area with the establishment of a PTAC office in the Aurora Chamber of Commerce building. The Colorado Office of Economic Development and International Trade, which manages the Small Business Development Center program, also provides financial support to PTAC.

The collaboration among Dennis and the military-installation small-business program managers has continued; they meet for coffee and talk about other possible collaborations and how to change presentations and materials.

In 2013, PTAC's overwhelming success was acknowledged in special state legislation appropriating money for state support and setting up a bipartisan task force to look at ways to sustain PTAC's operations in the future.

Dennis summarizes the success this way. "All of the parties have gotten payback—every one of them. What has made this successful is we are a community. We are very open, and while sometimes in federal government there is no sense of mutual benefit from these kinds of collaborations, we found one here. We all agree on a central purpose. We are here to promote the relationship between the business community and government."

Not only were none the team members in the PTAC story in a supervisory relationship, none were even in the same organization! Once the various program managers and PTAC talked about purpose, they saw a common goal. All of them had an interest in educating Colorado businesses about the government contracting process. Dennis Casey and PTAC were able to leverage those common purposes into a statewide opportunity: making Colorado businesses more competitive.

A useful purpose must inspire. The Arizona ProcureAZ project taught that as the magnitude of potential change expands, resistance may grow. Jean Clark's mantra about the transformational opportunity that the ProcureAz project provided is framed by an inspiring purpose. Port St. Lucie's goal to improve distressed housing, and its adjusted vision to make houses not just minimally renovated but attractive to purchasers, helped solve an issue with vendor participation in the project. One can imagine that opportunities existed for the team members to each help make the purpose vivid and remind project participants of its importance.

An ambiguous purpose can impede a group's progress. When Oregon's disaster-preparedness workgroup began putting the group's purpose on meeting agendas, it helped clarify the specific objective of the team: creation of intuitive procurement tools for use in disasters.

Team members can help clarify purpose. They lead by asking questions, suggesting ideas, and helping develop purpose statements that motivate, guide, and bind a team.[14] Team members stepping into leadership roles can enlist everyone's support in reviewing and revising purpose statements. They can use questions to test the clarity of purpose statements. They can act by offering to draft and coordinate the goal, objective, or other statement of purpose for the team's activity.

At the beginning of chapter 1, I quoted an anonymous meeting participant who asked, "How will we know we succeeded?" This anecdote brings up an important point about timing. In this particular group, there was an openness that invited very forthright comments. I have been in situations where such a question might have been taken less graciously. Likewise, sometimes a team gets off track and the formal leader can feel like she is being blamed for missteps. As we discussed in chapter 4, understand the group norms and the perspective of the formal team leader. If there is a designated leader on a team, some of these conversations may be better left for one-on-one discussions.

An alternative way to address a concern with ambiguous purpose is to go to the team leader individually, ask a question, and offer a suggestion. "It may just be me, but do you sense that some of the attendees may not understand the team's goal?" After a pause to invite response, if there is none, perhaps ask, "Do you think adding an introductory agenda item about the group goal would be useful?" This is a sensitive way to show leadership in clarifying purpose without embarrassing a formal team leader.

Teams come closer to aligning purpose when they are focused on well-defined objectives.[15] And there is plenty of work to go around in a team aimed at defining purpose—charter development, writing goals, and the like. In the Dallas Area Rapid Transit dashboard project, Jason Edds and Connie Arrington worked to clarify the purpose of the measurements. The stories about measurement in Rockland County, New York, and Miami-Dade County illustrate the importance of aligning with organizational objectives and management involvement in development of measurements to make them credible.

Compelling purpose has technical dimensions, like a charter in a project team. Purpose, however, also satisfies other intrinsic needs of groups. Teammates come to a team hoping to find fulfillment in most cases. They want to be around people that have values that align with their own. They want to fulfill personal motivations through contributions they make to the team.

Use Just Enough Structure to Help Organize Thinking and Action

The term "just enough structure" is borrowed from Bellman and Ryan (2009). While groups need structure to effectively perform as teams, there is a trade-off. Too much structure can impede creativity.

Teams need members who lead them through planning, problem solving, and diagnosis. There is an individual skill component to this. In fact, competence is one attribute of successful leaders both in teams and transformational leadership contexts.[16] The concept of competence also embraces the building of competence in others to act. Effective leaders are able to organize work to promote "ownership," build competence, define appropriate measures of successful performance, and set priorities.[17]

Effective leaders in groups help organize thinking.[18] Use caution, though. Perhaps more than any other activity, attempting to contribute leadership to the thinking of a group can threaten the self-image of members. People may not like behavior that could be construed as a challenge to their ability to think logically. So a light touch here is especially important.

Yet, procurement professionals sometimes need to intervene when the interests of the organization require. Kim Heartley-Humphrey is a case in point. Kim is the Chief of the Acquisitions & Contracting Services Division in the California Office of Systems Integration (OSI). I spoke with OSI's senior leadership team in connection with writing the OSI story told in chapter 3. Their best practices website was eye watering, but I had something on my mind to ask Kim. In front of her managers, I asked Kim how she got her voice heard when surrounded by so many IT professionals. Kim was quick to respond, "I jump in whether I'm invited or not." There was laughter in the room, followed by one of the best testimonials I have ever heard. Deborah Rose, OSI's director, added, "I don't know anyone in the state that can do what Kim does."

Kim, I learned, has deep experience in California information technology. She is well regarded as a thought leader able to help bring structure to agency thinking about information technology projects. People expect her to "jump in."

Developing that kind of credibility to shape others' thinking takes time. Fisher and Sharp (2009) counsel lateral leaders first to sharpen their own approaches to thinking. They generalize the process of disciplined thought into 4-D stages: data (discovering symptoms of problems); diagnosis (analyzing possible causes); direction (identifying possible approaches to solutions); and do next (planning the next steps towards the solution).

To them, the use of data involves looking for information that will help in subsequent decisions. Lateral leaders can help groups assess whether there is bias towards certain information, ill-advised reluctance to find other relevant information, or approaches to data that make it appear that the group is trapped in a certain point of view. On the data side of things, one indirect approach to helping a group face objective data is simply to ask, "Can you tell me what the facts are?" Used carefully, this is a question that can help a group focus on the objective facts and begin the process of assessing the data.

Teams can share the task of critically evaluating the logical progression of the group's reasoning. If you are a formal leader of a team, invite criticism of your own thinking. This may be one of the most effective ways to laterally lead and create the environment for mutual accountability for the team's work.

This book outlines various models that can be used to add structure to thinking and action at appropriate times. Teams can use members who are skilled at thinking expansion techniques (such as brainstorming), exploratory tools, and focusing skills like those discussed in chapters 6–7. Teams need skills in measurement, analysis, and managing risk and change. Teams need leaders competent in using tools to explore problems and opportunities and eventually selecting from among alternatives.

Take the Punta Gorda, Florida, story about Lean Sigma and their project to improve payables. While that initiative was consultant supported, Marian Pace had to model the importance of everyone's using tools like process mapping, fishbone diagrams, and criteria-based decision making. In team environments not having consultant support, there are resources available to help a team learn how use the tools. An opportunity to exercise lateral leadership perhaps?

Harry McCabe, the Colorado Department of Human Services contracts manager, was able to satisfy multiple objectives with his creative use of contract risk-analysis checklists. Teri Brustad and Carol Wills continue to mold the success of the Colorado Public P-Card Group while fighting off temptations to make the group more structured that it needs to be. Lisa King was a lateral leader who taught lawyers a thing or two about project management by organizing and adding structure to the annual procurement update. Kay Kishline and Thirza Kennedy were leaders in the Colorado State Purchasing Office who helped clarify the peer-review program so it achieved its purpose of building a peer network. And Linda Morris continues to add her quiet leadership to integrating adult-learning principles into Virginia's exceptional procurement training and certification program.

These are all examples of leaders using just the right structure. Team activities require time and resources, meaning there are opportunities to exercise leadership in building team competency and managing the team's work.

Sometimes adding structure gets people out of comfort zones. As we have noted throughout this book, there is a fine balance between promoting creativity and knowing when it is time to move to the focusing phases of a team's work towards a decision.

We end this section on structure with a topic that runs throughout the practice of public procurement: negotiation. Even though we did not use stories specifically illustrating the elements of effective negotiation, all of the leaders in these stories negotiated. Do you think Cheryl Shanaberger negotiated when the topic of advance payments to vendors using procurement cards came up? How about when Danielle Hintz engaged her procurement office in using appreciative inquiry to ask customers what they thought of the city of Longmont's procurement office? Or does Kim Heartley-Humphrey negotiate when she "jumps in" to a risk-management meeting regarding a new information systems project that has risks that procurement can help mitigate?

Of course, all of these involved negotiations. In fact, Heath and Heath (2013) offer an interesting perspective about negotiation that we do not often think about. To them, bargaining and compromise among stakeholders leads to better buy-in when decisions are made.

So we look at one final structured activity: negotiations. A lateral leader can contribute to helping a team negotiate by sharpening her skill and helping the team plan. Negotiation success is three-quarters planning and the rest execution.

Sharpen Your Negotiation Skills for the Team

We all negotiate! A team often is involved in negotiating: the procurement and project teams in this book for example may negotiate contracts with vendors, resources with using agencies, and various issues with stakeholders.

Find a negotiation model that fits the team. One common approach used by governments is Fisher, Ury, and Patton's *Getting to Yes* model. First introduced in 1981 by Roger Fisher and William Ury, the central premise is that through integrative (*win-win*) interest-based negotiation, one usually can

(continued on next page)

Sharpen Your Negotiation Skills for the Team, cont'd.

find a negotiated outcome that satisfies the interests of both parties. This approach is opposite to what sometimes is characterized as the more adversarial distributed position-based negotiation. In distributed, or win-lose negotiation, what is gained by one party is lost by the other. Car sales sometimes are characterized as win-lose negotiations: relationships do not matter, price is the focal point, and the negotiation is poisoned by mistrust. Integrative negotiation, on the other hand, is an interest-based inquiry to find solutions that benefit both parties.

Getting to Yes emphasized the importance of planning. Each party's interests must be understood regarding the various issues that arise. At the bargaining table, displaying sensitivity to other parties' interests is one way to foster constructive relationships. Be hard on the issues, not the people.

Issues and Interests. Interests differ for different issues, and in complex negotiations, sometimes multidisciplinary teams are needed for planning to effectively deal with the ranges of issues and interests. The full identification of the issues and complete analysis of interests underlying the issues help illuminate and educate in a way that permits agility at the bargaining table. For each issue, identify your own and the other party's interest. Also, time may favor one side or the other. Whose side is time on?

Communication. Business intelligence, or market research conducted prior to a procurement, may provide insight to the other party's key interests. Sometimes, however, questions at the bargaining table are used to learn the other party's interests. Some thought must go into developing lines of inquiry for use at the table to gain useful information.

At the bargaining table, statements may be made that can spiral a negotiation out of control—at one extreme—or more commonly, cement parties into intransigent positions. William Ury's *Getting Past No* (1991) offers practical advice for dealing with emotional outburst, "dirty tricks," fear of agreement, and other impediments to negotiations. His underlying theme is, "name the game," as in humorously wondering out loud whether the good cop/bad cop routine is being used on you. The book offers some simple rules for guiding your personal behavior: don't react, step to the "balcony"; don't argue, step to their side; don't reject, reframe; don't escalate, educate; and don't push, build them a golden bridge. These are guiding principles that are useful at the bargaining table.

Planning the opening is important, as well as planning how to say "no." Plan and practice the possible "no." Start with a yes (highlight common interests and what you find constructive, even if only the fact there is dialogue). Follow with a firm "no" and a reason. Then close with a tentative "yes" regarding what might be possible.[19]

Move Slowly Towards Commitment. The objective of negotiation is to achieve "commitment." Commitments, however, come in different forms. In a contract negotiation, a commitment is a written execution of an agreement. And parties reach commitment in different ways. Sometimes the negotiator at the table does not have the full authority to commit an organization. So ask questions during planning and at the table. Who can commit for you and the other side? Are there certain commitments your team is ready to make quickly?

Generally, commitment has to be achieved slowly as the parties build trust. Time has to be spent developing a relationship (and trust) between the parties so that eventually a commitment once reached is enduring. "Stepping to the other side" to understand the other party's interests is an effective way to see a problem from a different perspective.[20] For example, "I see that limitation of liability is very important to you; you use the term 'bet the company.' Help me understand better how this project could cause you to bet the company's financial future?"

Legitimacy and Standards for Agreement. Communication planning not only identifies questions for probing the interests of the other party. Planning the arguments used in the negotiation also is important. In contract negotiations, for example, advancing a proposed term is often met by a request to explain it. Being able to support positions persuasively is important, and it requires practice. Further, it is important to know who the audiences are. Sometimes a person not at the table—like a manager—has to be persuaded to accept an option. You are trying to "build a golden bridge" to agreement.[21] But this takes practice.

Options and BATNA. The best alternative to a negotiated agreement (BATNA) represents the plan of action if agreement cannot be reached. Often confused with the "bottom-line" (that requires agreement), the BATNA assumes a failed negotiation. The options and possible zone of agreement are defined in part by the "resistance point," those options that are less favorable than the BATNA. The considerations in developing the BATNA are the same for both sides, so forecasting the other party's BATNA is an important part of planning.

Negotiators still talk in terms of positions in negotiations. Opening positions, for example, typically are advanced early. The "aspire to" option is the most favorable position that can be advocated legitimately and often is used to frame the opening position. Parties often plan a "content with" option, known as the objective, that represents a reasonable, desired outcome that will fully meet expectations. The "can live with" option is a better description than the "bottom line." It practically serves as a trigger to reevaluate the wisdom of agreement. Comprehensive planning illuminates the possible options and their reasonableness and acceptability. At the table, when options are explored, follow Ury's counsel, "Don't reject, reframe," in order effectively to explore options.

The range of options is dependent on the perceived standards of agreement, like fair and reasonable pricing, existing constraints such as legal requirements, and the strength of the BATNA.

A party tries to improve its BATNA and indirectly disclose it to the other side if its BATNA is stronger. A threatened lawsuit represents an inelegant use of a BATNA. On the other hand, implying "other options" will be evaluated sometimes can be effective. The strength of the BATNA illuminates the "power" of a party. But power can easily spiral into contentiousness. Ury counsels, "Don't escalate, use power to educate."[22]

Relationships and Emotions. After *Getting to Yes*, Roger Fisher and co-author Daniel Shapiro, a psychiatrist, wrote *Beyond Reason*. They further explored the emotional dimension of negotiation. Diffuse emotional issues by expressing appreciation, preserving autonomy for the other side, finding commonality of interests or backgrounds (affiliation), and showing respect for the other side's status. Use statements and questions like, "I see your point," "Help me understand," "Yes, and," "Good point," "What would you do if you were in my shoes?", "How could we make it better?", and "I'm sorry, I didn't make myself clear."

Methods at the Table: Tactics and Strategy. Planning is the most important step in negotiation. But the team also needs to discuss certain tactical and strategic issues. How will the team deal with "dirty tricks"? Confront them? Who should be at the bargaining table? Who should control the agenda and the

(continued on next page)

Sharpen Your Negotiation Skills for the Team, cont'd.

document? How will the team signal "time out"? These are important issues that should be discussed with the negotiating team after planning.

A lateral leader can sharpen her negotiation skills and bring just enough planning structure to the table to help the team plan for negotiations.

As this book illustrates, there are specific models and tools that help a team organize thinking and acting. Use these tools to build just enough structure into the team's work. Can you find opportunities for leadership here?

Use Questions Effectively to Help the Team Learn

Humility is the antidote for hubris.[23] There may be no better way to demonstrate humility than to ask questions that show an authentic desire to learn.

The relevance of learning to leadership takes on dimensions of its own. Leadership itself can be learned. Kouzes and Posner regard leadership as an acquired capability, or learnable. One theme in their model of exemplary leadership is the importance of asking purposeful questions.[24]

Learning, in one respect, describes how we approach leadership itself. But learning also is a critical ingredient of successful teams. Effective leaders are active learners who create a climate for experimentation.[25] Questions reflect inquisitiveness, and inquisitiveness is a hallmark of successful people. And not being afraid to go where the answers lead is a part of the equation.

Good questions are the tools of good coaches, and in many ways lateral leaders coach.[26] Ask purposeful questions daily. Questions get others thinking and send messages about the purpose and focus of teams and larger organizations. Questions are useful to broaden perspectives, show respect for the opinions of others, and build support for decisions.[27]

Simply asking the question begins the process of change.[28] The state of Idaho began its journey into a transformational change to requests for proposals by asking questions about its evaluation methods. Why are people who aren't experts with the service spending so much time evaluating things that don't differentiate the good proposals from the bad? Not only do the questions build empathy through the respect they show for opinions of others, they start the process of defining the gaps between the present and future possibility. That starts the process of change.

Learning is best achieved through action, followed quickly by examination of the results and adjustments in strategy if necessary.[29] Review actions and conduct mid-course corrections as necessary. The minute a plan is underway there often are changes in circumstances. And changes in circumstances may require revisions to the project strategy.

An environment for experimentation and learning promotes continual reevaluation and adjustments to performance strategies and approaches. Port St. Lucie demonstrated inquisitiveness by testing the old assumptions about talking with vendors and later in diagnosing the causes for lapses in industry participation. Someone on the team had to lead that reexamination of the project, perhaps asking simple questions like, "What if?" followed by, "How about if we try talking to the vendors about why they are not participating?"

Generate small wins and learn from them. Small wins boost confidence.[30] As we learned in the chapter on change, we can build on small wins to help a team and other stakeholders see what is possible. Arizona used quick, small wins in successfully implementing early phases of the e-procurement system. The state of Idaho learned from successive uses of the Performance Information Procurement System. Incremental wins promote learning.

Oregon's WSCA lodging procurement team asked itself how the standard procurement model might be adapted to accommodate franchising in the lodging industry. The team found a creative solution. Questions of this nature do not need to be asked only by the formal team leader.

Inquiry and the use of questions recently have been associated with another capability of effective leaders: the ability to influence and persuade. Long associated only with salespersons, experts are revisiting the role of empathy in persuasion and influence in today's world of interconnected, flattened organizations.

Diagnose the Split Personalities of Influence and Persuasion

Thirty years ago, Robert Cialdini (1984) published his groundbreaking work on the science of persuasion. Long a classic among salespersons, Cialdini identified various levers of influence—some call universal principles—that were based on his scientific research.

The principle of reciprocity means that we tend to feel obligated to return favors. Under the principle of authority, we are influenced by authority figures and experts. The principle of consistency/commitment says that we try to align our actions, values, and communications. Another principle—liking—explains that we want to say "yes" to someone we like. The principle of scarcity means the less available a resource, the more we want it. The principle of social proof causes us to act like others with whom we identify.

The characterization of persuasion as having split personalities has to do with manipulation. In many peoples' eyes, these principles were weapons used by seedy salespeople trying to get us to comply with their wishes. Giving a small, promotional gift sets the stage for a larger "ask" later that would tap into reciprocity. A car dealer leaving a fake invoice on the table might be an authority ploy that makes the buyer think the offered sale price is related to actual invoice cost. A political campaign's accepting ten-dollar donations sets the stage for a larger donation solicitation, a deployment of the principle of consistency. A negotiation ploy to "take it or leave it" is a disguised use of scarcity. And the coffee-shop tip jar filled with dollar bills (placed there by the counter sales staff) tugs at our desire to be like everyone socially.

These principles are proven to work to influence people.[31] The leadership challenge is to use influence and persuasion techniques in ways that are not deceptive, manipulative, or inauthentic.

The application of the science of influence enjoyed a resurgence of celebrity outside of the sales world in 2008 and 2010 with the publication of three books: Thaler and Sunstein's *Nudge,* Patterson, Maxfield, McMillan and Switzler's *Influencer* (2008), and Heath and Heath's book *Switch* (2010). Those books were about change management, and the relevance of Cialdini's principles became crystal clear. The themes in fostering successful change and overcoming resistance—topics discussed in chapter 8—are closely related to the principles of persuasion.

(continued on next page)

Diagnose the Split Personalities of Influence and Persuasion, cont'd.

Nudge introduced the term *choice architecture* and how institutions like government can take steps that influence constructive behavior. *Influencer* grounded effective change on identifying vital behaviors and finding ways to change those behaviors. Connecting personal motivation to commitment and consistency sounded suspiciously like Cialdini. Harnessing peer pressure and finding strength in numbers did too. In *Switch*, Heath and Heath's admonition to "build habits" and "find the feeling" likewise paralleled Cialdini's findings on consistency and commitment. Heath and Heath's call to "rally the herd" drew on social proof as well.

The books added other elements to the Cialdini equation. In *Influencer*, changing the environment to make the vital behaviors easier was a key. So was leveraging both personal and structural motivation: configuring work areas so there is more open, informal communication is an example. Another example might be eliminating tired policies that get in the way of constructive change. Heath and Heath called this "scripting the critical moves" in *Switch*. They also found importance in shrinking the size of the change and growing (training) the people involved in change. In many respects, some of these principles were at the foundation of the success of Arizona's ProcureAZ e-procurement system implementation. The project effectively used the levers of influence to overcome resistance and manage change.

So maybe Cialdini's experiments about persuasion and *compliance* with requests are not so evil? It turns out they are not. Humility, authenticity, and resiliency also factor into the equation.

In 2012, Daniel Pink surveyed the current research on persuasion and adapted Cialdini's principles to the modern virtual and networked age. He concludes in *To Sell is Human* that empathy—what he calls *attunement*—improves the prospects of influence. We may not all be salespersons, but we all "move" people—their ideas, their behaviors, their choices. While competence in clearly defining problems and solving them goes hand-in-hand with Cialdini's authority principle, research also has shown that there are more factors at work. Humility, buoyant resilience and optimism in a sea of disappointments, and commitment to purposeful service increase influence. And using questions effectively is a theme throughout Pink's book as a way of demonstrating humility and improving persuasiveness and influence.

A lateral leader needs to be persuasive, and these principles identify characteristics that can be learned and practiced. Diagnose for yourself the split personalities of persuasion and influence. While there may still be risks that these tools can be used for deception and manipulation—especially in negotiation—the principles remain solid allies if applied authentically consistent with your values. So what if knowing how to effectively use the email subject line improves your *pitch*![32]

What are some constructive applications of the principles of persuasions and influence? Consider these:

- Structure a major project or procurement using a pilot with hand selected participants, and ask them to meet as a user group and explain the value of the project to the larger audience (social proof). Social proof can be used as a weapon, though, as when a vendor says, "Why won't you agree to the limitation of liability clause? Everyone else has."
- Recruit a user team by including in promotional announcements a notice that only select people are being asked to join the team (scarcity). But scarcity also can be a sword, as when a vendor says its offer is only good until the end of the day. Plan how to deal with a scarcity ploy if you confront its use.

- In a survey, first send a brief email explaining that you are developing a customer satisfaction survey and want one question answered, "How many minutes are they typically willing to commit to a survey?" Then follow-up later with those respondents to see if they might assist with testing the survey (commitment/consistency).

- Before beginning a tough negotiation, ask the opposing side about where they are from, how long they have been in their current position, and explore what you might have in common (liking).

- In a bid protest decision, get the help of an attorney to review/revise the draft decision to add some relevant legal precedent (authority). And when negotiating a dispute, consider having the attorney at the table.

- After a large procurement award, call an unsuccessful bidder, thank them for the time they spent in developing their proposal, and offer to spend some time with them to debrief the procurement and help them see where they might improve (reciprocity).

- During a difficult negotiation, offer to incorporate oral agreements in the draft and propose language that might promote agreement on tough issues (*Nudge's* choice architecture, *Switch's* "scripting the critical moves," and *Influencer's* "structural ability.")

The inquiry and use of questions we discuss here set the stage for empathy that is essential to building trust in teams. After all, if you exercise leadership by asking questions, you demonstrate humility, avoid hubris, and steer clear of destructive behaviors than can hurt team performance. And as we just learned, "stepping to their side" can improve your influence and ability to persuade.

Help Promote Collaboration and Feedback by Stepping to Their Side Often

Chapter 4 introduced empathy in the discussion of teams. Daniel Goleman (2002) is widely credited with having cemented the role of empathy in effective leadership with his groundbreaking work in emotional intelligence. Empathy for our purposes is the ability to see things from others' perspectives. Empathetic behavior is important to effective teams.[33] And being in touch with the concerns of stakeholders helps a team forecast the types of planning that can create an atmosphere conducive to lasting change.

Establishing trust through collaboration and relationship building permits the kinds of mutual exchanges and communication that is vital to a team. Developing trust requires work: seeing things from others' perspectives, addressing fears that might exist from expressing dissent, and knowing that people are motivated in part by being part of a group and may feel threatened by perceptions of dissension.

Be the first to trust. Show concern for others. Listen and demonstrate empathy.[34] Maintaining trusting, empathetic relationships with others in a team is the key to learning if there is resistance. Find out what other team members value, what special skills they can contribute in ways they enjoy. Do they have a role in the team that they consider consequential? Status remains an important factor in motivation, and continually assess whether roles are aligned with expectations and individual needs.[35]

One of the ways to gain another's perspective is to ask them for their ideas. But ask real questions. Loaded questions that are obviously masking an agenda can spur resentment, distrust, resistance, or even hostility. Approach questioning as what Edgar Schein (2009) calls "humble inquiry." Asking real questions motivated by genuine curiosity or desire to learn another's perspective begins to develop trust.

Remember, though, that the use of questions implies a second part of the exchange: listening. Be engaged in the listening. Clarify concepts that you don't understand, but don't interrupt. Acknowledge what is heard in a way that demonstrates that you heard. Don't be thinking of the reply or counterargument at the same time the explanation is being given.

Fisher and Sharp recognize, of course, that questions can threaten. They suggest including a rationale for a question in those situations where a question may seem surprising or unusual. Team members often have not been involved in the thinking leading up to the inquiry.

I heard an example of this in a conference call regarding a new mentoring program. The program would address the emerging challenges caused by aging professionals not knowing when their cognitive capacities had diminished so much they were no longer competent. The committee team lead and potential committee member had not previously met prior to the phone call. At one point, the potential committee member said, "I'd like to ask a difficult question, important to me because at this stage in my life I am concerned that I may not have anything relevant to contribute. So please don't take this the wrong way, but 'How old are you?'" The age question is widely considered inappropriate, and some context before the question is asked eliminates surprise and gives "permission" to object.

Trying to gain perspective from others on the team is a precursor to change. Change often is difficult and is accompanied by a range of emotions. Even in a team environment, members often face change and need to understand it, exercise some sense of control, and be able to forecast somewhat the future. They often have other jobs and demands on their time. Unless a team leader steps to their side to see their perspective, it is difficult to find out what the personal circumstances are that may be affecting their outlook on any change or team activities.

One of the central themes in Fisher and Sharp's book is the permissibility of sharing your own thoughts after you ask. But consider also inviting criticism. Better yet, criticize your own thoughts. Encourage an air of permissiveness in criticizing your ideas if you are seen as a team leader. It not only helps avoid groupthink, it helps develop trust in the group and assists you as a leader in understanding others' points of view.[36]

Fisher and Sharp devote an entire chapter to feedback in team activities. The way that feedback is given implicates the feelings of others, of course, and requires special care in keeping in tune with others' perspectives. They categorize feedback into two essential purposes: emotional expression of appreciation; and feedback for the improvement of skills. There are slight twists on the ways that effective feedback is given depending on the purpose.

Some feedback is appreciative, and general encouragement may be appropriate at times, especially in the early stages of team performance or after setbacks.[37] If a team member sees a particularly good example of a meeting led by another team member—especially in early phases of a team's life—laterally leading with appreciative feedback is uplifting and motivating. Fisher and Sharp recommend that leaders express their true feelings, "I was proud of how you handled that meeting." They also suggest that a specific example be added to the feedback, "The way that you framed the agenda item on measurement using a question really promoted creative dialogue; everyone participated."

Check in with the other person to make sure they are ready for feedback. "I thought the presentation was very well organized, and the attendees seemed engaged. How did you feel about it? Let me know if you would like to discuss some possible ways to make it even better." Moving too quickly into constructive review can be a bit demoralizing.

If feedback moves into what is commonly regarded as constructive criticism, remember to find positive elements of performance. Also remember to assess your own internal "story" about what happened. Your assumptions or conclusions may be incorrect, so remain open to explanations. And it is important to reinforce what goes well. Offer advice on how to leverage that success and make it even better.

When moving into suggestions for what could be done differently, keep the emphasis on the behavior, not the person. For example, consider a situation when a colleague cut off a meeting participant who was talking too much. You might feel like saying, "Even though you were short on time, you hurt Kris's feelings by cutting her off." An alternative way to provide feedback might be, "Instead of 'Kris, we don't have time for that,' consider something like, 'Kris, that's a good point. We've unfortunately run out of time, but let's discuss it after class.'" This diverts the criticism away from the individual and towards a constructive solution and specific behavior that can be practiced.

Some professionals may feel that asking for help signifies weakness. Sometimes the best way to "step to their side" is to ask for coaching or help yourself. Discuss with your team how you learn, and what kind of help you can use. Not only do you learn, you continue to foster an atmosphere of collaboration and feedback.

Feedback and criticism have potential to lead to conflict. But conflict is a necessary part of leadership. Conflict sharpens purpose and values. Conflict draws into focus the objectives and potential for alignment of interconnected groups.[38] Conflict often challenges loyalties and may be essential to adaptive change.[39] Teams are an excellent laboratory for learning about conflict.

Learn to Embrace Conflict

"Conflict, like trust and independence,
is also a necessary part of becoming a real team.
—Jon Katzenbach and Douglas Smith

Conflict is an essential part of leadership. Teams bring varying perspectives to a team's work. They can achieve what a single individual cannot. But conflict is a necessary outgrowth of the varying perspectives on teams. As the leadership context changes to larger organizations, community interest groups, and political groups, conflict forms a necessary ingredient to sharpening purposes and values.

Without constructive conflict, teams are at risk of "groupthink," where individual members censor their concerns and ideas are accepted without careful consideration or vetting.[40]

Conflict takes different forms and is managed using a variety of strategies. In mediation, for example, the topic of conflict spans the management of emotional flooding and anger, strategies for avoiding negative emotions, and methods of developing positive emotions. Emotional conflicts best can be avoided by dealing forthrightly with misperceptions and failure in communication. These techniques are designed to preserve the development of trust among team members. But in an emotional outburst, some means of freezing the situation first must be found.[41]

Take anger for example. A team probably should acknowledge that the diversity of perspectives and passion about issues could cause anger. The usual prescription for dealing with anger is to pause, don't react, acknowledge sincerely the feelings being expressed, and take a break or caucus.[42] Keep in mind the needs of the angry person: to vent, to be heard, to be understood. Be patient, attentive, and calm.[43] In a negotiation context, Ury (1991) advises to "go to the balcony."

Talk as a team about how to resolve conflict. The Colorado FAST team discussed self-directed team workbook exercises when new members joined the team or when events warranted their revisiting the norms. Harper and Harper's (1992) self-directed team workbook has exercises the team members complete individually and then discuss. The workbook guides the team though establishment of ground rules. Some are:

- Be aware when team member positions move toward "rigidity."
- Listen openly and don't cut off.
- Don't be "right" at all costs and believe only your way is best.
- Attack the problem, not the people.
- Be open and honest.
- Share the same information with everyone.
- Don't let individuals dominate meetings.

Strategies for avoiding escalation to unconstructive conflict apply to negotiations as well, at least where negotiators are genuinely interested in reaching agreement.[44] Practice saying no. As we saw in the negotiation discussion earlier in this chapter, there is a constructive way to express commonality of interest, say no firmly, and still leave room for agreement. Ury (2007) calls this the Yes! No Yes? model.

In team conflict, think of conflict as a group problem. Ascribe the issues to a system problem, not the problem of any one individual.[45] Sometimes, though, a private conversation with a disruptive individual might be needed, with constructive feedback given that focuses on behaviors that were disruptive and the reasons they were counterproductive.[46] Acknowledge that an underlying problem exists. Let them express their feelings. Define the problem and determine the underlying need. Find common areas of agreement, no matter how small, and agree on what action should be taken. Involve them in the buy-in and definition of the plan going forward. Then follow up with them in a couple of weeks.[47]

Sometimes the conflict goes unresolved. As a last resort, a team leader may deal with the offending team member in the presence of the team (a high-risk intervention), or the team member may have to be removed from the team. Contact your human resources department for assistance if conflict escalates to these levels.[48]

The approaches to teambuilding in chapter 4 are designed to avoid conflicts that escalate into full-scale wars. Use facilitative leadership so everyone participates. Make sure everyone has meaningful roles on the team. Use active and open listening, and respect differences of opinions. When feedback is given, make it thoughtful and focused on behaviors, not on the person's character. Don't attribute questionable motives to other members: focus on the problem or purpose. If a person's opinion is discounted, step in and support that person.[49] And share credit for team successes.

John Kotter (1993) reminds us to step to the side of bosses as well.[50] What are the conflicts that they face? What information do they need? Learn how they communicate. Some prefer written communication, followed up by oral briefings. Others prefer oral discussions that can be followed up by written summaries or other documentation. How do they view meetings, what is their idea of an effective meeting?

Kotter also suggests that you find out what their goals are, what expectations they may have. Senior executives in particular can feel isolated and have to make decisions that test loyalties, bump up against entrenched culture, and sometimes are painful.[51] Teams can help by stepping to the side of executives and senior management as well to get their perspective. Normally the formal team leader will have to manage those relationships for the team.

Trust is the common prescription for how teams succeed. Trust, however, is a product of shared experiences and relationships. Taking time to gain the perspectives of others around you, asking real questions, inviting criticism of ideas, and really listening to the feedback that is given, all create shared experiences that help foster trust in teams and between leaders and followers.

Help the Team Engage by Committing Your Time and Attention

"Leaders venture out: they don't sit idly by waiting for fate to smile on them. They are pioneers. . . . You need to search for opportunities by seizing the initiative and looking outward for innovative ways to improve."
—Kouzes and Posner (2012)

Effective leaders get personally involved, because people feel more connected to leaders having a personal stake in the outcome.[52] Model the way, say Kouzes and Posner (2012).

At its core, the contributions that are essential to team success require the commitment of time and attention. All deference to Woody Allen aside, 80 percent of success is not just showing up. As can be seen from the stories throughout this book, there is a need for thoughtful commitment of time in order to achieve success in a team.

Those around you can tell if you are not fully engaged. Creating a learning environment is roundly regarded as a key to effective leadership, but learning takes time. "Speed kills learning."[53]

At the same time, remember that when you lead through engagement, you create expectations. There is a credibility dimension in committing your time and attention to the activities of a team. As the process of asking questions begins, employees expect to see action.[54]

Engagement is an important element of lateral leadership.[55] Engagement means that every team member has a meaningful, consequential role. You try to find a role for yourself that is fulfilling on the team. You help others find roles that are challenging and that leverage their skills in meaningful ways. As this book shows, the types of contributions and roles vary widely and leave room for everyone to help.

Find ways to tangibly contribute to the activities needed for the team to succeed. Ideas are fine, but action is needed also. Count me among those who believe that a team leader must find consequential contributions to the team's work so there is a feeling of rough equivalence in work. Sometimes that contribution can include assuming responsibility for coordinating with interlocking teams or management. Arizona state employees appreciated Jean Clark's personal involvement in ProcureAZ. I suspect that much of Jean's time was spend coordinating with other stakeholders and senior executives and not working on purely technical issues like testing. But the teams found her contribution valuable.

Leaders commonly face the challenge of taking on too much, though. Fisher and Sharp suggest revisiting as a team how work is allocated. Delegation is one strategy, but it reallocates work. A team and its leader(s) should make work division a topic of discussion during the early stages of team formation.

There is a caution here. You've all been around formal leaders who assigned work largely based on line-of-sight. Those with desks near the office unfortunately received the most "taskers." The Colorado FAST team had its own challenges associated with shared leadership.

Shared Leadership in Colorado FAST

As we have seen, Colorado FAST was a self-directed team that served as the interface between the Colorado State Controller and departments, institutions of higher education, and agencies statewide. FAST had no supervisor; they shared leadership.

Everyone on self-directed teams assumes a leadership role in projects. One former State Controller identified the trade-off for management, however. Management has to learn not to go to the same individual for status updates and other coordination. According to Linda Bradley, "We tried use the weekly FAST meetings with the State Controller to meet the management needs for timely information about project status. And we used a whiteboard to visibly track project status and priorities." Still, there is increased commitment of time by management in working with self-directed teams.

Another "downside" to high performing teams is the propensity of other organizations to recognize the value of the team members and recruit them away. FAST was asked to train other agencies on effective use of teams, so they received a fair amount of exposure. FAST members enjoyed more than their share of promotions into other agency controller positions. One eventually became State Controller. Roger Cusworth was selected to be the controller for the Colorado School of Mines.

While Roger has not yet seen an opportunity at his university to use the FAST self-directed team model, he still applies his FAST experience. "I apply a lot of what I learned. I try to promote a team atmosphere, where people are encouraged to provide free, candid input. We are a team, and I value every one's contribution."

FAST had unique allocation-of-work challenges. Management needed timely, accurate information about project status, and leadership was shared. FAST worked on the issue constantly. As Roger Cusworth found, not all situations are suitable for self-directed teams.

All teams face their own flavor of work allocation issues. As a team member, take the initiative in laterally leading a discussion about how work is allocated among team members.

Contributions to the leadership of a team can take unexpected turns and forms. The classics of leadership theory identify one particular attribute of leaders: innovation or the ability to challenge the status quo. One may believe that internal government processes like procurement do not lend themselves to opportunities to demonstrate creativity. Sue Wheater from Montrose County, Colorado, proved otherwise. The *Art in the Procurement Manual* story I experienced first-hand!

Art in the Procurement Manual of Montrose County, Colorado

Do you have art in your procurement manual? Sue Wheater from Montrose County, Colorado, does!

In 2011, I visited Sue Wheater, Procurement & Contract Administrator in the Montrose County purchasing office. As I exited Sue's office, I looked down and saw what appeared to be a procurement manual, except it had colored artwork on the cover. I was intrigued. Sue explained that in 2009, Montrose County was developing a new procurement manual. She wanted people to read it. "I thought using artwork would make it more fun," Sue explained.

(continued on next page)

Art in the Procurement Manual, cont'd.

Sue contacted the Black Canyon Boys and Girls Club that had chapters in the surrounding community. Sue was invited to talk to the kids about county purchasing. According to Sue, "I talked with them about how we bought things from pencils all the way to big equipment. I was amazed at how attentive they were." Sue engaged the kids in a "request for posters" competition. She explained how the winners would be chosen and how the county would use the artwork. She made it simple but captured some essential elements of public bidding. "I brought a big manila envelope. I told them the date the artwork submissions were due, that the envelope had to have the date on the outside, sealed, and submitted by the due date."

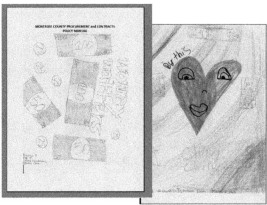

*Art work by the Black Canyon Boys and Girls Club, Colorado

Figure 10-2. Art in a Procurement Manual.

The kids produced the art, but evaluation was the hard part! Occasionally, Sue asked visitors from other county offices to look at the submissions and rate them. Finally, selections were made. The county's Administrative Services department then developed certificates with the winners' names, a first-rate product that was framed and embossed with a Montrose County gold seal. Sue also bought red, white, and blue award ribbons from the local Dollar Store. Armed with the certificates and ribbons, Sue went to the Boys and Girls Club meeting to announce the "source selection" decision and present the awards.

Sue explained to the kids how difficult the decision had been for the evaluation committee; they even had to bring in outside "experts." She remembers fondly, "The kids were gathered together. I started announcing beginning with the third-place winner and worked up. They were cheering! The kids who won beamed! The winners were proud that their artwork was featured on the cover and front pages of the manual, and that I was using their artwork in talks. The framed certificates were really a big deal."

Sue sent personal thank you letters to all those who "competed." The winners' artwork was included in the Montrose County's Procurement Manual. The first-place winner's artwork, shown in figure 10-2, was used on the cover. Other artwork was included throughout the manual.

When Sue gives presentations, she includes the artwork on her slides. The RFP contest achieved fame of a sort. When other counties' commissioners visited, Sue's commissioners brought them by to show them the procurement manual.

> Sue's project teaches a lot about intrinsic motivation, about how a small, creative project can mobilize people. But as good as those lessons were, there was one overarching, astounding achievement.
> "No bid protests!"

What are the lessons here? Sue committed a significant amount of her time and attention to this project. She framed the project with a purpose of improving community relations. Sue coordinated with her internal support offices to make them part of the project. Her project illustrates the power of surprise—art in a procurement manual—in getting ideas to stick. As was mentioned in the introduction, she actually got county commissioners, even those who were visiting, to look in her procurement manual!

Sue's story illustrates the utility of a story in getting us to remember an idea. It also teaches another lesson: the power of recognition. Celebrate accomplishments of the team.[56] Appreciation makes everyone perform better.[57]

Mostly, though, the Montrose story illustrates a unique scope of engagement. Other stories in this book show similar commitment. Terry Brustad and Carol Wills commit their time to making the Colorado P-Card Users Group a first-rate community. They dedicate their time and are not required to lead that effort. Lee Johnson developed brown bag training as a way to offer training opportunities in an informal setting and at the same time promote discussions about new state programs and initiatives. Matt Ackerman leveraged YouTube creatively to improve availability of the Washington Department of General Services contract training that already had won an award from NASPO for its innovation.

Sue Wheater modeled effective leadership. Other leaders whose stories are told in this book also demonstrated leadership through their contribution of personal time and attention. They fostered engagement by others.

Most of All, Choose to Help

This chapter integrates stories and lessons from this book by showing how they exemplify lateral leadership. We focused on the role of leadership in the success of teams and how you can contribute to moving teams towards a goal.

As has already been hinted, the concepts introduced by Fisher and Sharp do not end at the small group. In their next to last chapter, "What If You Are the Boss?", the authors include a comparative table to show how leadership contributions differ in groups where you are a member and those where you are a manager or executive.

Their conclusion? But for the fact that leaders with supervisory or managerial responsibilities have additional powers to decide or direct, there are no differences in the skills leaders need. The skills of asking good questions, offering ideas and suggestions, and modeling constructive behavior are essential tools for any leader. Lateral leaders and leaders with formal authority both have to work together with colleagues who often have better ideas. Even transformational leaders of large organizations or political movements can improve their personal skills and help the group formulate its purpose, think systematically from the problem through diagnosis to strategy and action, learn from experience by starting soon and reviewing often, become fully engaged in a challenging role needed by the group, and help foster a climate of mutual support and feedback up, down, and laterally.[58]

Transformational or adaptive leadership challenges may involve other issues that extend beyond the small-group, lateral leadership dimension. Large transformational political and social change sometimes involves irreconcilable, competing purposes. Some adaptive change is less about disciplined thinking and principled analysis and more about organizational culture, habits, and loyalties. Try as one does to remain empathetic and see things from other peoples' perspectives, some adaptive change and transformation involve loss that does not always have a win-win solution. And Luke (1998) reminds us that the interconnectedness and autonomy of community and political organizations raise collaboration to another dimension in public leadership.

But our focus in this book was on teams. Fisher and Sharp summarized their lateral leadership model using a final prescription, "Choose to help." Teams have needs. Members of teams have varying motivations, demands on their time, and responsibilities. You have opportunities to assist these collections of diverse individuals achieve their goals if you choose to take action. Your effectiveness as a lateral leader is measured by your contribution.

Opportunities to lead come in various flavors. In organizations like procurement offices with significant roles in maintaining internal controls, the chances to help may arise in unusual contexts. Take contract terms and conditions, for example. Procurement professionals often need help knowing when those clauses are appropriate or can be used. North Dakota's risk-management collaboration between the Procurement Office, Attorney General, and Risk Management Division is unique. I was not there to see that collaboration unfold—the story is told in chapter 8—but I know for certain someone had to take the lead in building that collaboration.

The California Office of Systems Integration is leading the way in cross-functional management of complex information technology projects. That office works its way through complex project management using flexible teams, defined roles, and exceptional learning approaches. When I spoke with former OSI members, I was astounded by their use of words like "mentoring" and the clarity of what their teams were striving to do to achieve successful information technology implementations, no small feat.

I never discussed with Sue Wheater her use of project management, team theories, "just enough structure," and empathy when she did her intriguing Request for Posters project. I imagine, though, that Sue paused occasionally to figure out how to commit her time meaningfully with the kids. She likely struggled a bit with how to simplify the complex world of procurement in ways that would be interesting to them. And more than likely, she thought about the rest of the team, the other county offices that supported her. "Do you have the time? Can you help?" I suspect that Sue knew that others were busy and tried to make the project as easy as possible on them. Talk about empathy and stepping to their side often! Sue chose to help the county foster strong public relations with the community. She enlisted the assistance of others in the county, but Sue led with her creativity, influence, and ability to frame and accomplish a consequential goal.

Sue Wheater's story stuck with me, and I suspect it stuck with some kids. To use Chip Heath and Dan Heath's model, Sue's story is simple, unexpected, emotional, credible, concrete and easy to tell. Her story is the "stickiest" among all those I tell.

Celebrate with me the notable achievements of colleagues whose stories are told here. Learn from them. As you move into other dimensions of leadership in your career, I hope lessons you learned here inspire you and help you continue to evolve leadership skills that can make larger organizations more effective. Always keep purpose in mind. Practice the art of the question. Use just enough structure. Step to their side often. Commit your time and attention. Choose to help.

Afterword: Creating Excellence

"Let's do it! Design it." —Kunjan Dayal, Sound Transit

◆

As this book reached its final stages, I wondered how it should end. The manuscript was complete and out for preview. Early reviews were encouraging. But I had an abiding sense that the final chapter hadn't been told.

Not much has been said about the division of parts in the table of contents: Part I: Expand. Part II: Focus. Part III: Sustain. As the deadline approached, the editor, publisher and I had a healthy dialogue about those parts, whether we should write short introductions to each part. We didn't.

But in the back of my mind, there was an overarching theme of creativity that went with these stories. The process of getting better as a team and organization is not a linear one, but there seem to be recurring patterns. Great groups have a period of expansion in thinking. At some point the team pivots and begins the process of exploration and focusing: often a decision is reached. Strategies for sustaining the efforts—learning and leadership—are important. In many ways, this book went through its own expand, focus, sustain cycle as we shut down the research, moved into editing, and thought about how to make the book more useful.

Then I spoke with April Alexander. April was quoted in a feature story in the February/March 2013 edition of *Government Procurement* magazine. When I picked up the magazine amidst piles of manuscript drafts and reference books, I saw an article titled, "The Route to Excellence." The story was about Sound Transit's path to achieving the pinnacle of awards in public procurement: NIGP's Pareto Award of Excellence. Sound Transit was only the eighth agency to receive the award since its inception in 2003.

The story was focused on the rigor with which agencies are evaluated for the Pareto Award. I saw in the story a reference to "street teaming" as a practice used in the agency. With "excellence" in the story title and "street teaming" in the backstory, it was a no-brainer. I had to know more.

As was my practice with these stories, I tried to find out as much as possible about the project before I asked their lateral leaders to spend time with me on the phone. The NIGP online resource library is a great place to find examples of best practices. When I searched for documents referring to Sound Transit, I found a 2010 procurement and contracts scorecard.

Armed with two things to talk about in particular, I called April in Seattle, and she graciously agreed to speak with me. In just 60 minutes, I reaffirmed the chapter 3 lesson: learn from the stars! You learn things that you simply won't find out unless you talk to them.

Sound Transit operates express bus, light rail and commuter train services in the Seattle metropolitan area. April leads the Materials, Technology and Services group in the Procurement and Contracts Division. I congratulated April on Sound Transit's achievement. I explained to her that the *Government Procurement* article had raised some interesting back-story possibilities that were relevant to *Seeing Excellence*. I sent her the book's introduction and table of contents—and the *Art in the Procurement Manual* story of course!

When we spoke, April had read that story. We spoke about creativity. Sue Wheater's story was a reminder for me that there are opportunities to demonstrate creativity in government. April agreed, and she shared her own story.

It started with frustration. Their purchasing function is fairly centralized, but they still provide tools to permit users to purchase the things necessary to do their jobs. Sound Transit does a lot of construction contracting, and as the agency moves into its fifteenth year, the procurement mission is moving more towards operations and maintenance. Small purchases become a mainstay of O&M.

April doesn't remember the specifics of the purchase issue that triggered the creative moment. But it involved the application of the small purchase thresholds and what users could and could not do to purchase. April tells the story best, "I was probably a little frustrated. I was talking to our previous director of Procurement and Contracts, Kunjan Dayal, about my frustration. I said something like, 'What I need is something right in front of them that shows the purchasing limits. I need a mouse pad!' Kunjan's response, "Let's do it! Design it.'"

And they did. The mouse pad is distributed to users and displays the Sound Transit logo. Named *Quick Guide,* the pad has the thresholds for purchase cards, informal quotes, written quotes, and the level at which Purchasing must be contacted. The Procurement and Contracting office telephone number is on the pad.

That small but powerful project illustrated the three parts of this book. April and her director expanded their thinking through a conversation. When she plopped the idea of a mouse pad, Kunjan pounced into an elegant "focusing" phase! The mouse pad closed the deal.

The pad sustained the idea also. April and I discussed how their solution—putting the thresholds right in front of everyone with a computer, meaning just about everyone who had any purchasing authority—was an illustration of principles covered in chapters 8 and 9. From a change management perspective, this change in the environment was akin to Heath and Heath's (2010) scripting the critical moves. And the surprise of seeing a mouse pad designed this way would help cement the importance of these issues, make them stick—just like Montrose County's art in the procurement manual got people looking inside their manual.

It didn't stop there. April's team found another innovative solution to a common problem. As the use of procurement cards grew, there was some concern about misuse. Not from intentional fraud, but employees in the field often had the procurement cards in their wallets alongside their personal cards, creating an opportunity for unintentional misuse.

April explained the solution that the P-card program and Kunjan devised. "We created a procurement card sleeve. The rules for procurement card uses—transaction limits and a list of restricted items, for example—are on the sleeve. And the sleeve had the added benefit of physically distinguishing the card from others they may have had in the wallet."

Again, while this solution seems simple, it is an excellent example of what Thaler and Sunstein call *choice architecture* in their book *Nudge* (2008). In Sound Transit's case, the agency used a physical device, a sleeve, to set a *default* in the choices. The default for someone opening their wallet is to go to the more accessible personal credit card. The sleeve requires conscious activity (removing the sleeve) in order to use the agency card. While chapter 8 highlighted large projects involving enterprise-wide change management challenges, chapters 9 and 10 also showed that influencing peoples' behaviors uses similar strategies.

I had already uncovered way more in terms of best practices than I ever imagined when the call started. Then April and I talked about her agency's "street teaming."

Sound Transit has real customers in the traditional sense, and Sound Transit's CEO has a laser focus on the customers and the importance of teams.

April explains, "Our CEO started the street teaming. The idea was that when we started new transit service, we would go out to where the customers were. We helped new riders figure out the ticket vending machines, for example. Everyone was strongly encouraged to participate. Employees even gave up weekends sometimes."

April soon saw the value. "One day, when I was street teaming, I met a man in a wheelchair. He thanked me for expanding the service. The buses that he could take to the airport required him to transfer and were more difficult for him to access. With light rail, he was able to roll his chair right on and go directly to the airport. It was then that I realized that I was part of—and important to—something bigger. I was amazed at how he felt that we, as an agency, had directly impacted his quality of life in a positive way. But listening to him and talking to him gave me something invaluable that I would not have felt if it had simply been relayed to me that we were impacting peoples' lives. I was able to feel his excitement, to see his eyes tear up a little. I was able to connect to and feel the difference that the everyday work that I, in particular, was doing was meaningful. We were not simply buying things. When our team returned to our offices on Monday morning, I think each member of the team had their own, personal 'wheelchair' story. A feeling of being a part of something that was making a difference in people's lives."

Wow. We don't always get to connect to our customers in such a personal way. You have to find opportunities. I was intrigued with stories April told me about the great culture at Sound Transit. New employees are welcomed by the CEO in public employee meetings. She also has some fun. As April tells the story, "Our CEO asks for someone to toss Sound Transit hats towards new employees. Nobody else in the room catches the hat; they swat at it to keep it from touching the ground until the new employee can catch it. The CEO's message is that it takes teamwork to keep that hat from hitting the ground." Creativity rears its head again!

April and I talked about the scorecard and agreed how I would clear this story with her agency. But I asked one final question. "Not every procurement professional is going to have such an innovative culture, one that promotes creativity. Are there lessons here for the rest of us?" I asked. April was quick to answer, "Yes. Go see your clients. You likely will find out something about your operation that can be improved. Better yet, you'll realize that procurement is an important part of what your organization does."

Sound Transit provides a wonderful example of the expanding, focusing, and sustaining lessons in this book. As for the role of lateral leaders like April, her director, and especially the CEO, not much more needs to be said. They could have written chapter 10.

Another chapter of this book is being written—by the procurement professionals it showcases. They will continue to create excellence.

In writing this book, I was awestruck by the resourcefulness, dedication, and caring that these stories illustrated. I'm not sure why I was so surprised, but I was reminded just how good this profession is.

Your projects are laboratories for leadership, project management, continuous improvement, and learning. As I close this manuscript one final time, I'll reflect on some patterns I've seen.

Action is a key to success. Just begin. As April Alexander says, begin with the client. Go to the client's office. Don't just call. Go visit. When I practiced criminal law as a defense attorney in the Air Force, I always visited the scene of the crime. Terrible analogy, I know; our procurement offices aren't pushing those boundaries! But I learned that going to the location opens perspectives you never get otherwise. You will learn something.

The Japanese have a name for this principle, *genba*, meaning "real place," or as Heath and Heath (2013) explain, the place where the action happens. Japanese detectives call the crime scene the *genba*. Japanese quality management practitioners are taught to go the factory floor to see problems first-hand and talk with those living them. Go to the client's *genba*.

Take someone with you. The stories here involve collaboration, the no-kidding key to success. Taking one person with you begins to frame opportunities with someone else who cares. It sows the seeds of teams that grow later.

Start with a single question for the client. What one thing can we do (or stop doing) to help you? That begins the process of change.

After that conversation, go back to your office and talk with your colleague about what you learned. How does the gap look, the one between reality and what the client thinks the future should look like? Then start closing the gap.

Finally, keep learning. One of my favorite quotes, attributed to poet Dorothy Parker, was attached to an email from a client: "The cure for boredom is curiosity—there is no cure for curiosity." This book was the product of curiosity, not just my own. The stories show a commitment to continual learning and figuring things out.

My personal expand and focus phases are over now that this book has been written. The sustain part is up to each of you. Go create excellence. Put a little more art in your procurement process and watch what happens as a result!

Endnotes

Introduction

1   George, *Lean Six Sigma*, 133-141.
2   See http://www.accountability.wa.gov/leadership/lean/default.asp. The site has examples of value stream mapping, a seven step problem-solving process based on the Toyota Production System, and examples of other tools.
3   The NASPO George Cronin Award for Procurement Excellence is described and its past winners identified at http://www.naspo.org/content.cfm/id/cronin_award.
4   Steve Demel, "Embracing 'Lean' – It's all About the Process," *Government Procurement* (Atlanta: NIGP/ Penton Media, February/March 2013).
5   Tague, *Quality Toolbox*, 36.

Chapter 1

1   Ronald Heifetz recommends this question among other as useful for getting leaders to think about adaptive change. Heifetz, *Adaptive Leadership*, 171-172.
2   Stephen R. Covey, *The 7 Habits of Highly Effective People* (New York: Simon & Schuster, 1989).
3   Edgar Schein, *Organizational Culture and Leadership*, 80-88.
4   Katzenbach and Smith, *Wisdom of Teams*, 62.
5   NIGP, *Online Dictionary of Procurement Terms*.
6   NIGP, *Online Dictionary of Procurement Terms*. See also Kerzner's (2009) definition of project management.
7   Available at http://www.nigp.org/eweb/docs/Research/ValuesGuidPrin.pdf.
8   NIGP, *Online Dictionary of Procurement Terms*.
9   NIGP *Values and Guiding Principles*, available at http://www.nigp.org/eweb/StartPage. aspx?Site=NIGP&webcode=abt-ppv_gp.
10 NIGP, *Online Dictionary of Procurement Terms*.
11 Whitney andTrosten-Bloom, *Appreciative Inquiry*, 109-110, 184.
12 Hackman, *Leading Teams*, 72-82.
13 Hackman, *Leading Teams*, 89.
14 Hackman, *Leading Teams* and *Collaborative Intelligence*.

Chapter 2

1   Whitney and Trosten-Bloom, *Power of Appreciative Inquiry*, 57.
2   McCue and Pitzer, *Fundamentals of Leadership and Management*, 103.

Chapter 2, cont'd.

3   NIGP, *Online Dictionary of Procurement Terms.*

4   Block, *Flawless Consulting,* chap. 7. Block's chapter 7 discusses important differences between internal and external consultants, many of which are covered by McCue and Pitzer (2005).

5   George, *Lean Six Sigma,* 138-139.

6   Gray, Brown and Macanufo, *Gamestorming,* 27-32.

7   Block, *Flawless Consulting,* chap. 19.

8   Tague, *Quality Toolbox,* 36.

9   Peter Block, *Flawless Consulting,* chap. 12.

10 The description of Appreciative Inquiry is from Whitney and Trosten-Bloom, *Appreciative Inquiry,* 146-149.

11 Whitney and Trosten-Bloom, *Appreciative Inquiry,* 247-250.

12 In 2013, WSCA's mission was assumed by the WSCA-NASPO Cooperative Purchasing Organization LLC, a subsidiary of NASPO. See www.wsca-naspo.org for a description of the new organization.

13 Niven, *Balanced Scorecard Step-by-Step,* 124-141. See also McCue and Johnson, *Strategic Planning in the Public Sector,* 52-56.

14 Kerzner, *Project Management¸* sec. 2.2 and 2.3.

15 In the mid-1980s, the British Standards Institute encouraged the International Organization of Standardization (ISO)—a worldwide federation of national standards bodies—to develop an international standard for quality systems. Over 25 countries were involved in the first development. ISO 9000 was revised in 1994 and again underwent significant revisions in 2000. ISO 9000 family of standards includes ISO 9000 (general principles and definitions), ISO 9001 (specified requirement for a quality management system), and ISO 9004 (guidelines for assessing and improving the effectiveness and efficiency of the system). The ISO standard in its present form departs from the previous versions by eliminating "quality" as a separate, bolted-on management structure in an organization. It also migrates away from the procedural focus in the previous versions. A whole consulting industry grew up around the ISO 9000 certification process. ISO 9000 certification is rare in governments.

16 Kerzner, *Project Management,* sec. 11.3.

17 Price, *Takeoff,* 15.

18 Stanley E. Portny, *Project Management for Dummies,* 3rd Ed. (New York: Wiley, 2010), chap. 18.

19 Kent Beck and Martin Fowler, *Planning Extreme Programming* (Boston: Addison-Wesley, 2001), p. xi.

20 David L. Bradford and W. Warner Burke, "The Future of OD?" from Joan V. Gallos, ed., *Organization Development* (San Francisco: Jossey-Bass, 2006), 853.

Chapter 3

1   The story of Sound Transit's Pareto Award Achievement is told in Larry Anderson, "Sound Transit's Route to Excellence," *Government Procurement* (Reston VA: NIGP, February/March 2013).

2   Patterson, Grenny, Maxfield, McMillan and Switzler, *Influencer,* chap. 2.

3   OSI's Best Practices website is at http://www.osi.ca.gov/.

4   California Health and Human Services Agency, Office of Systems Integration, *Request for Demonstration (RFD) #15531: State Systems Interoperability and Implementation Plan (SSIP) Project* (May 10, 2013).

5   Maoboussin, *Think Twice,* 97-99.

6   NIGP, *Online Dictionary of Procurement Terms.*

7   *Ibid.*

8   Tague, *Quality Handbook,* 116.

9   McCue and Pitzer, *Fundamentals of Leadership and Management,* 110.

10 NIGP's Public Procurement Principles and Practices can be found at http://www.nigp.org/eweb/StartPage.aspx?Site=NIGP&webcode=abt-ppv_gp.

11 See, e.g., Collision and Parcell, *Learning to Fly*, 82.

12 Senge, *The Fifth Discipline*, 158.

13 Senge, *The Fifth Discipline*, 58.

14 Senge, *The Fifth Discipline*, Appendix 2.

15 Mauboussin, *Think Twice*, 129.

Chapter 4

1   Davis and Davis, *Effective Training Strategies*, 289. See also Bellman and Ryan, *Extraordinary Groups*.

2   In SCOPEVision®, the kaleidoscope is the visual metaphor for teams.

3   Davis and Davis, *Effective Training Strategies*, 284.

4   See Hackman, *Leading Teams*, for example.

5   Hackman, *Leading Teams*, 117-119.

6   Hackman, *Leading Teams*, 54-59.

7   Katzenbach and Smith, *Wisdom of Teams*, 121.

8   Davis and Davis, *Effective Training Strategies*, 294.

9   Many of the ideas for this summarization, of facilitation in particular, are taken from Rees, *How to Lead Work Teams*. The summary of mirroring appears on pp. 189-191.

10 Hackman, *Leading Teams*.

11 See also Bellman and Ryan, *Extraordinary Groups*. Hackman, *Leading Teams*.

12 Hackman, *Leading Teams*.

13 http://www.naspo.org/documents/Meeting_the_Challenges_of_World_Class_Procurement_FINAL.pdf

14 Niven, *Balanced Scorecard Step-by-Step*, 74.

15 I learned the value of stepping out of a meeting by mistake. I was leading a virtual webinar meeting from a school district office. Towards the second half of the meeting, a fire alarm went off. I apologized but told the virtual meeting participants that I had to leave the building. The meeting was recorded, so I was able to listen to what was said. I was delighted to see that there was even more engagement when I left; it reinforced for me the need to watch how directive I am in meeting, perhaps unintentionally impeding others' participation. We can't set off a fire alarm, but a team leader's stepping outside of a meeting occasionally may promote more engagement by other members.

16 Hackman, *Leading Teams*, 105-107, 171-174.

17 Heifetz, *Practice of Adaptive Leadership*, 147.

18 Lencioni, *Five Dysfunctions of a Team*, 210.

19 Goleman, Boyatzis and McKee, *Primal Leadership*, 180.

20 Rees, *How to Lead Work Teams*, 43

21 Heifetz, *Practice of Adaptive Leadership*, 145-148.

22 Hackman, *Leading Teams*, 184-185.

23 Hackman, *Leading Teams*, 213.

Chapter 5

1   Katzenbach and Smith, *Wisdom of Teams*. Lencioni, *Five Dysfunctions of a Team*.

2   Price, *Takeoff!*, 28.

3   Price, *Takeoff!*, 44.

4   Price, *Takeoff!*, 15.

5   NIGP, *Online Dictionary of Procurement Terms*.

Chapter 5, cont'd.

6   NIGP, *Online Dictionary of Procurement Terms.*

7   Price, *Takeoff!*, 49-50.

8   Mike Cohn, *Succeeding with Agile: Software Development Using Scrum* (Boston: Pearson Education, 2010), 292.

9   Frederick P. Brooks, Jr., *The Mythical Man-Month: Essays on Software Engineering*, 2nd Ed. (Addison-Wesley Longman, 1995).

10 Wysocki, *Effective Project Management*, 229.

Chapter 6

1   NASPO Research Brief, *Benchmarking Cost Savings & Cost Avoidance* (September 2007), available at http://www.naspo.org, link to Research and Publications, Whitepapers & Issue Briefs.

2   There might have been some value to tracking the number of cases from a workload perspective. No doubt the simple ratio also promoted discussion between senior department lawyers and other executives about these cases. In that sense, there might have been some value to using the data as a vivid, visual display of our office's mission.

3   Hubbard, *You Can Measure Anything*, 23.

4   Hubbard, *You Can Measure Anything*, 31.

5   Berkun, *Art of Project Management*, 211-212. Berkun believes that the phenomenon of data paralysis is symptomatic of the belief that if there were enough data, the decision would resolve itself.

6   Hubbard, *You Can Measure Anything*, 102-103.

7   Hubbard, *You Can Measure Anything*, 41-43.

8   Hubbard, *You Can Measure Anything*, 138.

9   Hubbard, *You Can Measure Anything*, 21-26.

10 Given the low number of protests in any agency, the author questions whether the mathematical ratio of successful to total protests is a valid measure of procurement quality. The numbers of protests may be process measures that reflect workload trends, however.

11 Niven, *Balanced Scorecard Step-by-Step*, 213.

12 Hubbard, *You Can Measure Anything*, 32.

13 Kaplan and Norton, *Balanced Scorecard.* Niven, *Balanced Scorecard Step-by-Step*, 5.

14 This summary of balanced scorecard is taken from Niven (2008).

15 McCue and Pitzer, *Fundamentals of Leadership and Management*, 28.

16 Scholtes, Joiner and Streibel, *Team Handbook*, pp. xvii – xx.

17 Mauboussin, *Think Twice*, 94-95.

18 NIGP, *Online Dictionary of Procurement Terms.* NIGP has a partnership with Spikes Cavell who promotes a tool called MEASURE to assist agencies in recording and reporting of delivered savings to their agencies. The online tools capture, collate, analyze, and report savings and efficiencies delivered by the procurement function.

19 NASPO Research Brief, *Benchmarking Cost Savings & Cost Avoidance* (September 2007), available at http://www.naspo.org, link to Research and Publications, Whitepapers & Issue Briefs.

20 Niven, *Balanced Scorecard Step-by-Step*, 65.

21 Hubbard, *You Can Measure Anything*, chap. 12.

22 Hubbard, *You Can Measure Anything*, 227-228.

23 Ullman, *Making Robust Decisions.* Ullman maintains that averaging scores in a matrix injects error because it does not account for uncertainty in decision making. Moreover, there is a regression to the mean, so that judgments by more knowledgeable individuals are marginalized by the averaging of scores.

24   Tague, *Quality Toolbox*, 370-372. Scholtes, Joiner and Streibel, *Team Handbook,* p. 4-10.

25   Hubbard, *You Can Measure Anything*, 222-224. The discussion of effective criteria is taken from Ullman, *Making Robust Decisions*, 144-152.

26   Ullman, *Making Robust Decisions*, 144.

27   A sample evaluation plan used in the Colorado attorney general's timekeeping procurement is available on the NIGP Resource Library. Search for "Colorado Evaluation Plan." The plan has definitions of evaluation standards.

28   Hubbard, *You Can Measure Anything*, 222-224.

29   Hubbard, *You Can Measure Anything*, 214-220.

30   Hubbard, *You Can Measure Anything*, 66.

Chapter 7

1   Scholtes, Joiner and Streibel, *The Team Handbook*, p. 5-15.

2   Tague, *Quality Handbook*, 330-334.

3   The phases of thinking show up in various publications. Tague's *The Quality Toolbox* generally uses an expanding and focusing description. Gray, Brown and Macanufo's *Gamestorming* is based on game theory and uses three phases of opening (divergence), exploring (emergence), and closing (convergence).

4   Tague, *Quality Handbook*, 15. The other basic tools of quality management are the cause and effect diagram (Ishikawa or fishbone chart), check sheet, control charts (used to show variation in manufacturing processes), histogram, Pareto chart, and scatter diagram.

5   Tague, *Quality Handbook*, 256.

6   Wright (2007) identifies alternatives in Appendix D of her book, *Risk Management in Public Contracting*: The Four Ps (place, procedure, people, policies) or the Four Ss (surroundings, suppliers, systems, skills).

7   Fisher and Sharp, *Lateral Leadership*, 80-93.

8   Davis and Davis, *Effective Training Strategies*, chap. 7.

9   Ullman, *Making Robust Decisions*; Mauboussen, *Think Twice*.

10   Heath and Heath, *Decisive*.

11   Berkun, *Art of Project Management*, 200-201.

12   Lehrer, *How We Decide*, 144. Lehrer uses the term "choking on thought."

13   Gladwell, *Blink*.

14   Lehrer, *How We Decide*, chap. 7.

15   Lehrer, *How We Decide*, 245.

16   Heath and Heath, *Decisive*, 160-161.

17   Example taken from Lehrer, *How We Decide*.

18   Lehrer, *How We Decide*, 246.

19   A.D. Dijksterhuis, "On Making the Right Choice," *Science* (2006), cited in Lehrer, *How We Decide*.

20   Kahneman, *Thinking, Fast and Slow*.

21   Heath and Heath, *Decisive*, 165-166.

22   Mauboussin, *Think Twice*.

23   Lehrer, *How We Decide*, 254.

24   Lehrer, *How We Decide*, 247.

25   Lehrer, *How We Decide*, 253.

26   The Walt Disney story was told by Belsky, *Making Ideas Happen*, 76.

27   Heath and Heath, *Decisive*, chap. 5.

28   Lehrer, *How We Decide*, 247.

Chapter 7, cont'd.

29 Mauboussin, *Think Twice*; Gawande, *Checklist Manifesto*.

30 Ullman, *Making Robust Decisions*, 43.

31 Berkun, *Art of Project Management*, 204-207.

32 Berkun, *Art of Project Management*, 207-208.

33 The story of Joseph Priestly and Benjamin Franklin is told in Heath and Heath, *Decisive*, 20-22.

34 Tague, *Quality Handbook*, 200.

35 Gray, Brown and Macanufo, *Gamestorming*, 241; Tague, *Quality Toolbox*, 233.

36 Tague, *Quality Handbook*, 505.

37 Tague, *Quality Handbook*, 235.

38 Ullman, *Making Robust Decisions*, chap. 2-3.

39 Ullman, *Making Robust Decisions*, 153-157.

40 Ullman, *Making Robust Decisions*, 163.

41 Ullman *Making Robust Decisions*, 249.

42 Ullman, *Making Robust Decisions*, 254.

43 Ullman, *Making Robust Decisions*, 249.

44 Ullman, *Making Robust Decisions*, 154.

45 Ullman, *Making Robust Decisions*, 245.

46 A responsible bidder or offeror is a contractor, business entity, or individual who is fully capable to meet all of the requirements of the solicitation and subsequent contract. The bidder or offeror must possess the full capability, including financial and technical, to perform as contractually required. NIGP, *Online Dictionary of Procurement Terms*.

47 I am a fan of debriefings after contract award, although there are some risks that can be mitigated. See Richard Pennington, "Legal Pro: Untying the Legalistic Straightjacket," *Government Procurement* (Atlanta: NIGP/Penton Media, June/July 2012).

48 Available at http://www.e-publishing.af.mil/index.asp. Search for "Tongue and Quill."

49 Daniel Kahneman, Dan Lovallo and Olivier Sibony, "Before You Make That Big Decision," *Harvard Business Review* (June 2011), 52-60.

50 Mauboussin, *Think Twice*, 141.

51 Berkun, *Art of Project Management*, 220-222.

52 Ullman, *Making Robust Decisions*, 96.

Chapter 8

1 NIGP, *Online Dictionary of Procurement Terms*.

2 Flanagan and Norman, *Risk Management and Construction*.

3 Wright, *Risk Management in Public Contracting*, 2.

4 Wangemann, *Subcontract Management Manual*, 99, 131, 423.

5 NIGP Public Procurement Principles and Practices, "Technology in Public Procurement," available at http://www.nigp.org/eweb/docs/Practices/TechnologyPublicProcurement.pdf.

6 Wright, *Risk Management in Public Contracting*, 29.

7 Wright, *Risk Management in Public Contracting*, 1.

8 COSO, *Enterprise Risk Management*, 110.

9 COSO, *Enterprise Risk Management*, 88.

10 Cooper, Grey, Raymond, and Walker, *Project Risk Management Guidelines*.

11 Cooper, Grey, Raymond, and Walker, *Project Risk Management Guidelines*, 22-26.

12 Wright, *Risk Management in Public Contracting*, 54.

13 Cooper, Grey, Raymond, and Walker, *Project Risk Management Guidelines*, 41.

14 Klein, *Power of Intuition*, 98-118.

15 Heath and Heath, *Decisive*, 206-208.

16 See also Gray, Brown, and Macanufo, *Gamestorming*, 117.

17 Cooper, Grey, Raymond, and Walker, *Project Risk Management Guidelines*, 49-50, 85.

18 COSO, *Enterprise Risk Management*, 51.

19 Cooper, Grey, Raymond and Walker, *Project Risk Management Guidelines*, 81.

20 See the model Risk Management Plan used by OSI available at http://www.bestpractices.osi.ca.gov/sysacq/documents.shtml.

21 Cooper, Grey, Raymond, and Walker, *Project Risk Management Guidelines*, 76.

22 Cooper, Grey, Raymond, and Walker, *Project Risk Management Guidelines*, 77.

23 McCue and Johnson, *Strategic Procurement Planning*, 165-168.

24 See, generally, Fewings, *Construction Project Management*, 204-206.

25 Cooper, Grey, Raymond, and Walker, *Project Risk Management Guidelines*, 323; Wright, *Risk Management in Public Contracting*, 260.

26 http://www.nd.gov/risk/files/Manuals/Guidelines-Managing_Contractual_Risk.pdf.

27 See North Dakota Project Management Guidebook, Risk Management Supplement (December 7, 2009), available at http://www.nd.gov/itd/files/services/pm/risk-management-guidebook.pdf.

28 Wright, *Risk Management in Public Contracting*, 60-62.

29 Cooper, Grey, Raymond, and Walker, *Project Risk Management Guidelines*, 322.

30 Heath and Heath, *Switch*, 253-254.

31 Robert I. Sutton and Robert L. Kahn, "Prediction, Understanding, and Control as Antidotes to Organizational Stress," Jay Lorsch ed., *Handbook of Organizational Behavior* (Englewood Cliffs NJ: Prentice Hall, 1987), 272-285.

32 Rick Mauer, *Beyond the Wall of Resistance* (Austin TX: Bard Press, 2010).

33 Wendy Mack, presentation to the Pikes Peak ASTD Chapter, March 13, 2012.

34 Tague, *Quality Toolbox*, 268-270.

35 Richard Pennington, "The Anatomy of Change: Georgia's State Procurement Transformation," *Contract Management* (Washington DC: April 2011), 20. The complete story of the Georgia initiative is told in Sharon McMahon, *Smart Government: Bureaucracy with a Business Brain* (Macon GA: Mercer University, 2010).

36 Heath and Heath, *Switch*, chap. 1; Kotter and Cohen, *Heart of Change*, 29-30.

37 Kotter and Cohen, *Heart of Change*, 60.

38 Kotter and Cohen, *Heart of Change*, 26.

39 Kotter and Cohen, *Heart of Change*, 84.

40 Price, *Takeoff!*, 29.

41 Patterson, Grenny, Maxfield, McMillan, and Switzler, *Influencer*, 173-175.

42 Cialdini's "weapons of influence" were reciprocity, commitment and consistency, social proof, liking, authority, and scarcity.

43 Cialdini, *Influence*; Patterson, Grenny, Maxfield, McMillan, and Switzler, *Influencer*.

44 Heath and Heath, *Switch*, chap. 3.

45 Heath and Heath, *Switch*, chap. 2.

46 Find the "positive deviants." Patterson, Grenny, Maxfield, McMillan, and Switzler, *Influencer*, 35-43.

47 Heath and Heath, *Switch*, chap. 6.

48 The state's policies regarding contract risk are in the "Review and Approval" policies found at http://www.colorado.gov/dpa/dfp/sco/contracts/contractpolicies.htm.

Chapter 8, cont'd.

49 Gawande, *Checklist Manifesto*, 100.

50 Gawande, *Checklist Manifesto*, 67.

51 Gawande, *Checklist Manifesto*, 79.

Chapter 9

1   The state of South Carolina has an excellent summary of knowledge management principles in its Knowledge Management Guide published by the Budget and Control Board at http://www.ohr.sc.gov/ OHR/wfplan/KnowledgeManagementGuide%289-2012%29.pdf.

2   Collison and Parcell, *Learning to Fly*, 142.

3   Collision and Parcell, *Learning to Fly*, 133-142.

4   Collision and Parcell, *Learning to Fly*, 136.

5   Belsky, *Making Ideas Happen*, 196.

6   Collision and Parcell, *Learning to Fly*, chap. 9.

7   Belsky, *Making Ideas Happen*, 207.

8   Shore and Warden, *Art of Agile Development*, 91-97.

9   Klein, *Power of Intuition*, 61.

10 Art Kleiner and George Roth, "How to Make Experience Your Company's Best Teacher," *Harvard Business Review* (July – August 1997).

11 Heath and Heath (2008) use SUCCES as an acronym for the elements of sticky ideas: simple, unexpected, credible, concrete, emotional, and communicated using stories.

12 Price, *Takeoff!*, 40. See also Stephen Denning, "Telling Tales," *Harvard Business Review* (May 2004), 122.

13 Stolovich and Keeps, *Telling Ain't Training*, 165, 173, 202.

14 Davis and Davis, *Effective Training Strategies*.

15 Von Krogh, Ichijo, and Nonaka, *Enabling Knowledge Creation*, 19-22.

16 NASPO Research Brief, *Responding to an Aging and Changing Workforce: Attracting, Retaining and Developing New Procurement Professionals* (March 2008), available at http://www.naspo.org, link to Research and Publications, Whitepapers & Issue Briefs.

17 Ikujiro Nonaka, "The Knowledge-Creating Company," *Harvard Business Review* (November - December 1991), pp. 96-104.

18 Von Krogh, Ichijo, and Nonaka, *Enabling Knowledge Creation*, 25.

19 Cross, *Informal Learning*.

20 Leimbach, Michael P., and Ed Emde, "The 80/20 Rule for Learning Transfer," *Chief Learning Officer*, (December 2011), p. 64 (citing examples of post event emails to send out tips and reinforce the learning experience).

21 Edmondson, Amy C., "The Competitive Imperative of Learning," *Harvard Business Review* (July - August 2008), p. 60.

22 Hackman, *Leading Teams*, 152.

23 Von Krogh, Ichijo, and Nonaka, *Enabling Knowledge Creation*, 23-25.

24 Trautman, *Teach What You Know*, 132, 136.

25 *Ibid.*

26 Davis and Davis, *Effective Training Strategies*, chaps. 12 and 13.

27 McCain and Tobey, *Facilitation Basics*, 30. Using a mixture of media and experiences is consistent with an evolving theory called interleaving. Varying the learning subjects and locations has been shown be more effective than concentrated studying in one place for an extended period of time on one topic before moving to another.

28 This is a summary of principles from Trautman (2007).

29 Von Krogh, Ichijo, and Nonaka, *Enabling Knowledge Creation*, chap. 6.

30 Von Krogh, Ichijo, and Nonaka, *Enabling Knowledge Creation*, 143-146.

31 Davenport and Prusak, *Working Knowledge*, 38-39.

32 Collison and Parcell, *Learning to Fly*, 225.

33 Larry Anderson, "E-Learning at a Bargain Price," *Government Procurement* (Atlanta: NIGP/Penton Media, October/November 2012).

34 Chris Grebisz, "In Practice: Want Learning to Stick? Chunk It," *Chief Learning Officer* (August 2012), p. 37.

35 Stolovitch and Keeps, *Telling Ain't Training*, chap. 6.

36 McCain and Tobey (2004) say that the best facilitators are subject matter experts, putting procurement professionals squarely in the center of effective training. Their book is aimed at subject matter experts. McCain and Tobey, *Facilitation Basics*, 2, 158.

37 McCain and Tobey, *Facilitation Basics*, 23.

38 Stolovitch and Keeps, *Telling Ain't Training*, 55-57.

39 Stolovitch and Keeps, *Telling Ain't Training*, chap. 5.

40 Leonard and Swap, *Deep Smarts*, pp. 206-208.

41 These observations on how the program could have been improved are based largely on the model by Steve Trautman (2007).

42 See also McCain and Tobey, *Facilitation Basics*, 24-26.

43 Stolovitch and Keeps, *Telling Ain't Training*, chap. 6.

44 Davis and Davis, *Effective Training Strategies*.

45 Leonard and Swap, *Deep Smarts*, pp. 235-236.

46 Klein, *Power of Intuition*, 232-237.

47 http://workforceplanning.wi.gov/category.asp?linkcatid=1507&linkid=17&locid=14.

48 Leonard and Swap, *Deep Smarts*, chap. 8.

49 An overview of TVA processes and tools for preventing knowledge from "walking out the door" is available at http://www.tva.gov/knowledgeretention/pdf/overview.pdf.

50 Leonard and Swap, *Deep Smarts*, 34-39.

51 Gray, Brown and Macanufo, *Gamestorming*, 228. A community of practice describing the process and history of the World café is at www.theworldcafe.com. Another technique at promoting conversation and giving participants control of the learning is known as *open space technology*. There are few requirements, only that there be a single, compelling theme. The theme is written on a flip chart and a few minutes taken for individuals to write specific discussion topics. Normative group techniques are used quickly to group the topics. The objective is to have one topic for each table in the room. Multi-voting can be used to set priorities where there are more topics than tables. A single law, the "law of the two feet," frames the discussion. The law means that participants are free to join or leave a discussion at any time, although there are various versions of the join/leave norms in different descriptions of open space. Discussions are held for discrete periods of time, followed by a break, and then discussions are reconvened, so participants can join several during the seminar. A leader stays at each table while participants rotate. I saw this work very effectively in a meeting of independent publishers where they had a fairly common experience level. The Harrison Owen's user guide can be found at http://www.openspaceworld.com/users_guide.htm.

Chapter 9, cont'd.

52 Using movement and a mixture of media and experiences is consistent with an evolving theory called interleaving. Varying the learning subjects and locations has been shown be more effective over the long term than concentrated practice in one place for an extended period of time on one topic before moving to another. See UCLA professor Robert Bjork's video describing interleaving research at http://www.youtube.com/watch?v=l-1K61BalIA.

53 Kouzes and Posner, *Leadership Challenge*, 201-202.

Chapter 10

1 Burns, *Leadership*, 185.

2 Kotter, *What Leaders Really Do*, reprint of "Power, Dependence, and Effective Management," *Harvard Business Review* (July – August 1997).

3 McCue and Pitzer's *Fundamentals of Leadership and Management in Public Procurement* (2005) surveys different leadership theories.

4 McCue and Pitzer, *Fundamentals of Leadership and Management in Public Procurement*, 50-63.

5 Burns, *Leadership*, 442.

6 NIGP, *Online Dictionary of Procurement Terms*.

7 The early writings of John Kotter (1999) contained transactional themes. While his later writings placed leaders at the center of change, Kotter had also espoused as valuable various transactional skills: negotiation and manipulation (what now is referred to as the science of persuasion.) Kotter, *What Leaders Really Do*, 40-42, 115; Cialdini, *Influence*. Kotter forecasted more empathetic themes in leadership as well: the importance of reciprocity and credibility, for example. Kotter, *What Leaders Really Do*, chap. 5, reprint of "Power, Dependence, and Effective Management," *Harvard Business Review* (July – August 1997).

8 Bellman and Ryan in *Extraordinary Groups* (2009) use the term "leading with a light touch" to characterize constructive, facilitative leadership behavior.

9 Rees, *How to Lead Work Teams*, part two. Bellman and Ryan (2009) call this shared leadership. Hackman (2002) suggested that while effective teams most often have a recognized leader, team members can share leadership roles in achieving effective team performance. Hackman, *Leading Teams*, 231.

10 Bellman and Ryan (2009) identified other characteristics of great groups: shared leadership; just enough (but not too much) structure; full engagement by the team members; the embracing of differences; unexpected learning; and strengthened relationships. But compelling purpose is a cornerstone, however, because the group purpose has to be aligned with the intrinsic motivations that cause people to join and perform in groups.

11 Burns' (1978) study of values and moral leadership aligns with this book's admonition to keep purpose in mind. Bellman and Ryan (2009) found higher purpose to be an element of effective teams as well.

12 Kouzes and Posner, *Leadership Challenge*, 116-117.

13 Kotter, *What Leaders Really Do*, reprint of "Leading Change," *Harvard Business Review* (1995).

14 Fisher and Sharp, *Lateral Leadership*, 74.

15 Luke (2008) found that objectives take on special importance in public leadership contexts. Community and political groups may have different values and purposes. Making progress on controversial issues can be stymied if aligned purpose in a moral sense is the goal. Instead, Luke counsels to focus on outcomes as the purpose, realizing that the values underlying and methods to achieve the outcomes may be different. Luke uses reduction of teenage pregnancy as an example: the groups interested in the issue have widely varying moral purposes but they may agree on the outcomes that need to be achieved. There is a lesson here also for teams that are stuck. Conflict arising out of disagreements

about how to reach the objective sometimes can be constructively channeled by focusing on the outcomes that need to be achieved.

16 Burns devoted an entire chapter to planning as one dimension of effective leadership. Burns, *Leadership*, chap. 3. Kouzes and Posner (2012) found competence of leaders to be among the top four characteristics of effective leaders (along with honesty, inspiration, and forward thinking). Kouzes and Posner, *Leadership Challenge*, 34-35.

17 Kouzes and Posner, *Leadership Challenge*, 21, 252-261.

18 Fisher and Sharp, *Lateral Leadership*, chap. 4.

19 Ury, *Power of a Positive No*.

20 This paragraph is a synthesis of Fisher, Ury, and Patton, *Getting to Yes*, and Ury, *Getting Past No*.

21 Ury, *Power of A Positive No*, chap. 4.

22 The options and BATNA paragraphs were a synthesis of Fisher, Ury, and Patton, *Getting to Yes* and Ury, *Getting Past No*.

23 Kouzes and Posner, *Leadership Challenge*, 339-342.

24 Kouzes and Posner, *Leadership Challenge*, 78, 83-84, 185-186, 244-246. Ronald Heifetz (2009) uses questions almost exclusively to probe adaptive leadership that touches change implicating organizational culture, competing loyalties, and conflicting purposes.

25 Kouzes and Posner, *Leadership Challenge*, 201-205.

26 Kouzes and Posner, *Leadership Challenge*, 266-267.

27 Kouzes and Posner, *Leadership Challenge*, 81-83.

28 Whitney and Trosten Bloom, *Appreciative Inquiry*.

29 Fisher and Sharp, *Lateral Leadership*, chap. 5.

30 Kouzes and Posner, *Leadership Challenge*, 189-209; Heifetz, *Practice of Adaptive Leadership*.

31 For 50 scientifically proven ways to see how the principles of persuasion and influence manifest themselves, see Goldstein, Martin, and Cialdini, *Yes!*.

32 Pink, *To Sell Is Human*, 166-168, 179-180.

33 Other leadership studies highlight empathy or related concepts as important to leaders' success. Burns (1978) used the work "empathy" in discussing a comprehensive model for leadership, his theory of transformational leadership. The extent to which leaders and followers achieve a common purpose, and the relationship established between the leader and followers is forged using relationships that may be characterized as empathetic. No leaders can truly lead unless they can respond to the wants of followers.

34 Kouzes and Posner, *Leadership Challenge*, 8.

35 Fisher and Sharp, *Lateral Leadership*, chap. 2.

36 Fisher and Sharp, *Lateral Leadership*, 30.

37 Coaching is the term used to refer to this kind of support during team performance. In early team performance before performance really begins, teams often are in mild conflict, a little rudderless, and need encouragement. Hackman, *Leading Teams*, 176-191.

38 Luke, *Catalytic Leadership*.

39 Heifetz, *Practice of Adaptive Leadership*.

40 Scholtes, Joiner and Streibel, *Team Handbook*, p. 7-3.

41 Moore, *Meditation Process*, 172-202

42 Moore, *Meditation Process*, 180-181.

43 Human Resources at University of Berkeley, *Guide to Managing Human Resources: Chapter 15, Managing Conflict*, available at http://hrweb.berkeley.edu/guides/managing-hr/interaction/conflict.

44 Luke (1998) describes the *Getting to Yes* interest-based negotiation model as a way to manage conflict.

Chapter 10, cont'd.

45 Scholtes, Joiner and Streibel, *Team Handbook*, p. 7-8.

46 Scholtes, Joiner and Streibel, *Team Handbook*, pp. 7-9 – 7-11.

47 Human Resources at University of Berkeley, *Guide to Managing Human Resources: Chapter 15, Managing Conflict*, available at http://hrweb.berkeley.edu/guides/managing-hr/interaction/conflict.

48 *Ibid.* See also Scholtes, Joiner and Streibel, *Team Handbook*, pp. 7-10 – 7-11.

49 Scholtes, Joiner and Streibel, *Team Handbook*, p. 7-22.

50 Kotter *What Leaders Really Do*, chap. 6, reprint of "Managing Your Boss," *Harvard Business Review* (May-June 1993).

51 The title of Heifetz's second book on adaptive leadership was, *Leaders on the Line: Staying Alive Through the Danger of Leading* (2002). Heifetz reminds us of another dimension of empathy. In adaptive challenge situations broadly implicating culture, competing loyalties, and conflicting purposes, there can be loss and pain. While stepping to their side in a team environment promotes team trust, leaders who are promoted to executive levels in many cases have to revisit empathy. There may be situations where there is no win-win and people suffer. Empathy in that context means as a minimum understanding the fear and doing what can be done to help people understand, forecast, and to the extent possible control some aspect of the change. See also Luke, *Catalytic Leadership*, chap. 9.

52 Kouzes and Posner, *Leadership Challenge*, 315.

53 Leonard and Swap, *Deep Smarts*, p. 230.

54 Schein, *Helping*.

55 Fisher and Sharp, *Lateral Leadership*.

56 Kouzes and Posner, *Leadership Challenge*, 23-24.

57 Fisher and Sharp, *Lateral Leadership*, 179.

58 Fisher and Sharp, *Lateral Leadership*, 199.

References

Rather than opting for an alphabetical listing of all references, the references are organized using the four parts of the book: Introduction; Expand the Team's Thinking; Focus the Team's Attention; and Sustain the Team's Efforts. The reference appears only once even though it may be cited various places in the book. Where I thought a reference particularly valuable, a brief note is included.

Introduction

Continuous Improvement and General Resources

Deming, W. Edwards. *Out of the Crisis.* Cambridge MA: MIT, 1986. Although Deming reportedly did not want his name associated with the Total Quality Management movements in the late 1990s, he is widely regarded as the father of TQM.

George, Michael L. *Lean Six Sigma for Service.* New York: McGraw-Hill, 2003. George recounts to story of the use of Lean Six Sigma by the city of Fort Wayne, Indiana.

McCue, Clifford and Barbara Johnson. *Strategic Procurement Planning in the Public Sector.* Herndon VA: NIGP, 2010.

National Institute of Governmental Purchasing Inc. (2012). *Online Dictionary of Procurement Terms.* Herndon, VA: NIGP. Retrieved from Online Dictionary, available at www.nigp.org, select <Resource Library> <Publications>.

Pyzdek, Thomas. *The Six Sigma Handbook: A Complete Guide for Green Belts, Black Belts, and Managers at All Levels.* New York: McGraw-Hill, 2003. This 830-page reference book has how-to explanations of tools commonly used by Six Sigma teams (including project management) and a comprehensive explanation of DMAIC: Define, Measure, Analyze, Improve, and Control.

Scholtes, Peter, Brian Joiner, and Barbara Streibel. *The Team Handbook*, 3rd. ed. Madison WI: Oriel, 2003. Perhaps the best single volume on teams and problem-solving.

Tague, Nancy. *The Quality Toolbox*, 2nd. ed. Milwaukee: Quality Press, 2005. A tool chest of analytical techniques used by quality management professionals, including brainstorming and the tools used by the city of Punta Gorda in its Lean Six Sigma project.

Expand the Team's Thinking

Purpose, Opportunities, Best Practices, and Teams

Bellman, Geoffrey and Kathleen Ryan. *Extraordinary Groups: How Ordinary Teams Achieve Amazing Results*. San Francisco: Jossey-Bass, 2009.

Hackman, J. Richard. *Leading Teams: Setting the Stage for Great Performances*. Boston: Harvard Business School Publishing, 2002.

———. *Collaborative Intelligence: Using Teams to Solve Hard Problems*. San Francisco: Berrett-Koehler, 2011.

Harper, Ann and Bob Harper. *Skill-Building for Self-Directed Team Members*. New York: MW Corporation, 1992.

Katzenbach, Jon R. and Douglas K. Smith. *The Wisdom of Teams: Creating the High-Performance Organization*. New York: McKinsey, 2003. First published in 1993 by Harvard Business School Press.

Lencioni, Patrick. *The Five Dysfunctions of a Team: A Leadership Fable*. San Francisco: Jossey-Bass, 2002.

———. *Death By Meeting*. San Francisco: Jossey-Bass, 2004.

Parker, Glen M. *Team Players and Teamwork*. San Francisco: Jossey-Bass, 2008.

Scholtes, Peter, Brian Joiner, and Barbara Streibel. *The Team Handbook*, 3rd. ed. Madison WI: Oriel, 2003. A good guide for teams and problem solving, with descriptions of the major tools; perhaps the best single volume on teams.

Whitney, Diana and Amanda Trosten-Bloom. *The Power of Appreciative Inquiry: A Practical Guide to Positive Change*, 2nd ed. San Francisco: Berrett-Koehler, 2012.

Focus the Team's Attention

Project Management, Measurement, Analysis, and Decision Making

Belsky, Scott. *Making Ideas Happen: Overcoming the Obstacles Between Vision and Reality*. New York: Penguin, 2010.

Berkun, Scott. *The Art of Project Management*. Sebastopol CA: O'Reilly, 2005.

Fewings, Peter, *Construction Project Management: An Integrated Approach*. Abingdon, Oxfordshire UK: Spon Press, 2005.

Gladwell, Malcolm. *Blink: The Power of Thinking Without Thinking*. New York: Little, Brown and Company, 2005.

Heath, Chip and Dan Heath. *Decisive: How to Make Better Choices in Life and Work*. New York: Crown Publishing, 2013.

Hubbard, Dennis W. *How To Measure Anything: Finding the Value of Intangibles in Business*. Hoboken NJ: John Wiley & Sons, 2010.

Kahneman, Daniel. *Thinking, Fast and Slow*. New York: Farrar, Straus, and Giroux, 2011.

Kahneman, Daniel, Dan Lovallo, Olivier Sibony. 2011. *Before You Make That Big Decision*. Harvard Business Review 89(6) (June):50-60.

Kaplan, Robert S. and David P. Norton. *Balanced Scorecard: Translating Strategy Into Action.* Boston: Harvard School Review Press, 1996.

Kerzner, Harold. *Project Management: A Systems Approach to Planning, Scheduling, and Controlling*, 10th Ed. New York: John Wiley & Sons, 2009.

Klein, Gary. *The Power of Intuition: How to Use Your Gut Feelings to Make Better Decisions at Work.* New York: Double Day, 2003. Klein is credited with giving us the *pre-mortem* described in chapter 8 on risk management.

Lehrer, Jonah. *How We Decide.* New York: Houghton Mifflin Harcourt, 2009.

———. *Imagine: How Creativity Works* (New York: Houghton Mufflin Harcourt, 2012)

Maubossin, Michael J. *Think Twice: Harnessing the Power of Counterintuition.* Boston: Harvard Business School, 2009.

Niven, Paul R. *Balanced Scorecard Step-by-Step for Government and Nonprofit Agencies*, 2d Ed. New York: Wiley, 2008.

Price, Dan. *Takeoff: The Introduction to Project Management Book That Will Make Your Projects Take Off and Fly!* Manitou Springs CO: Winning Ways Management, 2005.

Project Management Institute. *A Guide to the Project Management Body of Knowledge*, 4th Ed. Newport Square PA: PMI, 2009.

Rees, Fran. *How to Lead Work Teams: Facilitation Skills,* 2d. Ed. San Francisco: Jossey-Bass/Pfeiffer, 2001. Especially good treatment of meeting management and facilitation.

Shore, James and Shane Warden. *The Art of Agile Development.* Sebastopol CA: O'Reilly Media, 2008.

Ullman, David G. *Making Robust Decisions: Decision Management for Technical, Business, and Service Teams.* Oxford UK: Trafford Publishing, 2006. This book uses the author's proprietary decision-making software (*Accord*) in many examples, but the book has useful discussions of considerations in complex decision-making processes.

Wysocki, Robert K. *Effective Project Management: Traditional, Agile, Extreme*, 5th Ed. Indianapolis: Wiley Publishing, 2009.

Sustain the Team's Efforts

Risk and Change Management, Learning, and Leadership

Bennis, Warren. *On Becoming a Leader.* Philadelphia: Perseus, 2009.

Block, Peter. *Flawless Consulting: A Guide to Getting Your Expertise Used.* San Francisco: Pfeiffer, 2011.

Burns, James MacGregor. *Leadership.* New York: Harper & Row, 1978.

———. *Transforming Leadership.* New York: Grove/Atlantic, 2003.

Cialdini, Robert B. *Influence: The Psychology of Persuasion.* New York: HarperCollins, 1984, 1994, 2007. Widely considered a classic in the research of persuasion and influence.

Collison, Chris and Geoff Parcell. *Learning to Fly: Practical Knowledge Management from Leading and Learning Organizations.* London: Capstone Publishing, 2004. The chapters on peer assists, after-action reviews, retrospects, and communities of practice are particularly strong.

Committee of Sponsoring Organizations of the Treadway Commission, *Enterprise Risk Management—Integrated Framework* (2004), available at http://www.coso.org/erm-integratedframework.htm.

Cooper, Dale F., Stephen Grey, Geoffrey Raymond and Phil Walker. *Project Risk Management Guidelines: Managing Risk in Large Projects and Complex Procurements.* Chichester UK: John Wiley & Sons, 2005.

Cross, Jay. *Informal Learning.* San Francisco: Pfeiffer, 2007.

Davenport, Thomas H. and Laurence Prusak. *Working Knowledge.* Boston: Harvard Business School, 1998.

Davis James R. and Adelaide B. Davis. *Effective Training Strategies: A Comprehensive Guide to Maximizing Learning in Organizations.* San Francisco: Berrett-Koehler Publications, 1998.

———. *Managing Your Own Learning.* San Francisco: Berrett-Koehler Publications, 2000. These two books go hand-in-hand. The 1998 book takes a trainer perspective and explains seven training strategies: behavioral, cognitive, inquiry, mental models, group dynamics, virtual reality (simulation), and holistic (experiential). The 2000 book follows these strategies but from the perspective of the learner and offers suggestions on how the learner can best utilize the strategies.

Fisher, Roger and Alan Sharp. *Lateral Leadership: Getting It Done When You Are Not The Boss*, 2nd Ed. London: Profile Books, 2009, originally published under the title *Getting It Done: how to lead when you're not in charge.* New York: Harper Business, 1998.

Fisher, Roger Fisher, William Ury and Bruce Patton. *Getting to Yes: Negotiating Agreement Without Giving In*, 3rd Ed. New York: Penguin Books, 2011. This negotiation classic, now in the third edition, brought us win-win negotiation, interest-based bargaining, and the best alternative to negotiated agreement.

Fisher, Roger and Daniel Shapiro. *Beyond Reason: Using Emotions As You Negotiate.* New York: Penguin Books, 2005. This book out of the Harvard Negotiation Project adds practical "at the table" dimensions for dealing with emotion: appreciation, autonomy, affiliation, status/roles.

Flanagan, R. and G. Norman. *Risk Management and Construction.* Oxford: Blackwell Publishing, 1993.

Gawande, Atul. *The Checklist Manifesto: How to Get Things Right.* New York: Metropolitan Books, 2009.

Gladwell, Malcolm. *Tipping Point.* New York: Little, Brown and Company, 2000.

Goldstein, Noah J., Steve J. Martin and Robert B. Cialdini. *Yes! 50 Scientifically Proven Ways to Be Persuasive.* New York: Free Press, 2008.

Goleman, Daniel, Richard Boyatzis and Annie McKee. *Primal Leadership: Realizing the Power of Emotional Intelligence.* Boston: Harvard Business School Press, 2002.

Gray, Dave, Sunni Brown and James Macanufo. *Gamestorming: A Playbook for Innovators, Rulebreakers, and Changemakers.* Sebastopol CA: O'Reilly Media, 2010.

Harvard Business School Press & Society for Human Resource Management. *The Essentials of Negotiation.* Boston: Harvard Business School Publishing, 2005. An excellent, comprehensive text that cover selected negotiation contexts including vendors and consultants, legal disputes, and employment.

Heath, Chip and Dan Heath, *Made to Stick.* New York: Random House, 2008.

———. *Switch.* New York: Random House, 2010.

Heifetz, Ronald. *The Practice of Adaptive Leadership: Tools and Tactics for Changing Your Organization and the World.* Boston: Harvard Business School Press.

Kotter, John P. *What Leaders Really Do.* Boston: Harvard Business Review, 1999. Compilation of six Harvard Business Review articles on leadership by John Kotter along with a 1999 introduction.

———. *Leading Change.* Boston: Harvard Business School Press, 1996.

Kotter, John P. and Dan S. Cohen. *The Heart of Change.* Boston: Harvard Business School Press, 2002.

Kouzes, James M. and Barry Z. Posner. *The Leadership Challenge*, 5th ed. San Francisco: Jossey-Bass, 2012.

Leonard, Dorothy and Walter Swap. *Deep Smarts: How to Cultivate and Transfer Enduring Business Wisdom.* Boston: Harvard Business School Publishing, 2005.

Luke, Jeffrey. *Catalytic Leadership: Strategies for an Interconnected World.* San Francisco: Jossey-Bass, 1998. Written for the public leader, this book in many respects bridges the gap between technical/transactional leadership and adaptive/transformational leadership theories.)

McCain, Donald V. and Deborah D. Tobey. *Facilitation Basics.* Alexandria, VA: ASTD Press, 2004. This book is aimed at subject matter experts who train; the authors believe that subject matter experts make the best facilitators despite special challenges for experts to train effectively.

McCue, Clifford and Jack T. Pitzer, *Fundamentals of Leadership and Management in Public Procurement.* Herndon, VA: NIGP, 2005.

Moore, Christopher W. *The Mediation Process: Practical Strategies for Resolving Conflict.* San Francisco: Jossey-Bass, 2003.

Nonaka, Ikujiro and Hirotaka Takeuchi. *The Knowledge Creating Company: How Japanese Companies Create the Dynamics of Innovation.* Oxford: Oxford University Press, 1995. Widely regarded as a classic in knowledge management that explained the difference between explicit and tacit knowledge.

Patterson, Kerry, Joseph Grenny, David Maxfield, Ron McMillan, and Al Switzler. *Influencer: The Power to Change Anything.* New York: McGraw-Hill, 2008.

Pfeffer, Jeffrey and Robert I. Sutton, *The Knowing-Doing Gap: How Smart Companies Turn Knowledge Into Action.* Boston: Harvard Business School Publishing, 2000.

Pink, Daniel. *To Sell Is Human: The Surprising Truth About Moving Others.* New York: Riverhead Books, 2012.

Schein, Edgar. *Helping: How to Offer, Give, and Receive Help.* San Francisco: Barrett-Koehler Publishers, 2009.

———. *Organizational Culture and Leadership* (San Francisco: Jossey-Bass, 2004)

Senge, Peter M. *The Fifth Discipline: The Art and Practice of the Learning Organization.* (New York: Random House, 2006. Widely regarded a classic, the book is about systems thinking and learning organizations.

Stolovitch, Harold D. and Erica J. Keeps. *Telling Ain't Training*, 2d Ed. (Danvers MA: ASTD Press, 2011) (Now in its second edition, this is the text used by the NIGP for instructor training and certification)

Thaler, Richard H. and Cass R. Sunstein. *Nudge: Improving Decisions About Health, Wealth, and Happiness.* New Haven: Yale University Press, 2008.

Trautman, Steve. *Teach What You Know: A Practical Leader's Guide to Knowledge Transfer Using Peer Mentoring*. New York: Prentice Hall, 2007. Practitioner author's peer-mentoring model to teach one-on-one teaching strategies.

Ury, William. *Getting Past No: Negotiating Your Way from Confrontation to Cooperation*. New York: Bantam Books, 1991. In the framework of *Getting to Yes*, Ury offers practical framework for dealing with difficult negotiations and "dirty tricks"; one of the better books to supplement *Getting to Yes* with advice on what to do "at the table."

———. *The Power of A Positive No: Save the Deal, Save the Relationship—and Still Say No.* New York: Bantam Books, 2007. Introduces more useful Ury advice and an approach to saying "no": the Yes! No Yes? model.

Von Krogh, Georg, Kazuo Ichijo, and Ikujiro Nonaka. *Enabling Knowledge Creation.* Oxford: Oxford University Press, 2000.

Wangemann, Mary. *Subcontract Management Manual.* New York: Wolters Kluwer, 2010.

Wright, Elizabeth. *Risk Management in Public Contracting.* Herndon VA: NIGP, 2007.

Zachary, Lois J. *The Mentee's Guide: Making Mentoring Work For You.* San Francisco: Jossey-Bass, 2009.

Index

About the Author

Richard Pennington, J.D., CPPO, C.P.M. is a retired U.S. Air Force Colonel who began his career flying B-52s and ended it as a judge advocate specializing in federal procurement. He was a Colorado state purchasing director and director of the Colorado division of finance and procurement, where SCOPE was born as a continuous improvement model. He later served as counsel in the Denver government contracts department of McKenna Long & Aldridge, LLP.

After two years consulting, researching, and writing *Seeing Excellence*, Richard returned to the practice of law in April 2013 as General Counsel for WSCA-NASPO Cooperative Purchasing Organization LLC. WSCA-NASPO is the nonprofit subsidiary of the National Association of State Procurement Officials that supports cooperative purchasing by the states and the consortium known as the Western States Contracting Alliance.

Richard teaches for NIGP and writes for *Government Procurement* and *Contract Management* magazines. His articles and blogs also can be found on the websites of American City & County and the Colorado Bar Association.

Richard is a graduate of the United States Air Force Academy, the University of Denver College of Law, and The George Washington University (Government Procurement Law). In 2005, he was selected as Manager of the Year by the Colorado State Managers Association. He was the 2009 recipient of NASPO's Giulio Mazzone Distinguished Service Award. Richard lives in Denver, Colorado, with his wife Maggie.

Richard primarily teaches for the national associations highlighted in *Seeing Excellence*. If you are interested in knowing more about *Seeing Excellence*, where it can be purchased, and how the ideas in the book evolve, please visit www.seeingexcellence.com.

CPSIA information can be obtained
at www.ICGtesting.com
Printed in the USA
FFHW012214120919
54844873-60556FF